Cambridge Studies in Social Anthropology

General Editor: Jack Goody

42

TRADERS WITHOUT TRADE

For other titles in this series turn to page 189

Traders without trade

Responses to change in two Dyula communities

ROBERT LAUNAY
Department of Anthropology
Northwestern University

CAMBRIDGE UNIVERSITY PRESS

Cambridge
London   New York   New Rochelle
Melbourne   Sydney

Published by the Press Syndicate of the University of Cambridge
The Pitt Building, Trumpington Street, Cambridge CB2 1RP
32 East 57th Street, New York, NY 10022, USA
296 Beaconsfield Parade, Middle Park, Melbourne 3206, Australia

First published 1982

Printed in Great Britain at
the University Press, Cambridge

Library of Congress catalogue card number: 82-4500

British Library cataloguing in publication data

Launay, Robert
Traders without trade: responses to change in
two Dyula communities.—(Cambridge studies in
social anthropology; 42)
1. Dyula (African people)—Social conditions
I. Title
966.6'8   DT545.42

ISBN 0 521 24179 0

BO

To Babouna, with love

Contents

vii

Contents

Figures, maps and tables

Figures

Maps

Tables

ix

Preface

In the summer of 1969, while I was still an undergraduate at Columbia University, I had the remarkable good fortune to spend two months in Ouagadougou, Upper Volta. Through Lady Barbara Ward Jackson, I had been awarded an Albert Schweitzer Travelling Fellowship in order to study the processes of urbanization there. With all the enthusiasm of a novice, I set out to live with an African family. Through a series of fortuitous circumstances, and with the assistance of Elliot Skinner, then American ambassador, and of Françoise Héritier and Roger and Suzy Platiel at the Centre Voltaique de la Recherche Scientifique (C.V.R.S.), I found a room in the compound of Saïdou Dao. Saïdou, as I soon learned, was a Dyula whose father had emigrated from Ivory Coast. The Dyula are a mobile people; frequently dependent on the hospitality of others, they are masters of the art of offering it themselves. Saïdou and his family were no exception. With hindsight, I can say that my first (and all too brief) trip to the field was thoroughly amateurish. I cannot claim to have learned a great deal about urbanization in Ouagadougou, but my chance encounter with a charming host left me with the determination to return to Africa, this time to study the Dyula in their home territory in northern Ivory Coast.

This book is the fruit of that determination. I spent over twenty-one months among the Dyula in northern Ivory Coast, from January 1972 to December 1973, thanks to a fellowship from the National Science Foundation and a Euretta J. Kellet Fellowship from Columbia University. The initial result of my labors was a Ph.D. dissertation for the University of Cambridge written under the invaluable supervision of Jack Goody. At the time, it seemed to me the best way to synthesize the material which I had managed to glean in the field. With several more years' hindsight, I have returned to the same data from a somewhat different perspective. As a result, about half of this book consists of a revision, in some instances a substantial one, of parts of my dissertation, while the rest is entirely new.

I owe a heavy debt of gratitude to all my colleagues who have read and commented on all or parts of my dissertation and drafts of this book: Esther

Preface

Goody, Marc Augé, Meyer Fortes, Tim Weiskel, Joseph Berland, and, above all, Jack Goody, who has been a consistent source of inspiration and encouragement. I would also like to thank the faculty and staff of the Department of Anthropology at Northwestern University for their support during the preparation of the manuscript, and Len Paplauskas of the Office of Research and Sponsored Programs of Northwestern for helping to fund the expenses involved. A host of others have kindly provided encouragement and assistance: Susan Allen-Mills and Louise Sanders of Cambridge University Press; Andrea Dubnick, who typed the final draft; Jane Taylor, who proofread it and kindly 'picked nits' in my English; Antonio Quintanilla, who prepared the maps and diagrams; and Robert Pickering, who photographed the cloth portrayed on the front cover.

But my greatest thanks of all must go to all those Ivoirians without whose continued help and sympathy my research would never have been possible. First of all, I thank those officials of the Parti Démocratique de la Côte d'Ivoire (P.D.C.I.), particularly Fatogoma Coulibaly and Mory Kounandy Cisse, who, when my wife and I arrived, totally bewildered, in Korhogo, immediately set themselves to find us a place to stay, and were throughout our sojourn of continued and precious assistance. Tidiane Dem, whose fund of knowledge about the history of the region is apparently inexhaustible, was of similar help. No words of thanks for the hospitality of my hosts in Korhogo and Kadioha, Al Hajj Valy Cisse and Fetegue Cisse, could be sufficient. Their wives deserve similar gratitude. Nor could I have gone without the real and enduring friendship of a host of other members of the Cisse family: Mory Kounandy, Ladji, Sitafa, Vamara, Basory, Sabati, Bakamory, Fadua, Karamoko Fatoma, Banambi, to name only a few. The fact that I was a guest of the Cisse in both Korhogo and Kadioha meant that I enjoyed a particularly privileged relationship with them and with their families. But I am also indebted to a large number of Dyula in both communities, and in particular to the late Bassirima Saganogo, to Sory Diane, to Karamoko Suware, and to Massa Dambele.

I have far from exhausted the list of all those who, by their friendship, guidance and assistance, have made this volume possible. I hope that all those whose names I have omitted will not take this as a token of ingratitude.

Finally, my wife Catherine deserves a special mention, for bearing with me both in the field and afterwards, in conditions which were often difficult to endure. In times of difficulty and even of despair, her persistence has made this book possible.

xii

1

Introduction:
The people and the problem

> . . . I am as you are, a Julietto, which signifies a Merchant, that goes from
> place to place . . .
>
>   Buckor Sano to Richard Jobson,
>   *Gambia, 1621*

The Dyula

In the various dialects of the Manding language, the word *dyula* has several
meanings. Some of these are of unquestionably recent vintage; indeed, they
are unintelligible outside the modern colonial and postcolonial contexts.
But at least two meanings of the word are far older. By far its most universal
meaning, and almost certainly the oldest, is 'an itinerant trader'. For the
most part, the word referred specifically to Moslem traders who spoke one
of the dialects of Manding as a first language.

   The extensive participation of Manding-speaking peoples in trade has a
very long history, dating at least as far back as the medieval empire of Mali,
the predominant power in the Western Sudan from the thirteenth to the
sixteenth centuries (Levtzion 1973:63). However, certain groups of
Manding-speaking traders, for instance the Marka and the Diakhanke,
trace their origins even further back to the Soninke empire of Ghana which
flourished in the ninth to eleventh centuries A.D. Originally, these Manding
traders were collectively known as the Wangara. In the words of the
seventeenth-century chronicler Mahmoud Kati: '. . . the Wangara and the
Malinke are of one origin, but "Malinke" denotes warriors, whereas
"Wangara" signifies merchants who ply their trade from country to
country' (Kati 1964:65). The word *wangara* was also used to designate one
of the gold-producing regions of the Western Sudan, possibly Bambuk
(Bovill 1968:119; Levtzion 1973:155); indeed, gold was one of the staples
of the trans-Saharan trade whose control formed the basis of Mali's
hegemony. The quest for gold accounts for two waves of Manding
expansion. The first, during Mali's heyday, was towards the Senegambia to
the west. The second, triggered by the disintegration of the empire, was
towards the south, at first in the direction of the Akan goldfields, and later
towards other forest regions which could supply the Western Sudan with
cola nuts (Levtzion 1973:94–102). Sixteenth-century Portuguese sources
mention the presence of the Wangara at various points along the West

1

African coast, not only in the Senegambia but also at Elmina on the Gold Coast (Levtzion 1973:165–8). The Wangara traveled even further afield: the Kano Chronicle attributes the introduction of Islam among the Hausa to the Wangarawa (Palmer 1963, vol. 3:104).

The name *Wangara* continues to be used in modern Ghana to refer to Manding-speaking Moslems. However, particularly in the Manding-speaking world, it was eventually replaced by the word *dyula*. Richard Jobson, an English merchant who visited the Gambia River in 1621, provided the first written mention of the word in his account of a conversation with one Buckor Sano, whom Jobson reckoned the richest trader in the region (Jobson 1968:116). Buckor Sano's use of the word is particularly enlightening, for he refers not only to himself, but also to the Englishman Jobson, as a *Julietto*. Compared to the word *wangara,* this use of the word *dyula* represents an important shift in meaning: whereas *wangara* referred exclusively to Manding-speaking traders from Mali, *dyula* could be used to refer to any trader, regardless of his origins and language. A term which simultaneously denoted ethnic category membership and professional status had been replaced by one which placed a clear emphasis on profession alone.

However, in some parts of West Africa, the word *dyula* could also be used to refer specifically to ethnic category membership. This second meaning to *dyula* was far more localized; roughly, it extended over areas east of the Bandama and Bagoué Rivers in parts of the modern nations of Mali, Upper Volta and Ivory Coast (Person 1968:97). In these regions, all native speakers of Manding called themselves Dyula, whether they were actively engaged in trade or not. There existed a crucial difference between those Manding-speaking communities where *dyula* was an exclusively professional category, and those where it was also a broader ethnic category. It was only a professional term in those areas where Manding-speakers constituted most, if not all, of the local population – areas characterized by a relative linguistic and cultural uniformity, though even here traders constituted a distinct 'subculture'. (Mahmoud Kati's distinction between the Wangara and the Malinke suggests that such subcultural differences were already a feature of the social organization of the Malian empire.) Those Manding-speaking communities who called themselves Dyula lived as minority enclaves among peoples linguistically and culturally different from themselves, peoples such as the Senufo, the Kulango and the Abron.

Those communities who labeled themselves Dyula were quite aware of the other and more usual meaning of the term. Any individual calling himself a *dyula* might either mean that he was a professional trader or simply that he was a native speaker of Manding. In any particular context,

Introduction

there was not likely to be any doubt which meaning was intended. However, in a more fundamental sense, these minority communities of Manding-speakers, by calling themselves *dyula*, were explicitly identifying themselves as a people of traders. Despite the fact that not all Dyula were traders, this identification made perfect sense. In the first place, in those regions where they settled as immigrant minorities, Manding-speakers enjoyed a virtual monopoly of local trade. This monopoly was made possible by the fact that the Dyula were only a small portion of a wide network of Manding-speaking traders and an even wider one of Moslem traders throughout the Western Sudan and beyond. Precisely because the Dyula did not assimilate to their neighbors, but rather conformed to cultural norms accepted elsewhere within West Africa, they served as useful intermediaries between local populations and other regions with which they traded. As such, immigrant Dyula were not only tolerated, but often welcomed, particularly by local chiefs with whom they collaborated on numerous occasions. Secondly, revenues from trade were one of the main sources of subsistence in these Dyula communities. In other words, trade provided a livelihood for many members of Dyula communities as well as the very *raison d'être* for their separate existence as representatives of a minority culture.

Koko quarter

When I set out for the field in 1972, it was my intention to study the Dyula both as traders and as a people. In particular, I was interested in determining how they had adapted their precolonial system of trade to modern social and economic conditions. Other West African peoples who had specialized in trade before the colonial period – the Hausa and the Kooroko for example (Abner Cohen 1965, 1966, 1969; Amselle 1971, 1977) – had successfully made the transition. I assumed that the same would be true of the Dyula.

Soon after my arrival in Ivory Coast, I set out for the town of Korhogo. The town seemed to me an appropriate place in which to begin. It was located in a region with a long history of Dyula settlement, with important precolonial centers of trade situated both to the east (Kong, Bouna and Bondoukou) and to the west (Tingrela, Tiong-i and Boron). Compared to these other towns, precolonial Korhogo was a minor place indeed. However, during the colonial period, it had been chosen as the administrative center for much of the entire northern region of Ivory Coast; it remains by far the largest town in the region, and one of the largest in the country. Despite the fact that it is not located along the major rail and road networks leading out from the capital, it seemed by its very size a likely candidate for a place where trade would continue to be an important activity for part of the

3

population. In any case, I was by no means committed to staying in Korhogo; it simply seemed the best place to begin searching for a community in which to conduct field research.

I began my search immediately upon arriving in town. With hindsight, I can now say that I was surprisingly lucky. In the first place, I found a Dyula community with incredible speed: I arrived in town on a Sunday, and moved into what were to become my permanent headquarters on Tuesday! I owe an immense debt of gratitude to a number of individuals for the efficiency of the help I received in establishing myself this rapidly. I was directed on Monday morning to the veterinarian's office, which was doubling at the time as the local headquarters of the Parti Démocratique de la Côte d'Ivoire, the unique and official party of Ivory Coast. The local party officials were taken entirely by surprise by my request to settle into a Dyula community. However, I insisted that I knew what I was doing – an assertion which proved even less true than I imagined at the time – and they promised to decide what to do with me on the following day.

They held absolutely true to their word. One of the party officials, Mory Kounandy Cisse, party secretary for the town of Korhogo, was himself a Dyula. He had arranged in the meantime to make a room available for my wife and myself in the house of his elder full brother, Al Hajj Valy Cisse. (I found out soon afterwards that this was Al Hajj Valy's personal room, which he was to give up for my benefit with overwhelming generosity for nearly two years.) The party officials could not have made a better choice for me. Throughout my stay, my hosts made every possible effort to help me with my research, however incomprehensible it may have seemed to them. Indeed, it is a host's responsibility in Dyula society to act as an intermediary between his 'stranger' and the rest of the local community, but it is also expected that the 'stranger' act through his hosts rather than take direct initiatives. One cannot change hosts within any one community without giving serious offense, so that a responsible host is an essential asset to any newcomer, and an irresponsible one a nearly irremediable disaster.

But perhaps my greatest stroke of good fortune was the nature of the community in which I unsuspectingly found myself. The name of the quarter in which I was living is Koko, which means 'across the stream' in Dyula; indeed, Koko quarter is separated from most of the town, and particularly the center, by an inconsequential little brook which can easily escape the notice of the casual visitor. (In fact, the locution *koko* is relative; 'across the stream' is by definition on the other side, so that Dyula residents of Koko quarter usually use the name to refer, not to their own home, but to the rest of the town!) The use of a stream as a boundary to divide a town or village into two distinct parts is a frequent phenomenon in the region, and many villages also have their own *koko* quarters. One of the most frequent uses of the boundary is to separate the Dyula part of a town or village from

4

the Senufo part; the Senufo form the majority of the population of the region. This was the case for Korhogo in the nineteenth century, when Koko was essentially the Dyula quarter of a large village that was the capital of a small Senufo chiefdom.[1] As with most modern African towns, Korhogo's rapid growth tended to erode or superannuate the social referents of many earlier spatial boundaries. However, most of this growth has taken place on only one side of the stream – the Senufo side. While it is true that Koko quarter has received a certain number of recent immigrants, most of its residents trace their descent to inhabitants of the nineteenth-century village.

Within Koko itself, there exists a distinct Dyula quarter, entirely composed of Dyula who are indigenous to the town. This remains the site of the Friday mosque for all the Moslems of the town, a vestige of Koko's precolonial status as *the* Moslem quarter, despite that fact that more imposing if not more aesthetic mosques are to be found across the stream. The Dyula of Koko continue to hold rights over the office of *imam* for the town mosque. The Dyula quarter has not escaped the trappings of modernity. Land has been parceled out into privately-owned plots, and cement houses are rapidly replacing the traditional mud huts. Surprisingly, in spite of all this, the Dyula quarter has by and large retained its traditional subdivision into clan wards. By a fortunate accident (fortunate for an anthropologist, in any case), the Dyula part of Koko has maintained an identity as a distinct community of the 'indigenous' Dyula residents of Korhogo. Spatially, and in many respects socially, its structure remains the same as that of a large Dyula village.

Koko is not, of course, a village. It is in many respects an integral part of the modern town. Many residents of Koko work across the stream, and all of them have extensive networks linking them to residents of other parts of town. Yet its identity as a 'traditional' community in the eyes of its own members as well as in those of an anthropologist make it a particularly interesting, if relatively rare, type of urban community. Compared to Koko, Korhogo 'across the stream' partakes of that amorphousness typical of any modern town anywhere in the world. Many anthropologists have been able to study the ways in which individuals adapt to the conditions of modern urban life. But in Koko I was able to study the adaptation of a whole community, as if a village could be grafted onto a town.

As opposed to many immigrants to Korhogo, the Dyula of Koko quarter consider themselves inhabitants, not only of the town itself, but of the region as a whole. They maintain extensive and important ties of kinship and friendship with Dyula in the surrounding villages, ties which antedate the colonial period. My hosts had particularly strong ties with a number of such villages, including Kadioha, a large all-Dyula village, 50 km or so to the southwest of Korhogo, from which their grandfather had emigrated in the nineteenth century. I visited Kadioha with my hosts on a number of occasions, and eventually spent several months there on my own. The comparison between these two Dyula communities, one in the village and one in the town, was illuminating in a number of respects. Of course, anthropologists have rightly emphasized the dangers of hasty comparisons of social behavior in town and village settings.[2] However, the special nature of Koko, whose Dyula inhabitants perceive themselves as members of a 'traditional' community, makes such comparison relatively easier. Indeed, the example of Kadioha highlighted those respects in which the Dyula of Koko structured their social relationships in the same way as did villagers. Perhaps the most insidious temptation in making such a comparison would be to consider Kadioha as 'traditional' and Korhogo as 'modern'; to assume that one community was changing 'faster' than the other. Both communities have experienced radical changes in the recent past. The crucial difference lies rather in the simple fact that Koko is, after all, very much a part of town. First of all, this influences individual strategies for coping with change. Whereas a villager must necessarily migrate in order to obtain wage labor or gain access to important consumer markets for certain services he can provide, the townsman is more likely to be able to find what he needs at home. More importantly, the very identity of the Koko Dyula *as a community* depends on the relations of individuals and the community as a whole with those on the other side of the stream. Kadioha will retain its identity as a Dyula village as long as people continue to live there. Koko, on the other hand, is faced with the prospect of another kind of disappearance; it could become like the rest of town, with one side of the stream a mirror image, perhaps in miniature, of the other. In a certain sense, the Dyula of Koko have their cake and eat it too. They can act as residents of a town and residents of a village at the same time in the same place. But such a feat can hardly be accomplished effortlessly.

Responses to change

So far, I have dwelt on my good fortune in finding such exceptional hosts and such an unusual community as Koko, and extraordinarily rapidly at that. But I doubt whether any anthropologist can rely forever on beginner's luck, and I was certainly no exception. I had come to Korhogo to study precolonial and modern patterns of trade. Not surprisingly, information about precolonial trade was rather limited. I had to rely on the reminiscences of old men about the activities of their fathers and in some cases their grandfathers. There were few men indeed who were both willing and able to provide me with any details, and there were even fewer checks on the accuracy of the material that I managed to glean. But my real problem was gathering information on modern trade: it simply did not exist, at least in the form I was seeking. That is not to say, by any means, that there was no trade in Korhogo – quite the contrary – nor even that there were no Dyula traders in Koko. But, whereas the Dyula of Koko and their cousins in villages such as Kadioha enjoyed a virtual monopoly over trade in the nineteenth century, they had irremediably lost this control by the time that I arrived in the field. The overwhelming majority of Dyula who still earned a living by trade in Koko were operating on an extremely small scale. In the not-too-distant past, it had not been unusual for Dyula with other occupations to engage in trading ventures on the side; this was now increasingly rare. There were large-scale traders in Korhogo . . . but they were mostly across the stream. It became increasingly clear that any study of continuities between pre-colonial and modern trade was not going to bear much fruit.

I was faced with a difficult choice. On one hand, I could abandon the Dyula of Koko and try to build up a network of contacts with traders across the stream. Otherwise, if I wished to stay in Koko, I would have to find another focus for my research. I chose to remain, feeling that it would be easier to find another problem than to find another set of people to study, especially given the congeniality of my hosts. I had by that time collected a considerable amount of information about marriage in Koko, and more kept coming my way whether I sought it or not. So, in my hurry to find another topic of research, I chose marriage. In particular, I set out to determine how the changes which the Dyula of Koko and Kadioha were experiencing were affecting marriage patterns. In retrospect, I believe this focus was too narrow. The question remains an important one, but it is only one facet of two more general and, in a real sense, fundamental problems. First, how are the Dyula of Koko and Kadioha adapting to their loss of control over the region's trade? Second, how are the Dyula of Koko adapting to their community's incorporation into a modern town? In a sense, my attention was turned back to the question I had wanted to answer before setting out for the field: how have precolonial patterns of social interaction been adapted to modern social and economic conditions? But I had erroneously assumed that these patterns were, both now and in the past, intimately connected with a system of trade. Instead, I found I had to explain the paradox: how can there be 'traders' without trade?

Of course, any discussion of change necessarily involved a diachronic dimension. To say that 'modern' conditions involved 'change' is either a truism, or, for want of evidence, an unwarranted assumption. Simply to state that the Dyula have lost their regional trade monopoly and that Koko has been incorporated into a modern town is not enough; it still needs to be shown that these changes have had a fundamental effect on the nature, if not the structure, of Dyula social relationships. In short, it is necessary to describe Dyula society as it was before the colonial period in order to assess the effects of any later changes. Such a description can only take the form of a hypothetical reconstruction, and as such can only be tentative. The task is all the more difficult because of the lack of written historical documentation, at least as far as primary sources are concerned. European exploration of the region began at the very end of the nineteenth century, a very brief prelude to its incorporation into the French colonial empire. The only exception was Rene Caillé, who passed through Tingrela, considerably to the east of Korhogo, in 1829, on his way to Timbuktu. The next European visitor was to be Binger, who arrived in Kong in 1888. His account of the town remains the single outstanding description of Dyula society before the advent of colonial rule. But, despite their relative proximity, Kong and Korhogo must certainly have been very different places before the colonial period. The former was a great trading town, whose population, estimated by Binger (1892:198) to be 15 000, was entirely Dyula. The latter was the seat of a former Senufo chiefdom, whose Dyula population was a minority, if an important one. That we have no comparable description of Korhogo is hardly surprising; the very importance of the site is almost entirely a function of the colonial period. It remains possible that there are extant local histories, written in Arabic, of Dyula communities in the region of Korhogo. A number of such texts have been discovered in Ghana (Hodgkin 1966), for example; I was assured by Dyula informants that similar texts had indeed existed in the past, and that some copies might still be extant, but my attempts to uncover them bore no fruit. However, my quest was hardly exhaustive, and there remains hope that some texts will eventually be brought to light. In any case, my own sources remain almost exclusively oral.

The first part of this book will be devoted to a brief reconstruction of Dyula society in Korhogo and Kadioha before the colonial period. Chapter 2 traces the history of Dyula immigration to the region, and discusses the nature of the symbiosis of the Dyula, as a minority, with their Senufo neighbors, both chiefs and agriculturalists. Chapter 3 examines the division of labor within the Dyula community in terms of the organization of the three economic activities held in most esteem by the Dyula: warfare, Islamic scholarship and trade. These two chapters attempt to delineate the nature of the social and economic 'niche' which the Dyula occupied in a multi-ethnic society before the advent of colonial rule. Chapters 4 and 5 discuss the principles of 'traditional' Dyula social organization. Chapter 4 deals with kinship, and particularly with the *kabila* or 'clan ward', the fundamental unit of Dyula social organization; Chapter 5 discusses the structure of marriage choices and the reasons for preferential marriage within the clan ward. Unlike most of the features of the precolonial Dyula economy, these aspects of social organization are still very much a part of modern Dyula society. Their description relies essentially on my own first-hand observations, rather than on reminiscences, and one might object that it is an unwarranted assumption that these features existed in similar form in the precolonial period. However, the Dyula insist that they did, and I shall argue that Dyula social organization was in fact a successful adaptation to the economic and social niche which the Dyula occupied in the Korhogo region in the nineteenth century and before.

The rest of the book deals with the changes which have taken place since the beginning of the twentieth century and their effects on the Dyula communities of Koko and Kadioha. Chapter 6 explains how the Dyula communities of the region lost their control over local trade, and how the transformation of Korhogo into a modern urban center has affected the relations of the Dyula of Koko with their neighbors across the stream. Chapter 7 describes the various strategies which the Dyula of Koko and Kadioha have utilized in order to carve out a new economic niche for themselves: the adoption of new occupations; migration away from the home community, and usually the region; and Western education. The next two chapters deal specifically with the response of the Koko Dyula to their incorporation into a larger urban community. Chapter 8 deals with the community's own sense of its distinct identity and the way that this affects the relationships of its members with other residents of Koko, with the town across the stream and with other Dyula in the region. Chapter 9 is specifically concerned with Islam and how the ideologies of religious tradition and reform have been used to express and maintain the Koko Dyula community's sense of identity. Chapter 10 reconsiders Dyula kinship and marriage in the modern context. This problem is particularly interesting in two respects. In the first place, the Ivoirian Civil Code of 1965 has expressly sought to legislate 'traditional' forms of social organization out of existence. Secondly, a consideration of those aspects of the kinship system which continue to operate, as opposed to those which have been abandoned, raises the general issue of the adaptation of 'traditional' structures to changing circumstances.

This last problem – the persistence, and indeed the very notion, of 'tradition' – is the subject of the concluding chapter and, ultimately, of the book as a whole. For, in a sense, the very idea of 'tradition' is misleading. It connotes a blind commitment to the past, a stubborn refusal to adapt, a denial, one might say, of the present, and, by implication, of the future. The Dyula have never been partisans of this kind of blind commitment. After all, they are by their own definition a people of traders, and traders cannot, in a very literal sense, afford such blindness. They must be responsive to change, if only changes in market conditions, in order to survive. And if the Dyula of Koko and Kadioha have abandoned trade, this is again because of their awareness of change and the need to adapt.

Yet the Dyula still consider themselves 'traditional'. If they can nevertheless adapt to change, it is because 'tradition' is, for the Dyula, very much a thing of the present rather than of the past. 'Tradition', in this sense,

Introduction

is a means of supplying meaning, and if the present acquires its meaning in terms of the past, it is equally true that the past takes on meaning in terms of the present. This book is a record of 'tradition' as well as of 'change' in Dyula society – two notions which we in the West label, perhaps too hastily, as opposites.

PART I

The legacy of the past

2

Dyula and Senufo

The modern nations of sub-Saharan Africa are all artificial creations, by-products of the partition of the continent at the Berlin Conference of 1885. While almost all of them are characterized by very considerable cultural diversity, Ivory Coast is even more heterogeneous than most. The country is bisected by an ecological frontier: the northern half of the country is savanna, the southern half tropical forest. Roughly speaking, this also corresponds to a cultural frontier. Modern Ivoirians frequently think of themselves as 'northerners' or 'southerners', though 'north' and 'south' are each characterized by further basic cultural divisions. Underlying this diversity, a system of affinities links the peoples of different regions of Ivory Coast with their neighbors living across modern borders. The peoples of southwestern Ivory Coast, speakers of Kru and Mande-fu languages, resemble many of the inhabitants of modern Liberia and Sierra Leone. The Akan-speakers of the southeast have their counterparts in southern Ghana. The inhabitants of the northwest, the Malinke (or Maninka, as they call themselves), are Manding-speakers as are their neighbors in Guinea and Mali. The central and eastern parts of the north are populated mostly by speakers of Voltaic languages, with homologus in parts of Mali, Upper Volta and northern Ghana. It is in this part of Ivory Coast that we also find those Manding-speakers who call themselves the Dyula.

The arrival of the Manding in northern Ivory Coast, even in the northwest where they are now in a majority, is a relatively recent phenomenon. Their homeland, the country of 'Mande', seat of the empire of Mali, lies farther to the north. The southward expansion of the Manding was a slow process, and the earliest immigrants occupied territories both to the east and to the west of modern Ivory Coast. To the east lay the Akan goldfields, which had attracted the attention of Manding traders by the fifteenth century and accounted for the foundation, in the fifteenth or sixteenth century, of the Manding trading town of Begho in what is now northern Ghana (J. R. Goody 1964:210; Person 1964:332). The gold trade also stimulated a demand in the Western Sudan for cola nuts, which grow only in the forest.

13

The legacy of the past

The cola trade, rather than the gold trade, spurred the expansion of the Manding to the west of Ivory Coast. This early wave of migration left linguistic traces both in the west and in the east, where one finds languages closely related, but not identical, to Manding – Kono and Vai in Sierra Leone, Ligby along the border of Ghana and Ivory Coast (J. R. Goody 1964:195–6; Person 1964:328). As early as this, a few of these 'Proto-Dyula', as they have been called, migrated to the region of Korhogo as well. The Dieli – the local 'caste' of leather workers – still speak a language distinct from both Dyula and Senufo, and which Person (*ibid.*) has identified as related to Ligby. Indeed, the Dieli, unlike other 'castes' in the region, are assimilating themselves into the larger Dyula group, and have been doing so since the nineteenth century if not earlier. This early Dieli immigration was a very restricted phenomenon, compared to what was to come later.

The arrival of the modern Dyula in north-central Ivory Coast seems to have taken place in the seventeenth century (Person 1964:332). The Dyula claim that, on their arrival, the region was occupied only by those Senufo who speak the Fodonon dialect and whom the Dyula call the 'Sono'. Dyula oral traditions concur that the first three Dyula settlements in the region were the villages of Dyendana, Faraninka and Boron, appropriately known as *Sono gba saba*, 'the three Sono hearthstones'. Dyendana and Faraninka are both located a short distance from Korhogo; Boron is considerably to the southwest. The three villages were situated along the trade route linking the Western Sudan and the forest, and ultimately the Atlantic Coast. Boron and Dyendana both became the capitals of chiefdoms, the very first to emerge in the region. The nature and extent of their hegemony remain unclear; undoubtedly, one of the primary functions of the chiefs was to maintain the security of the trade route.

The very existence of this route attracted further Dyula immigration. Whereas the original settlements, the 'three Sono hearthstones', were new village sites whose occupants were uniformly Dyula, later settlers sometimes chose to reside in pre-existing Senufo villages rather than founding their own. For example, members of the Tegeri clan moved into the old site of the Sono village of Pundya, later to become the village of Kadioha. The site, directly along the route from Dyendana and Faraninka to Boron, was an eminently logical choice. Dyula who moved into Senufo villages tended to live some distance apart from their neighbors in a separate section, not infrequently as far as a kilometer away from the Senufo. Both types of Dyula community – independent villages and separate quarters within mixed villages – remain common throughout the region.

Two series of events in the beginning of the eighteenth century radically affected the future of the region. Around 1730, the Baoule occupied the territory due south of Korhogo. For the most part, the Akan-speaking

14

Dyula and Senufo

peoples of Ivory Coast and Ghana either live in the forest or straddle the ecological frontier. However, the southernmost reaches of the savanna are located due south of Korhogo, and the Baoule chose to settle precisely in these reaches (see Map 1). The Baoule did not allow Dyula traders to traverse their territory, effectively cutting them off from their supply of cola in the forest. The Baoule traded in certain commodities with the Dyula, but never in cola (Chauveau 1972:2–8). As a result, the trade route through the 'three Sono hearthstones' ceased to be very profitable; trade routes both to the east and to the west led to nearer sources of cola. As far as long-distance trade was concerned, the whole region around Korhogo was condemned to remain a backwater.

In the meantime, two chiefdoms emerged to the east: Nafana and Kong. Quite possibly, these new chiefdoms were modeled on Boron and Dyendana. Oral traditions link both of their founders with the 'three Sono hearthstones'; Signele Tondosama of Nafana is said to have sojourned in Boron, Lassiri Gombele of Kong in Faraninka (Bernus 1960:247–50). Lassiri Gombele was killed in a *coup d'état* and a Dyula, Sekou Wattara, came to power in Kong. This marked a radical shift in the regional balance of power. A number of military expeditions were dispatched from Kong during the reigns of Sekou and his sons, bringing Kong into conflict, not only with its immediate neighbors, but with more distant and powerful rivals such as Ashanti (Bernus 1960:248–60). Undoubtedly, the basis of Kong's power was its access to horses, imported or raided from the north. Horses do not breed well as far south as northern Ivory Coast, but they survive well enough to constitute a formidable military asset, providing the strategic advantage of mobility to the armies who possess them (see J. R. Goody 1971). Unlike the 'three Sono hearthstones', Kong was not situated north of the Baoule region. It was consequently much closer to the forest, and its access to both gold and cola nuts assured the wealth needed to exchange for horses.

Some of the armies which set out from Kong in the mid-eighteenth century seem to have been only very loosely, if at all, under its control. One of these, led by Dyangarawuru Wattara, settled in the village of Pundya on its return from a campaign in the southwest. The earlier Dyula settlers of Pundya previously lived side by side and apparently at peace with their Senufo hosts. The arrival of a Dyula army was to disturb this equilibrium, and serious disputes arose between Dyula and Senufo in the village. The Senufo, feeling themselves outclassed if not outnumbered, decided to move the site of their village a few miles to the northeast, where the present village of Pundya is still to be found. The old site of Pundya, now entirely inhabited by Dyula, came to be known as Kadioha – paradoxically a name of Senufo origin signifying a typical form of greeting in the Fodonon dialect. The Senufo of Pundya retained certain ritual prerogatives over the site, and were called in to perform certain rites, in particular the expiatory rites for any blood shed in the fields.[1] From Kadioha, Dyangarawuru extended his control over Dyula and Senufo in neighboring villages, including Pundya, and Kadioha became the seat of another chiefdom in the region, with Boron as its neighbor to the southwest.

Slightly later, another army set off from Kong, led by Nanguin Coulibaly. Unlike Dyangarawuru's army, the bulk of the group, and probably Nanguin himself, consisted of Senufo who spoke the Kiembara dialect. According to oral traditions, this army wandered around the region for some time, visiting various chiefdoms – including Kadioha – until it settled at the site of Korhogo, in about 1750 (Bernus 1961; Person 1961:474). Nanguin founded a chiefdom which superseded the authority of nearby Dyendana.

By the end of the eighteenth century, the region had acquired the major social and political features which the French were to find a century or so later. The whole territory was divided up among a relatively large number of small chiefdoms, some of which, like Korhogo and Kadioha, trace their origins to Kong, though Kong never seems to have established any effective hegemony over the region. Almost all of these chiefdoms were under the authority of Senufo chiefs. The first French survey of the administrative district of Korhogo in 1908[2] listed a total of twenty-eight chiefdoms, of which only three – Boron, Kadioha and Ngandana – had Dyula chiefs. Both Boron and Kadioha are in the extreme southwest corner of the district. Boron, the only chiefdom without any Senufo inhabitants at all, was exceptional. Ngandana, a small chiefdom in the far northwest, right by the border with modern Mali, was the only one of the three with a majority of Senufo inhabitants.

The Senufo population of the region was itself marked by considerable linguistic and cultural, as well as political, diversity. Aside from the original inhabitants, speakers of the Fodonon dialect, the modern préfecture of Korhogo includes speakers of the Kiembara, Nafara, Bonzoro, Kouflo, Tanga, Kafibele and Tagbon dialects of Senufo (S.E.D.E.S. 1965, vol. 1:11). Speakers of any one of these frequently find it difficult or impossible to understand the others. With the exception of pockets of Fodonon-speaking autochthons, Senufo subjects and their chiefs spoke a single dialect in any chiefdom; neighboring chiefdoms might also share the same dialect.

If all these chiefdoms were small, some were, after all, larger than others: of the twenty-eight chiefdoms listed by the French in the 1908 survey, six had fewer than 1000 taxable (i.e. adult) inhabitants; fourteen had between 1000 and 5000; four between 5000 and 10 000; three had approximately 15 000; and only one – Korhogo – was larger, with over 22 000.[3] Despite these differences in scale, no one chiefdom or group of chiefdoms controlled the balance of power in the region. Warfare between chiefdoms within, as

16

well as outside, the region was by no means uncommon, but patterns of allegiances prevented the larger ones from gobbling up their smaller neighbors. Until the end of the nineteenth century, the region seems to have been characterized by the relative stability of its political boundaries.

Both linguistic and political boundaries impeded the development of a broad pan-regional or pan-ethnic sense of identity among the Senufo. Indeed, the very term 'Senufo' is of Dyula origin. The Senufo call their own language *Siena-re*; *Siena fo* (*fo* means 'to speak' in Manding) or *Senufo* can be translated as 'those who speak Siena'. The adoption of the term as a broader ethnic label was a by-product of French colonization, since the early French explorers and administrators in the region relied principally on Manding-speaking interpreters who familiarized them with the Dyula term.

Significantly, the Senufo did not think of themselves as such, whereas the Dyula did. For the ordinary Senufo, the largest social unit with which he normally identified was his chiefdom. Frequently, inhabitants of neighboring chiefdoms spoke dialects which he could only understand partially, if at all. Of course, the Dyula were also subjects of these chiefdoms, and most could speak at least one Senufo dialect. They were necessarily conscious of the linguistic, political and often cultural differences which divided their Senufo neighbors. However, for the Dyula, the fundamental division lay, not between one chiefdom and another or between one Senufo dialect and another, but between the global categories of 'Dyula' and 'Senufo'. The very real differencies which existed between various Senufo groups in the region, while not negligible, paled into insignificance in comparison with the differences between themselves and the Senufo as a whole. As the term *Siena fo* implies, linguistic differences were important. If bilingualism has always been a feature of local Dyula society, and is not uncommon among Senufo (at least nowadays), the distinction between *native* speakers of one language or the other remains a fundamental one for the Dyula.

This linguistic distinction was only one symptom of an underlying complex of deeper social and cultural differences. The word the Dyula still use most frequently to refer to their neighbors is not *Siena fo*, but rather *banmana*, which strictly speaking denotes a 'pagan'. Like the very name 'Dyula' itself, the label *banmana* was polysemic. In its most general sense, it applied to any of the peoples living in the 'northern' savanna who did not consider themselves Moslems; this included not only many Voltaics but also native Manding-speakers, the Bambara and many of the Malinke.[4] But locally, *banmana* and *Siena fo* were synonymous. Before the twentieth century, it was a foregone conclusion that all Dyula were Moslems and that all Senufo were 'pagans'. In most cases, the reverse was also true: Moslems were Dyula and 'pagans' were Senufo. There were only a few exceptions: for example, the Dieli leatherworkers were definitely 'pagans', but not Senufo. Even today, despite large numbers of Senufo converts to Islam, the

Dyula of Korhogo normally refer to *Siena-re* as *banmana kan*, literally 'the pagan language'.

The Dyula and Senufo languages were considered equivalent, not only to the Moslem and 'pagan' religions respectively, but also to other underlying cultural distinctions. In particular, the Senufo are matrilineal, whereas the Dyula have a strong ideology of patriliny. Not all patrilineal peoples are Moslems by any means; the Dyula were well aware of the existence of 'pagan' Manding-speakers who nevertheless remained culturally much closer to their own way of life than to that of their Senufo neighbors. However, matriliny was considered by its very nature incompatible with the practice of Islamic laws of inheritance. Dyula informants expressed particular distaste at the fact that nephews might also inherit the wives of their maternal uncles and, still worse, have certain rights of sexual access before their uncles' deaths. In short, while the Dyula are aware that 'pagans' are not necessarily matrilineal, the fact that their Senufo neighbors were matrilineal was taken as further evidence of their 'paganism'.

In any case, Senufo were considered 'pagans' and Dyula 'Moslems' virtually by definition. Paradoxically, this facilitated rather than impeded the process of cultural borrowing. Practices that elsewhere might be considered 'pagan' were adopted by certain Dyula without calling into question the principle that ethnic category membership and religion were coincidental. In particular, one of the most spectacular features of Senufo society is the *poro*, or initiation society; much of the sculpture for which the Senufo are justly famous is associated with *poro* activities. The *poro* was a central institution of Senufo religion as well as of political organization. One might hastily conclude that graven images and secret rites would have seemed anathema to Dyula Moslems, another fitting symbol of the 'paganism' of their neighbors. Nowadays, most Dyula have adopted this point of view. Yet, not very long ago, some Dyula also participated in *poro* activities, although Dyula and Senufo branches of the *poro* were kept strictly separate.[5] Initiation society rituals, considered 'pagan' in other parts of West Africa before the colonial period, and more recently in modern Korhogo, were formerly considered acceptable for certain Moslems in the region.[6]

Clan names were another marker distinguishing Dyula from Senufo. Only five such names were indigenous to the Senufo of the Korhogo region. The Dyula, on the other hand, had a much larger fund of patronyms, or *dyamu*. However, there existed a more or less standardized system of equivalencies between Senufo and Dyula clan names (Holas 1966:78). Whereas the Dyula had adopted the Senufo *poro*, clan names were diffused in the opposite direction.

Despite the undeniable importance of cultural borrowing in both directions, the distinction between Dyula and Senufo constituted a fundamental social fact. Admittedly, for the Senufo, dialectal, cultural and political differences between Senufo groups were equally, if not more, important in establishing any individual's identity. Subjects of other chiefdoms, speakers of other dialects of *Siena-re*, even members of 'caste' groups were all, like the Dyula, essentially 'different'. Thus the Dyula of precolonial Korhogo shared Koko quarter with members of other groups, the Fodonon and the 'castes', all of them separated spatially from the chiefdom's Kiembara-speaking majority. The Dyula were also aware that not all Senufo were alike. But, in a real sense, these differences were of secondary importance. The 'Dyula/Senufo' distinction defined their primary identity within the region.

The question remains: why did this distinction remain so important? Why didn't the Dyula assimilate to their Senufo neighbors? The history of the region clearly shows that the answer is not self-evident; groups could and did assimilate to their neighbors, retaining little but the memory of a distant or not-so-distant past. Some of the Dieli simply became Dyula; clan wards of Dieli origin also exist in Koko. The answer lies in the division of labor within the region. The categories 'Dyula' and 'Senufo' were each associated with a different set of tasks. The Senufo were, by and large, agriculturalists, in particular subsistence agriculturalists. The major occupation of the ordinary Senufo was to grow his own food; anything else was secondary. There were only two classes of exceptions to this rule. First, there were practitioners of 'casted' occupations (*fijembele*): woodcarvers (*kulebele*), blacksmiths (*fonombele*), brass casters (*kpeembele*) and gunsmiths (*cedumbele*) (Richter 1980:14–15).[7] Members of these groups are also practiced subsistence agriculture, craft activities being largely confined to the dry season. Chiefs – the second exception – did not themselves farm, their own fields being tilled by their subjects. Despite these exceptions, both Senufo and Dyula readily acknowledged that the Senufo were essentially a farming people.

The very name Dyula indicates that they were, by contrast, a people of traders. This did not in fact mean that no Dyula ever farmed. Slaves, who adopted the ethnic identity of their masters, were frequently set to work in the fields. Nor was farming itself necessarily considered demeaning by free Dyula. A Dyula who cultivated a crop with the express intention of selling it was, in a real sense, a trader. Circumstances might also constrain a free Dyula to grow food for his own consumption rather than for the market. This was not shameful; it was simply assumed that no self-respecting Dyula would indulge in such activity had he any other acceptable choice available. The three avenues to prestige among the Dyula were warfare, Islamic scholarship and trade. Growing one's own food was fit for slaves, or for those unfortunate individuals who could not support themselves while devoting their full attention to one of the other activities.

19

The legacy of the past

Table 1. *Dyula and Senufo adult population, Korhogo Region, 1908. (Source: Ivory Coast National Archives)*

Chiefdom	Total population	Senufo	Dyula	Percentage Dyula	Number of villages	Average population per village
Mbengue	8 970	8 000	970	10.8	45	199.3
Nielle	14 770	11 070	3 700	25.1	36	410.3
Ngandana	1 450	1 150	300	20.6	10	145.0
Korhogo	22 360	19 060	3 300	16.1	108	207.0
Kadioha	4 130	630	3 500	84.7	13	317.7
Boron	840	—	840	100.0	6	140.0
	52 520	39 910	12 610	24.0	218	240.9
Other chief-doms (22)	84 270	82 140	2 130	2.5	982	85.8
Total	136 790	122 050	14 740	10.8	1 200	114.0

Of these three activities, trade was the most important; it provided the wherewithal to support the other two. However, the arrival of the Baoule to the south of the region seriously restricted opportunities for trade. Major trade routes linking the forest and the savanna tended to bypass the region, to the profit of the Dyula communities situated either to the east (e.g. Kong, Bouna and Bondoukou) or to the west (e.g. Tingrela and Tiong-i) (see Map 1). Even so, the distribution of Dyula throughout the region shows that long-distance trade continued to be a real concern. Of the twenty-eight chiefdoms listed in the 1908 census (see Table 1), only six had a Dyula population in excess of 10%. These six chiefdoms alone accounted for 84.4% of the Dyula population of the region, but only 38.4% of the total population. The proportion of Dyula to Senufo varied very considerably from chiefdom to chiefdom throughout the region.

Map 2 shows that there were three distinct clusters of high Dyula concentration. Kadioha and Boron to the southwest had the highest densities of Dyula by far; indeed, no Senufo were to be found in the chiefdom of Boron, and they were a minority in the chiefdom of Kadioha according to French estimates.[8] This is hardly surprising. The southwest was nearest the source of cola nuts. The areas immediately to the south and southwest of Kadioha (including Boron) were entirely peopled by Manding-speakers. The chiefdom of Kadioha is situated right on the frontier between predominantly Manding-speaking and Senufo-speaking populations.

The chiefdoms of Mbengue, Nielle and Ngandana, in the extreme north of the region, constituted a second cluster. This cluster was perhaps the least affected by the Baoule occupation of the southern stretches of the

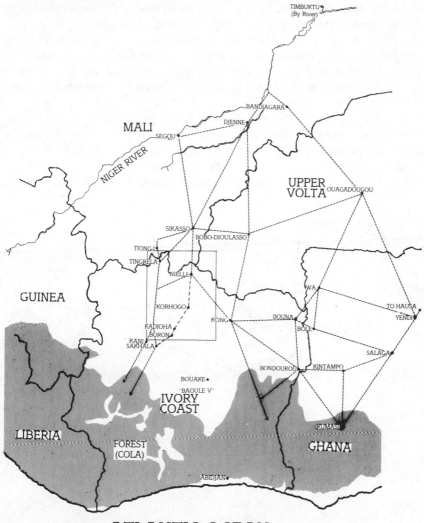

Map 1. Trade routes
  〜〜〜 Linking forest and savanna (source: Binger 1892:401)
  − − − (Trade route through Korhogo region – not cited in Binger)

savanna south of Korhogo. Binger, who passed through Nielle on his way to Kong, places it strategically with respect to major trade routes. He situates the village at a crossroad linking the town of Sikasso, to the north, with the two crucial north– south trade routes to the east and west (see Map 1). The route through Nielle may also have served as an east–west link between these two major axes; this was the route which Binger himself followed from Tiong-i to Kong.

The third cluster, in the chiefdom of Korhogo, lay along a trade route linking these other two clusters. However, this does not seem to have been a route of great importance by Binger's time, except to the Dyula residents of Korhogo chiefdom itself. It had, of course, seen better days, and explains the presence of two of the 'three Sono hearthstones' within the chiefdom. A

Map 2. Korhogo region, indicating centers of Dyula concentration in 1908

ring of Dyula villages arose around the site of Korhogo, the largest of these being Kapele, Waraniene and Katia. Only later, in the mid-nineteenth century, did the Dyula occupy Koko, in the village of Korhogo itself. The original occupants of Koko were in fact the Dieli, who by virtue of this fact still enjoy the right to the office of chief of Koko. Not surprisingly, few of the immigrants to Koko seem to have come from very far. Some trace their origins to neighboring Dyula villages such as Dyendana, Faraninka, Kapele and Katia. Others were from Kadioha and other, smaller Dyula villages under its control; still others came from larger Dyula communities not far away to the east – Kong and Kawara. At first sight, it seems puzzling that the chiefdom of Korhogo, poorly located with respect to long-distance trade, should have continued to attract Dyula settlers. However, not all Dyula trade was interregional. The Senufo themselves constituted a market, both for products which the Dyula produced and for those which they could import. Korhogo is situated in a zone of particularly dense settlement – 65 inhabitants per km^2 in 1963 (S.E.D.E.S.1965, vol. 1:20) – a zone which also included the neighboring chiefdoms of Napieoledougou and Sinematiali. According to the 1908 census, these three chiefdoms alone accounted for nearly 40% of the total Senufo population of the district. There were other, less densely populated chiefdoms close at hand, further enlarging the size of the local market. In fact, Dyula in all three clusters of regional concentration – north, center and southwest – exploited both forms of trade, local and long-distance. However, the character of each location affected the extent of reliance on one form or the other. Dyula in the north and southwest could profit from the flow of traders from outside the region passing through their communities. The Dyula in the center, on the other hand, had by far the largest local market.

Their dependence on trade and their allegiance to Islam (both of which tended to go hand in hand in the Western Sudan) also linked the Dyula to peoples and events outside the region. Not all traders and scholars traveled very far; the point, however, is that some did. Each Dyula community maintained a network of ties to others, both within and outside the region. The activities of trade and scholarship necessitated a freedom of movement, in the long as well as in the short term. Individuals could freely leave their home communities if they felt that another site offered more promising possibilities. Those who moved a relatively short distance away maintained their ties with the parent community; most of the Dyula clan wards of Koko are actively involved in the affairs of the villages from which their ancestors came. But those who moved further away let such ties lapse; many Dyula within the region remember the names and locations of ancestral villages which they have never seen, and whose inhabitants they have never met. Moslem traders and scholars from elsewhere, with rare exceptions Manding-speakers, were equally free to settle within the region if they so chose, and in certain cases were invited in by local Dyula. Such individuals were accepted into the local Dyula communities as a matter of course.

Their very identity as a people of Moslem traders meant that the 'ethnic boundary'[9] distinguishing the Dyula from other peoples was very rigid in some respects and very fluid in others. Within the region itself, the boundary was rigid indeed. With the exception of a few, numerically marginal 'castes', any individual could unambiguously be labeled as either Dyula or Senufo. Underlying this division was a system of complementary division of labor in which trade and subsistence agriculture (at least for its own sake) were considered essentially incompatible activities. But if the roots of this categorical distinction were economic, it also extended to the domains of language, religion and kinship. Yet beyond the confines of the region, this ethnic boundary could also be extremely fluid, for the Dyula were aware that they were also part of a larger world. Elsewhere, Manding-speaking Moslems might identify themselves by other names such as Maninka-Mory, Diakhanke and Marka. To the Dyula, such peoples were little different from themselves, and far 'closer' than any Senufo neighbors living just acoss the stream.

3

Warriors, scholars and traders

If the region as a whole was characterized by fairly intense ethnic specialization, with Senufo, Dyula and marginal groups of craftsmen each controlling different sectors, there was also a high degree of specialization within the Dyula group itself. Whereas, for the vast majority of Senufo, the primary occupation was the farming of staple cereals for subsistence, an individual Dyula was more likely to consider himself a warrior, a scholar or a trader. Yet it was possible for a Dyula to change his occupation, or to carry on more than one of these occupations at the same time. For example, a rich trader could arm his slaves, thereby commanding a small army with which to meddle in local politics or to wage war. On the other hand, he might turn over his business activities to his grown sons and spend his remaining days in the study of sacred texts. In such respects, Dyula social organization was extremely flexible. Despite this flexibility, however, these three occupations were not entirely equivalent. Of the three, trade was the most universal, as the very name 'Dyula' implies. Indeed, most Dyula engaged in trade of one form or another during at least part of their adult lives. But much of this trade was only of local importance; participation in the long-distance trade was the real mark of the specialized trader.

If any Dyula might become a trader, the same was far less true for the occupations of warrior and scholar. Warfare and scholarship were considered antithetical activities, and a reputation in one field almost precluded a reputation in the other. This antithesis was embedded in Dyula social organization, and was one of its fundamental principles. The whole of Dyula society was divided into two categories: the *tun tigi* (literally 'possessors of quivers') were the 'warriors', and the *mory* were the 'scholars'.[1] The most salient feature which distinguished the two groups was religion. The *mory* were (of course) orthodox Moslems. The *tun tigi* were quite lax in the practice of Islam; they were not very strict as concerns prayers and fasting, not to mention prohibitions on alcoholic beverages, all of which are essential tenets of Sunni Islam. Moreover, their religious observances were tinged with other practices many of which were borrowed

25

The legacy of the past

from their Senufo neighbors and which, to an orthodox Moslem, reeked of 'paganism'.

In preparation for the different activities which they would carry out during their lifetimes, the young 'warrior' and the young 'scholar' accordingly received different educations. Very early on, the young scholar was taught the Arabic alphabet, was then set to memorizing prayers and eventually long passages from the Koran. This process of study might continue indefinitely, as long as he found a master advanced enough to teach him. It was no anomaly to find a middle-aged man, or even an old man, who was still a 'student'. A 'warrior' started his education rather later in life, as an adolescent, within the initiation societies. These initiation societies were exclusively a *tun tigi* affair, although under certain circumstances a *mory* might undergo some of the ceremonies.[2] In these societies, a quite different set of principles from those embodied in the Koran were beaten into the initiates. These initiation societies were modeled quite consciously on the Senufo *poro*. However, each Dyula community, if it included any 'warriors', had its own sacred 'grove', and often several separate 'groves'. Thus all youths, 'warriors' and 'scholars' alike, received a long education which prepared them for their particular specialization. This specialized education reinforced the cleavage between the two groups, underlying the antithesis between the two occupations. This antithesis was also reflected in the distribution of high office among the Dyula. The Dyula in the region recognized two such offices: the chieftaincy, whether of a chiefdom or a village, was reserved in principle for a 'warrior'; the *imam*, on the other hand, was naturally a 'scholar'.

The division of labor in Dyula society was more complicated than this neat division into 'warriors' and 'scholars' might imply. Not all *tun tigi* practiced warfare by any means, and some *mory* were completely illiterate in Arabic. Traders might belong to either group, although 'scholars' participated in trade somewhat more actively that did 'warriors'. These categories were applied to whole kin groups, and so took no account of deviant individuals, of a man like Samory, a 'scholar' who began life as a trader and finished as a warrior (Person 1968). (Samory's case was paralleled, on a far less spectacular scale, by his ally Sabati Cisse in Kadioha.) As an accurate description of Dyula society, this division into 'warriors' and 'scholars' was incomplete, if not downright unreliable. Nevertheless, it cannot be dismissed out of hand. It formed an integral part of the Dyula model of their own society, one which survived at least until the colonial period, despite apparent inconsistencies. According to the Dyula, 'warrior' and 'scholar' as ideal types are irreconcilable. On a concrete level, this was expressed by two different patterns of ritual observance, and two different systems of education, all coexisting within one community.

Aside from this two-fold division, the Dyula were also divided into a

26

much larger number of discrete groups. These were the 'clans' or 'patronymic groups' which the Dyula called *dyamu*. There were quite a number of them to be found among the Dyula; there were more than fifteen in Kadioha alone, and they far from exhausted the list. In a very general way, the Dyula associated certain *dyamus* with either 'warrior' or 'scholar' status. For example, Cisse, Toure and Saganogo were felt to be 'scholarly' names; Wattara, Coulibaly and Kone tended to be associated with 'warriors'. Exceptions to such generalizations were so common that it is impossible to draw any systematic conclusions. In and of itself, *dyamu* accounted for very little in Dyula social organization; it was the basis of a restricted number of ritual observances such as certain food prohibitions and joking relationships. At best, because these names were so widespread, they provided one link between the Dyula and other peoples of the West African savanna. But the real importance of these names was apparent at the village level. Precisely because there existed a large fund of such names, they could easily be used to distinguish groups within a given village. As such, they divided up the social universe more completely than the global categories of 'warrior' and 'scholar'. Most Dyula settlements consisted of a number of discrete kin groups; the number of such groups could be quite large, as in Kadioha and Koko. Within the village, each such group was identified by its *dyamu* – the Wattara, the Dambele and the Konate of Kadioha, for instance. The system was not entirely without inconvenience, since two or even more unrelated groups might share the same *dyamu*: precolonial Koko had three different groups named Fofana and four named Coulibaly (not counting the Senufo ruling family across the stream whose members also called themselves Coulibaly). However, in most cases, knowledge of an individual's *dyamu* and his village sufficed to identify the group to which he belonged.

Such kin groups, at the village level, tended to be the primary units of specialization. The categories of *mory* and *tun tigi* were applied to each of these local kin groups as a whole. Individual deviants did not affect the status of the whole group, though over a long period of time, it was possible for the group to change from one category to the other, either adopting or abandoning initiation society rituals. The complexity of the division of labor within a Dyula settlement depended, to a large extent, on the size and importance of the settlement. Dyula settlements located at the site of an important market, or at the capital of a chiefdom, were likely to develop more elaborate patterns of specialization. Such was the case for both Kadioha and Korhogo. An isolated Dyula settlement, on the other hand, depended more completely on its own agricultural production for subsistence, leaving the inhabitants less time to devote to trade, warfare or religious studies.

A typical Dyula settlement, whether it consisted of a whole village like

27

Kadioha, or, like Korhogo Koko, a quarter within a village also inhabited by Senufo, was organized around a number of these discrete kin groups. These groups were called *kabila*s, after the Arabic word *qabila*, or 'tribe' (Delafosse 1955:324). The nucleus of the *kabila* consisted of the agnatic male descendants of a common ancestor. In most cases, this ancestor was the founder of the *kabila*; sometimes, other agnates later joined the founder or his descendants. All these core members shared a single *dyamu*. Residing with these agnatic core members were most of their wives and their unmarried daughters. Some women, particularly old women past their menopause, resided in their *kabila* of origin even if they were married outside. A number of other individuals resided within the *kabila*. An important part of the *kabila* often consisted of slaves and their descendants, who adopted the *dyamu* of their masters. Finally, a certain number of strangers (*lunan*) might also be found associated with the *kabila*. Such strangers might be cognatic or affinal kinsmen of core agnates; on the other hand, they were sometimes only friends, or even total strangers who had chosen to reside in the village. The descendants of such 'strangers', if they became numerous enough, eventually formed a *kabila* of their own, gradually dissociating themselves from their hosts (*diatigi*). However, as long as they remained within the village, this relationship between 'strangers' and 'hosts' was preserved, and was one basis for the formation of political factions within the village.

The proportion of slaves found within any given *kabila* was highly variable, depending as it did on the *kabila*'s wealth or political power. Slaves (*jons*) were divided into two quite distinct categories: *san jons*, or slaves bought or captured; and *worossos*, slaves 'born in the compound', the descendants of bought or captured slaves. These two groups enjoyed very different statuses. Bought slaves could be resold at the discretion of their masters; *worossos* could not normally be alienated from the *kabila*. Early colonial reports from Ivory Coast state that a bought slave was obliged to work five mornings a week for his master; a *worosso* needed to work only two mornings a week, and even this obligation tended to lapse after the third generation. Although such statements need not be taken at face value, it is certain that the amount of work expected from *worossos* was minimal as compared with that expected from bought slaves. But even bought slaves had a right to the time and opportunity to work on their own behalf, and it was possible for them to amass their own personal property. There was even a specific term, *jon ma jon*, for the slave of a slave; such cases were by no means unknown. It is difficult to assess what proportion of the total population consisted of slaves, but Caillé's (1968, vol. 1:346) observation for northwestern Ivory Coast almost certainly held true for the Korhogo region: 'A Mandingo who has eight or ten slaves is reckoned rich.' Slaves were unquestionably an important element of production in the Dyula economy; but there were certainly no vast concentrations of slaves, bordering on *latifundiae*, as were reported in other regions of West Africa (see Fisher and Fisher 1970).

Thus the male population of the typical Dyula village or quarter consisted of the agnatic cores of the various *kabila*s, to which were attached, wives, slaves and strangers. These *kabila*s varied in size; a few were indeed very large, but most were quite small. For the most part, they were unsegmented, or very minimally so; divisions into maximal, major and minimal segments, as in some African lineage systems, were a relatively rare phenomenon. Similarly, *kabila*s varied in their degree of economic and social specialization. In some *kabila*s, warfare, trade or scholarship was the overriding preoccupation of the bulk of the population; in other cases, the adult males were more evenly divided among the three occupations. Nevertheless, the relatively small size of most *kabila*s, probably not consisting of many more than 150 members, many of them children, made them apt units of specialization within any given community. The division of the community into *mory* and *tun tigi kabila*s further underscored this tendency towards specialization.

Accordingly, political, and often religious, leadership of the community was vested within a given *kabila*. The office of chief (*mansa* for a chiefdom, *dugu tigi* for a village) was always vested in a single *tun tigi kabila*. The office of *imam* (*alimamy*) was more variable. This office was not necessarily devoid of political authority, though the incumbent could not impose any formal jural sanctions. It is significant that *alimamy* was the title chosen by the conqueror Samory; early colonial reports from the Korhogo region also stress that the *imam* was sometimes more influential in a Dyula village than the actual chief. These offices of chief and *imam* summarize the dual division of Dyula society. One was, *par excellence*, a 'warrior' office, the other a 'scholar' office, yet both assumed leadership over the entire community.

In short, several major divisions underlay precolonial Dyula society. First and foremost was the regional division between the Senufo majority and the Dyula minority. The Dyula were themselves globally divided into 'warriors' and 'scholars'. At the village level, each village was further subdivided into various *kabila*s, and further still into 'hosts' and 'strangers' and freemen and slaves. All of these divisions played a large part in the organization of warfare and politics, of religion and of trade before the advent of the colonial period.

Warfare and politics

The practice of warfare was intimately linked to local politics within the Korhogo region. It was no accident that the office of chief was traditionally reserved for a 'warrior' *kabila*. The Senufo chiefs controlled a powerful instrument – the *poro* society. The *poro* not only included elaborate rituals to reinforce the authority of elders over their juniors, but it also constituted an effective power base for Senufo chiefs over their Senufo subjects. But chiefs, whether they were Dyula or Senufo, did not benefit from such an advantage over the Dyula. Not all of the Dyula recognized the authority of the initiation societies; only 'warriors' participated in their proceedings, while 'scholars' formed the majority in many Dyula communities, including those of Koko and Kadioha. Ultimately, political power among the Dyula rested on the ability to mobilize a more effective military force. A Dyula chief wielded no effective supernatural sanction with which to back up the legitimacy of his authority.[3]

The practical importance of warfare did not remain constant throughout the whole precolonial history of the region. Unfortunately, the political history of the region is not very well known. Nevertheless, it is tentatively possible to break down the history of the Dyula within the region into three main periods. The first period, beginning with the arrival of the Dyula, was one of military expansion. Its apogee corresponded to the height of the power of the state of Kong, and it culminated in the formation of numbers of relatively small chiefdoms throughout the area. The second period, the one about which least is known, seems to have been one of relative stability, marked by occasional wars between chiefdoms or between factions within any one chiefdom. Finally, at the end of the nineteenth century, politics in the region was overshadowed by the presence of two large armies from outside. The first army, based in Sikasso, capital of the state of Kenedougou, not far to the north of Korhogo, was led by Babemba Traore. The second army was led by Babemba's enemy, Samory Toure, and changed its theatre of operations several times during the period in question.

The first period was undoubtedly the golden age of the *tun tigi*. The Dyula warriors, aided by the horse, did not meet with any considerable opposition. They created their own enclave centered on the state of Kong, driving out or assimilating the original inhabitants. An enterprising warrior setting out with a band of mounted followers could establish an independent chiefdom on the periphery of Kong's sphere of influence. However, in the immediate vicinity of Korhogo, Kadioha was the only such chiefdom whose rulers maintained their Dyula identity while exercising control over Senufo as well as Dyula subjects. According to oral traditions in Kadioha, this Dyula overrule was by no means immediately accepted, and the Senufo of the region combined in an attack to drive them out. This attack was thwarted, according to the Dyula, with the help of the Moslem *djinn*s who live on the hill which looms behind the site of the village of Kadioha. In any case, the Dyula retained military control over the chiefdom. Opportunities for military conquest, given a minimum of men and materials, were at a peak

Warriors, scholars and traders

during this period, and there is some evidence that certain 'scholar' groups shed their Moslem orthodoxy at that time in order to become 'warriors'.

Once the area had been divided up into a series of small chiefdoms, there was much less opportunity for military expansion. The fact that no very major trade route passed through the region, at least after the arrival of the Baoule to the south, meant that there was little incentive to create a powerful, centralized state to control trade. War, as an occupation, declined in importance. It is hard to assess the extent of local wars in the region during this period, as their memory has tended to be eclipsed by the later campaigns of Samory and Babemba. 'Scholars' who participated actively in military expansion during the first period turned their attention back to trade and scholarship.

The end of the nineteenth century, marked by the rise of two nearby empires just before the French conquest, saw a resurgence of military activity within the region. At first Korhogo was brought into the sphere of influence of the nearby state of Kenedougou, which also, according to Person (1975:1564), subjugated Kadioha in 1893. (However, certain Dyula informants in Kadioha denied that this was the case.) The influence of Kenedougou was almost immediately eclipsed by that of Samory. The chief of Korhogo, Gbon Coulibaly, wisely allied himself with the conqueror, and the chiefdom was turned into a reserve of grain and reinforcements for Samory's army. In Kadioha, the chief was deposed by one of Samory's lieutenants, and an ally of Samory, the 'scholar' Sabati Cisse, was put in his place. Resenting the exactions of Samory's lieutenants, the Senufo subjects of Kadioha and of certain neighboring chiefdoms rebelled. Samory's army and its allies in Kadioha suffered heavy initial setbacks, but the balance of power was ultimately in Samory's hands, and both his authority and that of the Dyula of Kadioha were restored by 1896 (Person 1975:1746–7). French colonial rule succeeded too soon afterwards for the transformation to have had very lasting effects, but the sudden shift in the balance of power in the region was certainly beginning to make changes in Dyula society. The accession of a 'scholar', rather that a 'warrior', to chiefly office in Kadioha was certainly a sign of such change.

Throughout the three periods, warfare was not exclusively a political activity. Military or quasi-military activity could be deployed for purely personal gains, either through slave raiding or brigandage. Neither activity reached the pitch that was found in certain other parts of West Africa. Slave raids were not easily carried off between chiefdoms within the Korhogo region, as no chiefdom was large enough to overwhelm its neighbors. Occasional alliances between chiefdoms for the purpose of war certainly occurred from time to time, giving one side a temporary advantage, and the prospect of acquiring slaves during such a campaign was a strong incentive to join in. But systematic slave raiding cannot have been very practicable

31

until the arrival of Samory's and Babemba's armies, when Dyula from the region could join up with larger forces.

Brigandage – the looting of caravans or individual traders passing through the region – cannot have been too common either. The inhabitants of the region were themselves the principal users of the major trade route, and such brigandage was not usually carried out against one's neighbors. Brigandage was more widespread in Kadioha than in Korhogo, because Kadioha was closer to the source of cola nuts and therefore saw more through traffic. The principal victims were stragglers from caravans, whose goods were seized and who were subsequently sold as slaves. But brigandage was against the interests of traders, who profited from caravans passing through. Such brigandage could not have occurred on too large a scale, or caravans would simply have avoided the area. Thus the opportunities for exercising the warrior's profession, either by slave raiding or brigandage, were limited.[4]

Dyula military activity differed substantially in Kadioha, which had a Dyula chief, from that in Korhogo, which had a Senufo chief. Because they were independent, the Dyula of Kadioha were much freer to indulge in warfare. Moreover, the Dyula of Kadioha were faced with conflicts which pitted them against their own Senufo subjects, both in the early history of the chiefdom and during Samory's wars. The Dyula of Korhogo, on the other hand, were consistently allied with their Senufo chiefs, backing them on at least two occasions against fellow Dyula. All in all, the Dyula of Koko quarter contented themselves with a subordinate military role, which permitted them to live on good terms with their Senufo neighbors. The Dyula of Kadioha, on the other hand, enjoyed a completely dominant role; the price which they had to pay was the constant threat of armed resistance on the part of their Senufo subjects.

The balance of power within the village was particularly crucial in Kadioha, where the Dyula were in control of the chiefdom. In theory, this balance was regulated by the global division into the categories of 'warrior' and 'scholar'. Political and military power were supposedly concentrated in the hands of groups specialized in the arts of war. The history of Kadioha shows that, as usual, reality is more complicated than any simple model. Individual 'scholars' as well as whole 'scholar' groups sometimes took an active hand in either war or politics.

Dyula politics was marked by the division of a Dyula settlement into a number of discrete *kabila*s. In principle, all of these groups owed allegiance to the chief. In practice, each might attempt to assert its own independence, and even to assume political leadership over the whole village or chiefdom. The Dyula suffered from a definite lack of cohesiveness. In Kadioha, it was difficult for any one faction – including that of the chief – to gain a lasting advantage over rival factions within the village. Such enduring and usually unresolved rivalry within the village seriously impeded its military potential outside the village; the chief could not always count on other *kabila*s for support.

This problem of recruitment of support was fundamental in Dyula politics. Initiation societies provided a partial answer to the problem; this is certainly why they were the characteristic mark of 'warrior' groups. First of all, these societies inculcated a strong feeling of solidarity among all youths initiated at a single time. The whole process of initiation was long – no less than seven years – during which such solidarity was certain to develop. More importantly, all informants stressed that the guiding principle of the initiation societies was the systematic subordination of youths to their elders. Such subordination was absolutely necessary if the elders were to make all the decisions about sending the young men off to war. Clearly, an initiation society was a most useful tool for mobilizing warriors. Nonetheless, its usefulness was seriously hampered by the fact that a Dyula village or quarter might have not one, but several different and independent initiation societies. Kadioha and Koko each had no less than three. The fact is all the more striking because the majority in both Dyula communities were 'scholars', who did not participate at all in initiation society ritual. An initiation society might be associated with a single *kabila*, or on the other hand a group of *kabila*s, never more than three or four together. These societies reinforced the authority of 'warrior' elders over the youths of their own group, but not over those of other *kabila*s within the village.

There existed substantial differences in the power and influence of various *kabila*s within the village. A few, the chief's *kabila* among them, were in a relatively prominent position. Much of local politics consisted of factional rivalry between these few *kabila*s which competed amongst themselves for the support of the other *kabila*s in the village. Though the chief's *kabila* was, in principle, *tun tigi*, leaders of other factions could well be *mory kabila*s. This was the case in Kadioha, where the principle rivals of the chief's *kabila* were at various times the Suware and the Cisse, both 'scholar' groups. One means of recruiting support outside the *kabila* was the recruitment of 'strangers'. If initiation societies gave 'warrior' groups a more effective control over their own members, they were not necessarily better placed to attract clients from outside.

There existed yet a third means of recruiting an army – slaves. A rich man could buy slaves and, if necessary, equip them with horses and even guns. For this reason, a rich trader was always a potential political leader, and a possible rival to the chief. There is evidence that 'scholar' *kabila*s, whose free members did not always participate actively in battle, often sent contingents of slaves to fight on their behalf. In such cases, *worossos*, slaves 'born in the compound', were of substantial strategic importance. Such slaves, although they furnished relatively little work for their individual masters, were readily available as soldiers in the interest of the *kabila* as a whole. A rich *kabila*, whether of 'warrior' or 'scholar' status, possessed a greater number of bought slaves as well as of *worossos*, and all of these could be mobilized as warriors on behalf of the whole group.

Thus, certain *kabila*s were relatively specialized in war and politics. The division of the Dyula into 'warriors' and 'scholars' was only one factor in establishing this specialization. The presence or absence of outside military forces, whether these were of local Senufo or from outside the region, either enhanced or inhibited such specialization. The sheer size of a *kabila* was of no negligible importance, as was its wealth. Successful traders attracted 'guests', political clients of the *kabila*, and they also purchased slaves who added to the numbers of the descent group. The system of specialization that emerged was highly flexible, and depended on a host of particular circumstances; the accession of a 'scholar' to the office of chief in Kadioha at the end of the nineteenth century showed to what extent the system was liable to change. In spite of these changes, localized descent groups, the *kabila*s, never ceased to be the primary units of political and military power among the Dyula.

Scholarship

The Dyula, whether 'warriors' or 'scholars', all considered themselves Moslems (*silama*). Before the colonial period, adherence to Islam was probably the single factor that most clearly distinguished all the Dyula, as an ethnic category, from their immediate neighbors. The continued practice of Islam requires the presence of at least some men literate in Arabic. Moslem ritual requires the recitation of texts word for word in the original Arabic. The ordinary believer does not have to read, much less understand, Arabic. (The Dyula invariably learn to read Arabic – that is to say, to reproduce accurately the sound of any written word – before they learn the meaning of the individual words they recite.) But even the most ignorant of Moslems must be able to recite by rote those Suras and prayers which form an essential part of daily worship. These prayers in a foreign language could never be remembered, word for word, without the help of written texts, and of men capable of reading them.

Islam also has an extensive legal tradition. All human acts fall into one of five categories: essential duties, meritorious actions whose neglect is not punishable, indifferent actions, actions disapproved of but not forbidden and finally, forbidden actions (Levy 1962:202–3). Orthodox Moslems need to know which actions are essential and which actions are forbidden. This knowledge is contained within the Koran and the *hadith*s (tradition relating to the life of the Prophet Mohammed) and is systematically exposed and interpreted in the works of Moslem jurists. The term 'law' is

34

perhaps a misleading label for these various injunctions. A great deal of Moslem law, and certainly that part which was most rigorously applied by the Dyula *mory*, if not by the *tun tigi*, is exclusively concerned with the proper means of performing ritual. The proper performance of a wide variety of rituals depends on the knowledge of this corpus of Islamic law. Islam was the dominant ideology of traders in most of the West African savanna. The Dyula, in constant rapport with traders from other regions, needed to conform reasonably strictly to a pattern of ritual practice which transcended regional boundaries. Thus Dyula society required men who could not only recite, but also understand, Arabic, and who could thus interpret Moslem tradition to the rest of the community.

The dependence of orthodox Islam on trade meant that not all Dyula were equally concerned by its continued practice. Warriors, farmers and even petty traders who made their living by selling locally-produced goods to nearby Senufo, were less dependent on Islam than were the more important traders, whose business interests extended outside the region. Moreover, only a wealthy community could afford to maintain numbers of scholars who did not directly contribute to its subsistence. For both of these reasons, the most important centers of Islamic learning were also the most important centers of trade. Kong, the greatest of the Dyula trading towns had also the greatest tradition of scholarship. Elsewhere in Ivory Coast, the most learned scholars were often found in the towns which occupied a commanding position in the cola trade, near the edge of the forests. Bondoukou to the east and Sakhala and nearby Mankono to the west were all known for the excellence of their scholars.

The Korhogo region, bypassed by the most important long-distance trade routes, had a less flourishing tradition of scholarship. Nor were scholars evenly distributed among the Dyula communities of the region. French scholars and administrators showed an early interest in Islam in their African territories, partly because they feared that Islam might develop into an ideology of resistance to colonial rule. In their compilations, they identified the major centers of Islamic learning in the Korhogo region. Marty (1922:172–87) singled out in particular the Koko quarter of Korhogo as well as Kadioha. Of slightly less importance, Marty noted the village of Kapele, only 7 km outside Korhogo. His findings were confirmed by an administrative survey of Islam scholars carried out in 1931. Of forty-seven scholars listed in the Korhogo district, twelve were in Korhogo, nine in Kadioha and seven in Kapele; two other villages each had three scholars, one had two scholars and eleven villages each had a single scholar. Within the region, Islamic scholarship was concentrated very clearly in Kadioha, and in and on the outskirts of Korhogo. Still, the scholars of Korhogo and Kadioha were of importance only within the region; they were well aware of their limitations compared to the scholars of Kong, Bondoukou and

Mankono in Ivory Coast, or of Djenne and Segou on the Niger River.

Becoming a scholar of even local importance was a long and arduous process. It required years and years of study, especially as learning was not usually a full-time occupation. Young *mory* boys, and occasionally girls, commenced their education at the age of seven. First of all, they were taught the prayers and passages from the Koran that were necessary for daily worship; every Dyula had to learn at least this much, and in principle every adult was capable of teaching it. The next stage was the *kurana taran*, which consisted of memorizing the shorter Suras of the Koran. Girls were rarely taught beyond this stage; as far as the education of women was concerned, the Dyula were far less egalitarian than certain other West African Moslems (see Hiskett 1973:26). Much more important was the *kurana dyigi*, literally 'putting down the Koran'. This meant learning the whole of the Koran by heart. Many *mory* boys never got beyond this stage, which assured that they were capable of reciting accurately from a written text. Normally, it took three or four years of study before a boy 'put down the Koran' for the first time. Those who continued repeated this process, starting the Koran at the beginning again. They went through the Koran at least three, and as many as seven, times, each time picking up more and more of the meaning as they went along. These subsequent readings of the Koran took less time than the initial reading, but it was at least seven years before the student went on to other books. Once he had reached this stage, the student was relatively advanced and he proceeded at his own pace. The culmination of the student's career was the awarding of the turban (*dyalala*). Once awarded the turban, he became a scholar (*karamoko*) in his own right, with the right to train future scholars. The turban was rarely awarded to a man before middle age. On the other hand, pious old men and even women might be awarded the turban even with a mediocre level of scholarship, granted that they were not going to teach advanced students.

The *karamoko*s were ultimately responsible for the whole Dyula system of religious education. Any adult Dyula, or at least any *mory*, ought to have been capable of teaching a child the basic prayers and passages of the Koran. Very often, a *mory* father would begin the instruction of his own, and sometimes his brothers', children. Any man who had 'put down the Koran' several times was capable of teaching a child at least up to the first *kurana dyigi*. In a small *kabila*, one old man might assume the responsibility of teaching all the children of the *kabila*. There were also larger Koranic schools, where the master would teach children from other *kabila*s, and often from other villages. The master of such a school was often, but not necessarily, a *karamoko*; an advanced student, even if he did not have the turban, might ensure the running of such a school, and a learned scholar would in any case leave much of the business of teaching young children to his older pupils. The criterion of the turban is somewhat deceptive. It was awarded in preference to old men, and only to younger and even middle-aged men who were particularly brilliant students fully capable of teaching adults. As far as the education of children went, a younger teacher without a turban was often more learned than an older turbaned one, who may only have turned to scholarship as a major activity in his retirement from trade. Finally, at the top of the hierarchy were the important *karamokos*, those fully capable of teaching adults; within the Korhogo region, scholars possessing such qualifications were always few in number; advanced students sometimes left the region in search of a suitable master.

Teaching was not the only responsibility of the *karamokos*. They also presided over religious ceremonies, not only the rituals of the yearly and weekly calendar, but also life-crisis rituals, particularly funerals. One of their number, the *imam*, led the Friday prayer. Some *kabilas* also possessed daily mosques, in which all prayers were recited except at midday on Fridays; each daily mosque also had its *imam*, although the role was of considerably less importance. At no time did the Dyula ever have Moslem tribunals or judges (*qadis*) with authority to decide questions of Moslem law; disputes that could not be settled by common agreement among parties were always taken to the chief's court. But the scholars commanded considerable moral authority, and they were responsible for maintaining the principles of Moslem law within the community.

Education and the maintenance of Moslem law were not the only and certainly not the most remunerative activities of scholars. The activities of scholars fell into two distinct categories; *bayani karamokoya* was, in effect, the practice and interpretation of the Koran and Moslem law; *siri karamokoya*, on the other hand, consisted of divination, the manufacture of written charms and the like. (In Dyula, the word *siri* means 'to tie in a bundle', and refers here to the practice of sewing up written amulets to be worn by the user.) Divination was certainly not the monopoly of the literate, and anyone could become a diviner. The Dyula felt absolutely no qualms about consulting Senufo diviners. Conversely, the Senufo were an important market for the goods and services of Dyula scholars. The importance of scholars as diviners stemmed mainly from the fact that they could consult written manuals (see J. R. Goody 1968). Scholars also profited from the custom of giving *saraka* or 'alms'. All scholars practiced both *bayani* and *siri karamokoya*, theology and 'magic'. Nevertheless, individual scholars tended to specialize in one or the other, and a reputation in one field did not necessarily imply a reputation in the other. *Bayani karamokoya* was more 'respectable', and its practitioner relied on his reputation for piety and learning in the hope that these would attract him much 'alms'. The practitioner of *siri karamokoya*, on the other hand, subsisted on the outright sale of goods and services to his clients, many of whom were Senufo.

The legacy of the past

To the extent that scholars relied directly upon alms, or on the sale of goods and services, there was a limit to the number of scholars that a given community could support. There were, however, a number of other alternatives. Teaching, in and of itself, was not a remunerative activity. However, in certain cases, a teacher could profit from the labor of his students. This did not apply to children from the scholar's own *kabila*, perhaps not even to those from his own village, but primarily to students from abroad, who lodged and ate with their teacher. As Marty (1922:268) estimated that 60% of pupils were the teacher's own close kin, and another 20% distant kin or co-villagers, most scholars were unlikely to benefit from such an arrangement. Slaves might be given directly to the scholar as a form of 'alms'. Scholars could also invest what money they received in 'alms' or in payment for services by purchasing slaves. The labor, either of slaves or of his own pupils, freed a scholar from the obligation to work directly for his own subsistence, leaving him more time to devote exclusively to study.

Finally, a scholar might be supported, in whole or in part, by his own family. He might rely on younger brothers, grown sons or even nephews for subsistence.[5] But often this reliance on kinsmen, and especially on one's own grown sons, meant that only an old man could devote himself fully to the pursuit of learning. Such a system was amply sufficient to provide for the education of children within the *kabila*. They could easily be entrusted to an old man who had already retired from active life and who did not have to be a first- (or even a second-)rate scholar. However, such a system was grossly inadequate to provide education at a more advanced level; advanced students could only be taught by a man who had devoted most, if not all, of his active life to scholarship. The number of such men was rather severely limited by the resources available to the Dyula community.

Because of this limitation, scholarship, like warfare, was the specialization of a limited number of *kabila*s. A high proportion of men pursued their studies at an advanced level in only a few *kabila*s even among the *mory*. In Koko, these were the Diane and the Fofana; in Kadioha, they were the Haidara (*sharif*) and, to a lesser extent, the Saganogo and the junior branch of the Cisse. Perhaps the greatest of all specialized scholar *kabila*s was the Saganogo *kabila* of Kong (Wilks 1968:181–6). Such specialization entailed a particularly high degree of solidarity among the members of the *kabila*, as it required that much of the wealth of the group as a whole be channeled into the education of its members. Members of these *kabila*s rarely participated extensively, if at all, in long-distance trading. Such trading activity prevented individuals from devoting much time to study, and trading ventures could also constitute a considerable drain on the capital of the *kabila*. It was often necessary for members of specialized scholar *kabila*s to spend part of their lives earning money in another sector of activity such as petty trade or weaving. Such activities were less

38

profitable, but they left the younger men more time for learning. Even in the most specialized *kabila*s, full-time scholarship was often possible only for older men.

Trade

Long-distance trade in West Africa usually conjures up the notion of huge caravans crossing vast expanses of territory to peddle their wares. Such a romantic picture characterizes rather inadequately the Korhogo region in the nineteenth century. Large caravans were undoubtedly a common sight in the great trading towns such as Kong, Bouna, Bondoukou and Salaga, and along the principal routes that led to these towns. But the Korhogo region was not very centrally located with respect to the major routes, though it would be wrong to think that large caravans never passed through at all; indeed, the Dyula of the region participated in, and even dispatched, such caravans when they had the opportunity. Of course, it was always unsafe to travel alone even without merchandise or over a relatively short distance; one could always be sold as a slave by brigands waiting along the road, a by no means negligible risk. Insofar as traders preferred to travel in large numbers (at least ten or twelve), caravans of one sort or another were always the rule, both in the Korhogo region and elsewhere.

But these caravans were not necessarily major expeditions prepared to march for months on end before they reached their ultimate destination. In fact much, if not most, of the Dyula trade in the region was not long-distance trade at all. The bulk of the trade was concerned with goods produced, sold and consumed within the region. In large measure, the Dyula subsisted by producing for, and selling to, their Senufo neighbors. All sectors of Dyula society, 'warriors' and 'scholars' alike, participated in this purely local trade, though not to the same extent. For some, trade was indeed a full-time occupation. For others, trade alone was insufficient to procure subsistence. Individual Dyula tended to avoid the cultivation of staple crops for subsistence whenever possible, but it was not always possible. The hubs of Dyula social and economic life were the large centers such as Korhogo and Kadioha; in these villages, relatively few free Dyula cultivated staple crops extensively. In more isolated villages, where the Dyula had less access to a market for their wares, households had to grow most of their own food themselves. For such Dyula, trade was essentially a dry-season activity. Finally, in the larger centers, individual Dyula as well as whole *kabila*s preferred to devote their energies to warfare and scholarship rather than trade. However, it was not always possible to practice warfare, and the resources of the community limited the opportunities for engaging in full-time scholarship; in such cases, the individuals concerned had to fall back either on trade or farming for subsistence.

39

The legacy of the past

Another factor which determined the extent to which an individual might participate in trade (as well as scholarship) was slavery. An individual Dyula household had to rely on one of three means for procuring its own food. First, its free members could produce the food themselves, a solution which the Dyula preferred to avoid because it limited participation in the more prestigious activities of warfare, trade and scholarship to the dry season. Second, it could buy food from the neighboring Senufo; the Korhogo region was rich, from the agricultural point of view, and this kind of exchange was (and remains) very common. The disadvantage was that a large proportion, if not all, of the proceeds from trade had to be converted into food, preventing the household or individual from accumulating a large trading capital. Finally, the household could rely on slaves to produce its food. This was the ideal solution, but (like so many ideal solutions) was only open to those who could afford it. The production of food by slaves was organized in two ways. Slaves might live within the household, in which case they were expected to devote much of their working time to tilling their masters' fields. Such villages were entirely devoted to agriculture, and they periodically yielded a part of their crop to their masters. But there do not seem to have been very many such slave villages in the region except in the relatively brief period of Samory's campaigns. The fact that slaves 'born in the compound' did not have to work a great deal for their masters meant that the Dyula had to rely on bought or captured slaves.[6] If a household relied on slaves for the production of food, it had continually to procure a fresh supply.

Dyula trade depended both on the slaves and on the Senufo. Slaves were necessary for the production of foodstuffs; the Senufo were at the same time a market for Dyula goods, and a source of food in exchange for these goods. But the Dyula traders of the region, situated as they were off the major trade routes, could not rely exclusively on long-distance trade to procure goods for exchange. They had to produce such goods themselves, and most Dyula trading activity was concerned, not with buying items cheaply in one place and selling them dear in another, but with the production of goods for the local market, mainly tobacco and woven cotton cloths.

Initially, tobacco was probably a Dyula monopoly. If so, the Dyula did not retain this monopoly, but the Senufo did not produce enough to meet their own demands, and tobacco continued to be an item of the local Dyula trade. Most of this tobacco was made into snuff (*sara mugu*)[7] by Dyula women who pounded it in a mortar. Ground tobacco was mixed with a certain quantity of fat, probably shea butter. This was a delicate operation; if not properly performed, the mixture was ruined. Not all Dyula women were familiar with the techniques of snuff production, so the operation was in the hands of certain specialists. Growing the plants, on the other hand, was straightforward. Nor did tobacco cultivation require large fields; it was

40

often grown within the village in small plots adjacent to the compound. The Dyula grew two crops each year, one in the rainy season and one in the dry season. The latter crop required much more labor as the plants had to be artificially watered from wells or, more likely, from nearby streams. On the other hand, the dry-season crop was considered to be of superior quality, and undoubtedly yielded a higher price on the market.

The tobacco trade was ideally suited to the man who owned a few slaves. During the dry season, slaves could be relied on for the somewhat unpleasant job of watering the crops. Finally, when the crop was ready, the slaves were sent off to nearby market places to sell it. In short, slaves could do everything except, possibly, manufacture snuff. It was not uncommon for a small slave owner to move out into a Senufo village where he could sell directly to consumers. For the small slave owner, the tobacco trade offered two advantages; it required few special skills, and it involved few risks.

Much more important than tobacco, indeed the most important of all the Dyula trade goods by far, was cotton cloth. The Dyula participated massively in the weaving industry, and even today weaving is a major economic activity in Kadioha as well as in the Dyula villages on the outskirts of Korhogo. The weaving industry is virtually a symbol of the symbiosis of Dyula and Senufo in the region. The cotton was purchased from the Senufo, or grown by slaves. Weaving, on the other hand, was an exclusively Dyula occupation; only recently have a few Senufo taken it up. The surest means of identifying a Dyula village or quarter is still by its looms, situated in the shade provided by the trees in the village. As elsewhere in Africa, the cloth was woven in narrow bands which could easily be sewn together into an article of clothing or a rectangular blanket (see Johnson 1972). The time required to complete a single blanket depended on the intricacy of the woven pattern. An efficient weaver could finish a plain white blanket in one or two days, but a blanket with an elaborate design might take four or five days, if not more. Among the Senufo, such blankets were an important indication of wealth. The cloths were rarely worn – in general, the Senufo went almost naked – except as part of the costumes of secret society masks. The major use to which the cloths were put was in funeral ceremonies. Not only was the corpse wrapped in a shroud, but quantities of cloths were buried along with it. The number of these cloths varied with the rank of the deceased. Considerable quantities were buried with an elder, and even more with an important chief. More than thirty or forty cloths might be destroyed on such an occasion (Vendeix 1934:625). Thus the Senufo depended on Dyula production for an important part of their ritual and ranking systems; in turn, the Dyula depended heavily on the Senufo, both as food producers and as a market for cloths.

The production and commercialization of woven cloth differed significantly from the production of tobacco. If tobacco was ideally suited to cultivation by slaves, weaving was by and large a freeman's activity. The Dyula held that bought or captured slaves were too old to learn properly the technique of weaving; slaves 'born in the compound' could, of course learn these techniques, but the cloths they wove were sold for their own use, and not for their masters' benefit. This assertion conflicts with the reports of explorers who visited other Manding-speaking West African peoples. Park (1954:216) says of the Mandingo: 'As the arts of weaving, dyeing, sewing, etc., may easily be acquired, those who exercise them are not considered in Africa as following any particular profession, for *almost every slave can weave*, and every boy can sew' [my italics]. As nearby as Kong, Binger (1892:199) recorded the use of slaves in the weaving as well as in the dyeing of cotton cloth. If the Dyula weaving industry was not based on slave labor, we must look elsewhere than at any question of mere technical competence for the underlying reason. The answer may lie precisely in the fact that the Dyula of the region, located off major trade routes, depended much more heavily on weaving as a primary source of their wealth than did Manding traders elsewhere; Person (1968:120) stresses that weaving was 'le fondement de la domination économique des commerçants allogènes en pays Sénoufo.' Had the Dyula used slaves to augment the production of woven cloth, they would probably have flooded the market and seen the price of cloth diminish. It was more profitable for the Dyula to use their slaves to produce food, thus limiting their dependence on Senufo food production and permitting them to invest the profits from weaving in other forms of trade. By limiting the production of cloth to free Dyula and to slaves 'born in the compound', they were assured of a higher margin of profit. But the exclusion of bought slaves had important consequences for the organization of production in the weaving industry and the accompanying trade. In the tobacco trade, a trader could accumulate wealth by controlling the fruits of the labor of his slaves. In the weaving industry, this was only partly true, to the extent that slaves produced cotton and reduced the volume of the household's expenditure on subsistence crops. For the weaving itself, the trader had to rely on the labor of kinsmen, not on that of slaves.

The importance of controlling the output of several weavers becomes apparent when we consider the actual trade in blankets. Blankets for sale were usually transported by human porters. According to informants, a single porter could carry up to fifty blankets on his head; old men in Korhogo and Kadioha still remember having carried such loads. Obviously, such travel was slow, and the trader had to pay for food, lodging, etc. along the way. Binger (1892:313) estimated that such travel expenses might amount to as much as one-fourth of the total value of the merchandise. Consequently, it was not in a trader's interest to set out with less than a full load for each porter; otherwise, the 'overhead' costs of the journey would reduce the margin of profit on each blanket. In other words, it was only profitable to set out on a trading expedition once he had accumulated a sizable number of blankets. He could, of course, buy blankets from other weavers in the village or neighboring villages; this was quite a common practice, but required substantial initial capital. It was difficult for a weaver working alone to accumulate the requisite number of blankets. He had to provide food for the household, and he could only do this by growing it himself – but in this case, during much of the year he had no free time to weave – or by selling some of his blankets to other traders and using the proceeds to buy food in the market. If a trader could dispose of blankets woven by other members of his household, he could acquire the minimum number of blankets necessary for a single venture much sooner.

A number of kinsmen often pooled their resources in a single budget, under the control of the eldest among them. The most common units consisted of a father and his sons, or of several brothers under the leadership of the senior brother. This pooling of resources enabled the entire unit to amass a greater capital, whether in money or in blankets, which could be invested productively in the purchase of slaves, or in trading ventures. (Such capital could also be diverted to the training of scholars.) The most stable of these groups consisted of a father and his sons, and often lasted until the father's death. In a unit consisting of several brothers, or of an uncle and his nephew(s), junior members were much more likely to secede. The system conflicted, to a certain extent, with Moslem rules of inheritance whereby all brothers receive an equal share and sisters receive half the amount allotted to each brother. Any division of wealth at the father's death hindered the prospects for trade, which depended upon the accumulation of capital. Actual practice was something of a compromise: the entire capital, or part of it, was entrusted to a junior uncle or senior brother who continued to benefit for the time being from the labor of the individual heirs. Each heir, once he was married, and often not until he had a few children, would then receive his initial inheritance, and perhaps somewhat more, permitting him to go into trade for his own benefit. Moreover, many males married quite late in life, after thirty and sometimes even as late as forty. In the meantime, their labor was an important source of profit to one kinsman or another. It was in the interest of senior kinsmen to keep their juniors in a state of dependence as long as possible; on the other hand, junior kinsmen wanted to set themselves up independently. Thus the accumulation of capital in the weaving trade was linked to the exercise of authority within the joint family.

We have looked at the cloth trade only from the point of view of Dyula men, who were the weavers. But Dyula women also participated in the trade, in the preparation of the cloth. Two activities in particular were reserved for women: the carding and spinning of cotton into thread on the

43

one hand, and the collection of wild indigo and the dyeing of threads on the other. Meillassoux (1975:249–50) has estimated that one man could weave in a single day what it required six to eight women to spin. Women disposed entirely of the profits from such trade, and were free to use such profits to buy their own slaves. Slaves so acquired could also be put to work spinning or dyeing for their mistresses. Some women acquired a considerable capital in this way, and certain among them where richer than their husbands. The division of spheres of the economy into male and female did not prevent women from becoming successful traders.

The most prestigious branch of trade was still the long-distance trade. The staple commodities of the trade were cola and salt. The cola was bought in the southwest, primarily in Boron and Sakhala. The traders in these and neighboring towns bought cola directly from the Gouro on the fringes of the forest zone.[8] The Dyula sold the cola north of the region, in Sikasso and in other trading towns of modern Mali. In these towns, they bought bars of rock salt from the Sahara, which they sold in turn in the south for more cola nuts. A certain proportion of the cola nuts and salt was also sold for consumption within the Korhogo region itself. Horses (for warfare) and donkeys (as pack animals) were also purchased in the northern towns. The slave trade never seems to have been a mainstay of the region, and the direction of trade does not seem to have been consistent. Slaves were exported and imported, or traded to the north or to the south, depending on fluctuations in the supply and demand. A number of locally-produced items, mainly a variety of condiments, were also included in the long-distance trade. These were red peppers and ginger, and possibly shea butter and the seeds of the *nere* tree, which are used to enhance the flavor of sauces. Finally, certain cocoons (*tumbu forogo*) were collected around Korhogo – not, apparently, in Kadioha – and exported to Kong, and from there to Upper Volta, to be woven into a silk cloth of considerable value.

Any participation in the long-distance trade – except possibly the collection of cocoons – required the accumulation of an initial capital which must have been considerable. The fact that the region was off the major trade routes meant that the local Dyula could not establish a profitable position as 'landlords'.[9] This was less true in the southwest of the region, nearer the source of cola nuts. Boron in particular was a relatively important cola market. Kadioha, to the north of Boron, also had a few such 'landlords', but they catered only to the smallest-scale traders of the region who could not afford to travel further south. In Korhogo, 'landlords' made their appearance only in the twentieth century, with the development of the grain trade. For the most part, long-distance trade was limited to those who set off on expeditions or who could afford to send others off on their behalf.

In general, the starting capital necessary to participate in long-distance trade ventures had to be accumulated from the profits of one or other of the

44

local trades – tobacco, weaving or one of the women's trades (for indeed, some women were wealthy enough to invest in such expeditions). There were, of course, exceptions. Scholars, particularly if they enjoyed the patronage of an important chief, might receive enough gifts to engage in trade; this was the case of Sory Cisse, founder of the Cisse *kabila* in Korhogo. But ultimately, the cloth trade with the Senufo was the major source of income for the Dyula of the region, and only those profits which could be spared were channeled into long-distance ventures. The long-distance trader also required the labor of other individuals, whether slaves or junior kinsmen. Very often, the man who actually financed the venture did not set off on the expedition; the money was entrusted to a junior kinsman, or even to a slave, who handed over the profits on his return. The trader himself was free to devote his time to other activities, such as scholarship. The junior kinsman or slave in charge usually pocketed a certain portion of the profits, and was able to trade to a certain extent on his own behalf. A junior kinsman could thus accumulate a certain capital of his own which eventually allowed him to set himself up independently. A slave was also allowed to accumulate his personal capital, and could even invest in slaves himself. An important trader would require numbers of slaves to send off on expeditions as porters; the most important among them could send off whole caravans on their own, but most traders – even long-distance traders – could only rely on a few slaves. Accordingly, the small traders, who formed the overwhelming majority, contented themselves with shuttling goods between relatively nearby markets. Traders from Korhogo carried cola and salt back and forth between Boron, three days' journey to the southwest, and Sikasso, nine days' journey to the north. Traders from Kadioha went farther south than those from Korhogo, mainly to Sakhala, but they sold a larger proportion of cola to other traders within the region, rather than traveling all the way north to Sikasso.

Thus all trade in the region depended on the ability of individual traders to exploit the labor of others – either slaves or close kinsmen, and usually both – in order to accumulate the necessary capital to invest in any trading venture. Junior kinsmen, primarily sons and younger brothers, might either weave or act as porters and agents in the trade. The primary role of slaves was to cultivate foodstuffs, thus reducing the trader's dependence on proceeds from trade for subsistence, but slaves were also used to cultivate cotton for weaving and tobacco for sale, and as porters and even responsible agents in trading ventures. The labor of junior kinsmen was, in a certain sense, even more fundamental than the labor of slaves; only by exploiting the labor of kinsmen could a trader normally accumulate enough profits to invest in the purchase of slaves. Of course, the pattern varied in individual circumstances, and so a junior kinsman in the service of a particularly successful trader might accumulate enough capital on the side to set himself up in trade in his own right. There were, however, important limitations on the extent to which an individual could exploit the labor of others. First of all, *worossos*, slaves 'born in the compound', did not have to perform much work for their masters, and so the reliance on slave labor required the continual replenishment of the stock of bought or captured slaves. Also, junior kinsmen were perpetually seceding from the authority of their seniors, particularly after the death of the father. To a certain extent, the secession of younger brothers was compensated by the fact that a trader could increasingly depend on his own sons. Moslem laws of inheritance, on the other hand, which required that property be passed from father to child, and not from senior to junior brother, and further stipulated that each son receive an equal portion, was certainly a spur to the segmentation of the unit of production. As a result of these factors, accumulated fortunes often disappeared soon after the death of their owners; great trading dynasties were totally unknown in the region.

To the extent that traders relied on the labor of their junior kinsmen, warfare and scholarship were competing activities: sons, brothers or nephews engaged in one or other of these activities detracted from the size of the work force available to serve the interests of a senior kinsman who was a trader, and might even, in the case of scholars, be a drain on his capital. This is why scholarship was often the preserve of older men. An established trader could become a scholar, relying on junior kinsmen and slaves to keep up his business. This is also why *kabila*s specializing either in warfare or in scholarship, although they engaged in trade, did not assume a leading position in trading activities. For example, the young men of a 'scholar' *kabila* were often engaged in weaving, but, rather than devote their attentions to expanding the scale of their enterprise, they would be likely to sell their blankets to other traders and not engage in trading ventures themselves. On the whole, long-distance trade, like warfare and scholarship, also tended to be a speciality of certain *kabila*s. These were usually *mory*, or 'scholar', *kabila*s, but only a small proportion of their members, particularly old men, ever became advanced scholars.

For a *kabila* to assume a dominant position either in warfare, or in trade, or in scholarship, its younger men had to be devoted, in the majority, to one or other of these activities. A 'warrior' *kabila* depended on its young men as a military force. A 'scholar' *kabila* needed to deploy its resources towards the advanced training of its younger members, rather than accumulate capital. Finally, a trading *kabila* needed the labor of younger members in order that senior members might accumulate sufficient profits to invest in larger-scale trading ventures. Exceptionally, an inordinately large *kabila*, like the Cisse of Kadioha, might successfully devote its attention to all three spheres of activity. Even in this case, the senior branch was specialized in trade, the middle branch in politics and the junior branch in scholarship, and each one of these branches was as large, if not larger, than most other *kabila*s in the village. Even though the basic unit of production was the joint family and its slaves, and not the *kabila* as a whole, many *kabila*s tended to specialize in one particular sphere of activity. Small wonder that the social, as well as the economic and political, life of the Dyula hinged particularly around the *kabila*.

4

Clansmen and kinsmen

The 'kabila'

Anyone who spends a short time in a Dyula village or quarter cannot fail to notice that it is divided up into *kabila*s, or descent groups. Cissera (the Cisse quarter), Coulibaly-ra, Bakayoko-ra and so forth exist not only as social units, but as separate residential areas that can be plotted on a map. There are no physical boundaries between these quarters, and one runs right into its neighbor; but generally speaking, each descent group corresponds to a space within the village. A man's occupation, his religious practices, his political allegiance and his relationships with unrelated persons within his own village were all, until relatively recently, affected, though not absolutely determined, by his membership in a given *kabila*. The *kabila* dominates the ideology of social relationships among the Dyula; as such, it cannot but have an important, if not always consistent, effect on practice.

The importance which the Dyula accord to the idea of the *kabila* corresponds to an ideology of patrilineal descent. In principle, the members of a *kabila* are descended, through the male line, from a single common historical ancestor. There are, however, important exceptions to this general rule. The first exception consists of slaves, and descendants of slaves. Quite obviously, the slaves within a given *kabila* were not descended from the founding ancestor. Second and subsequent generation slaves (*worossos*) traced membership in a given *kabila* not through the male, but through the female, line. In other words, the child of two slaves belonged to the *kabila* of the mother, and not necessarily to that of the father. On the other hand, the legitimate child of a slave and a free person was always free. In the vast majority of cases, these unions were those of a man with his own slave woman. A slave woman was manumitted before she was married to her master, and her children were accorded the same status as any others. The legitimate children of a slave man and a free woman, on the other hand, belonged to the descent group of the woman's father. Such unions were indeed rare – I know of only one such instance – but this was a

48

means by which a man who had fathered only daughters could produce a legitimate male heir.

Another exception to the rule that members of the *kabila* are recruited through patrifiliation is the case of children born out of wedlock (*nyamogo den*). In principle, such children are debarred from inheritance in any descent group whatsoever. On the other hand, various descent groups can put conflicting claims to such children. Children born to a woman before her first marriage may be claimed by the woman's father, although they are generally claimed by the woman's first husband. In any case, the genitor, unless he ultimately marries the woman, has absolutely no legal claim to the child. Similarly, children conceived during adultery always belong to their mother's husband, and not to their genitor. On the other hand, an illegitimate child, whether he belongs to his mother's descent group or to her husband's, may be slighted as such, and may of his own accord seek out his 'real' father. If he is well treated by his genitor's descent group, he may choose to stay with them, and ultimately be integrated into their *kabila*. In short, while an illegitimate child is not supposed to inherit, his ambiguous status permits him a certain measure of choice in deciding to which *kabila* he ultimately belongs. Most *kabila*s are eager to increase the numbers of their descendants, and are often willing to ignore the origins of an illegitimate child, especially a male one, and permit him to inherit, in order to ensure his allegiance to the group.

Though a *kabila* may well trace as many as seven or eight generations back to the founding ancestor, and though some may date back to the eighteenth or even the seventeenth century, most *kabila*s are relatively small. Few include more than twenty married men, and many include fewer than ten, not all of whom are necessarily residing in the village at the time. It must be remembered that the Dyula, as traders, were very mobile. It was never exceptional for a man, especially a young man, to take up residence outside his home village. Often, such men returned to assume the prerogatives of elders within the village; but others who established themselves satisfactorily away from home never returned, and founded *kabila*s of their own. Those who established themselves relatively near the home village maintained close relations with their *kabila* of origin, and such relations have generally been preserved by their descendants. On the other hand, relations tended to lapse quite quickly if the new settlement was sufficiently far away to debar easy contact.

Whether the small size of most *kabila*s is the result of low population growth or of the emigration of individual members, or both, the fact remains that they are not usually large enough to show an elaborate degree of internal segmentation. Despite its patrilineal ideology, the Dyula *kabila* cannot be compared to the lineages found among certain other African peoples such as the Tallensi. Rather, except for close kin, the specific genealogical tie between two members is of very little importance. Despite the ideological importance of patrifiliation within the *kabila*, actual practice is much closer to that of the cognatic Gonja (see E. Goody 1973:215) than to that of peoples usually associated with the label 'patrilineal'.

On the other hand, a few *kabila*s have grown to exceptionally large proportions, containing over eighty married men within their numbers. The most notable examples in Kadioha and Korhogo are the Cisse *kabila*s, the Cisse *kabila* of Korhogo being an offshoot of the one in Kadioha. Both of these groups are divided into more or less clear-cut subdivisions, termed *lu* ('compound') in Kadioha, and *gba* ('hearth') in Korhogo. Both *kabila*s contain multiple levels of division, sometimes clearly defined, sometimes incipient, but in neither case does there exist any term to distinguish one level from another.[1] For example, the Cisse *kabila* of Kadioha is divided into three major named subdivisions: Kanangako, Lakafiera and Ludielima. Each of these subdivisions is said to descend from one of the three sons of the founding ancestors of the *kabila*, Ahamadu Cisse. Two of the three major subdivisions are further divided into smaller segments. Most of these minor subdivisions are, in fact, quite as large as most other *kabila*s in Kadioha. Although all members of a minor subdivision treat one another as close kin, most members of a subdivision of a *kabila* in Kadioha are unable to trace their genealogical links to one another, and the nature of such links is considered to be quite unimportant. In Kadioha, the significant facts of kinship are close kinship links – whether patrilateral or matrilateral or affinal – on the one hand, and membership of a *kabila* and one or other of its subdivisions, on the other. In actual practice, genealogies provide only a very loose model for social interaction, especially within one's own descent group. Although the Cisse *kabila* of Korhogo is itself an offshoot of the Cisse *kabila* in Kadioha, its pattern of segmentation is somewhat more complex. Its free members trace descent from three separate immigrants and not, as in Kadioha, from a single man. Because of its relatively recent (mid-nineteenth century) origins, more genealogical links are still remembered. Still, broadly speaking, it is organized along the same lines as the parent *kabila*.

It is important to stress that internal subdivisions are a feature of only a very small proportion of all *kabila*s, although these *kabila*s, by their very size, may comprise an important part of the population of any given community. In the vast majority of *kabila*s, the real or putative genealogical link between any two members is of minimal importance and is often unknown. An individual's status within his own *kabila* is principally defined with regard to other criteria: sex, generation, age and free or slave status. Offices within the *kabila* – as well as offices within the community at large vested in a given *kabila* – are assigned according to these criteria.

Women and slaves are debarred from holding most offices, with certain special exceptions. On the other hand, any freeman (*horon*) is liable, at least in principle, to hold office within the descent group. The principal such office is that of head of the *kabila*, or *kabila tigi*. In large *kabila*s, each subdivision also has its head, the *lu tigi* or *gba tigi*. The office of *kabila tigi* is automatically held by the senior freeman in the *kabila*, that is to say, the oldest man in the oldest generation. A person is automatically assigned to the next generation after his father's; a slave is assigned to the next generation after his master's. Thus a younger brother is always senior to his elder brother's sons, no matter what their respective ages may be. The *kabila tigi* is by no means the eldest man in the *kabila*; older men than he may well be his classificatory 'sons' or even 'grandsons'. As one middle-aged informant phrased it, explaining why he would never succeed to the office of *kabila tigi*: 'Some of my fathers are not yet born.' The candidate for the office of *lu* or *gba tigi* is chosen according to the same criteria of age and seniority. A corollary of this rule of succession is that a *kabila tigi* can never be deposed, for, at any given time, there is only one legitimate candidate for the office. It occasionally happens that a *kabila tigi* falls out with the rest of the descent group, and that he loses his authority, at least temporarily. In such cases, a *kabila tigi* may be ostracized by the rest of the *kabila* by common consensus. When this happens, the next in line of succession assumes all the functions of the *kabila tigi*. But this is only a temporary measure, and when the *kabila tigi* is reconciled with the rest of the descent group, he resumes his functions in office.

While the division of the *kabila* into discrete generations defines the order of succession to office, age is more important in terms of the day-to-day relations between members of the same *kabila*. Age is institutionalized among the Dyula by the existence of age groups, called *fla nya*. Each *fla nya* consists of all the persons born in a given *kabila* during a given period, roughly three years. There is a mild amount of joking between each *fla nya* and its *nya mogo* (the group that immediately precedes it), as well as its *ko mogo* (the group that immediately follows). Any such solidarity among age-mates – almost always between persons of the same sex – cuts cleanly across generational lines. It is true that these associations of age-mates have very few established functions. Still, relative age is very important within the *kabila*, and an older man is usually accorded more authority than a younger one, irrespective of their generations, unless the latter is an officeholder.

In short, while the Dyula *kabila* might be called a 'patrilineal descent group', the relationships between its different memebrs are determined more by age, sex, generation and free or slave status than by any purportive genealogical ties. Only a few *kabila*s are divided into subdivisions on anything resembling genealogical lines; even so, within these divisions,

51

relations between members are often based on extra-genealogical consider-
ations. As a result, the typical Dyula community is divided into any number
of relatively small groups, each consisting of up to twenty married men and
their families. These small groups are, for the most part, entire *kabilas*,
though a significant minority may, in fact, be subdivisions of larger units.
These small groups are in turn incorporated into larger ones, either the large
kabilas, or the *makafos*, groups composed of several *kabilas* of which one
is 'host' to the others.

This very system, in which relatively small and often quite autonomous
groups can combine to form larger units, allows for a wide range of
functional diversity. Indeed, it is very difficult to speak in general terms of
the functions of the *kabila*, much less of a larger group such as the *makafo*.
Because the Dyula are a trading, and not an agricultural, people, corporate
rights in land are of relatively little significance in many Dyula communities,
especially in the larger ones such as Korhogo and Kadioha. The *kabila* or
any' segment of it may perform any of a number of functions; on the other
hand, the functions performed by one group do not necessarily correspond
to the functions performed by its neighbor.

For instance, before the colonial period, some *kabilas*, or subdivisions,
were units of economic and political specialization; the majority of their
members engaged either in warfare, or in scholarship, or in long-distance
trade, and the human and material resources of the whole *kabila*, or of a
large part of it, could be deployed to the furtherance of these ends. Similarly,
a *kabila* might hold corporate rights over an office within the whole
community, for example, that of chief of a chiefdom or a village, or of *imam*
of the Friday mosque. A *kabila* might also have rights over an initiation
society or a daily mosque.

The wide variety of functions which the *kabila* and its segments are
capable of performing in different circumstances certainly contributes a
great deal to the adaptability of Dyula descent groups. Nevertheless,
though the structure and functions of different *kabilas* vary from case to
case, even within one village, there are still a number of functions which
every *kabila* performs for its members. These functions are embodied in the
head of the *kabila*, the *kabila tigi*, and reflected in his prescribed duties.
Such functions fall within two domains: the ritual domain, with the
organization of life-cycle rituals; and the jural domain, with the settlement
of disputes within the *kabila*.

Every *kabila* has rights over a certain ritual spot, where certain rituals
must be performed, and where assemblies may be held. A *kabila* may have
its own particular spot, or it may share a spot with other *kabilas* within the
same *makafo*. Such a spot might be a special ritual house, called a *bron*, or
might simply be a clearing. The *bron*, or ritual house, was often imbued with
various supernatural powers, and written charms were incorporated into the
walls during its creation. The *kabila tigi* and other officers of the *kabila*

each have a particular place in the *bron*. The place of the *kabila tigi* is particularly sacred, and it is believed that anyone other than the legitimate officeholder who sits in this spot will die. Even if the *kabila tigi* is temporarily ostracized, and the next in line of succession assumes his functions, he (the stand-in) is not permitted to occupy this spot. The other *kabila*s in the village, which always send representatives to any important ceremony, each have a particular spot in the house reserved for them. Finally, the elders sit apart from the junior members (including middle-aged men) of the *kabila*, who also enter by a separate door. Such ritual houses are no longer being built, or even kept in repair, in many communities such as Korhogo, where rituals take place in a particular clearing. Seating arrangements in such clearings are always quite informal, and no supernatural sanctions apply to any such spots. These ritual houses and clearings are always the sites of certain ceremonies that form an essential part of marriage and funeral rituals.

These rituals serve, to a large measure, as expressions of the solidarity of the *kabila*. The *kabila tigi* plays an active part in organizing such events. He is responsible for setting the date, for informing all the elders of his own *kabila*, and for notifying the heads of all the other *kabila*s in the village that they should send representatives. No ritual of any importance is complete without representatives from the other Dyula *kabila*s in the community. In most communities, every *kabila* always sends a delegation; only in the largest communities, such as Kadioha, representatives from many, but not all, other *kabila*s will be invited. Whenever a *kabila* performs such a ritual, almost all of the adult males of the *kabila* who are able to attend will be present. Neighboring Dyula communities, and *kabila*s related by kinship to those holding the ceremony, will also be represented by at least one member. Thus, the attendance at any of these rituals symbolizes not only the solidarity of the members within one *kabila*, but also the solidarity between various *kabila*s within one village, the solidarity between *kabila*s related by kinship ties and the solidarity between neighboring Dyula communities within the region.

Aside from such ritual functions, Dyula descent groups provide a framework in which decisions can be made in the jural as well as in the political sphere. Disputes within the *kabila* are quite frequent in Dyula society, all the more so because a high proportion of marriages take place within the descent group; thus both parties to a marital dispute are likely to belong to the same group. Traditionally, the chief of a village and, ultimately, of a chiefdom was responsible for settling disputes; today, such powers have also been assumed by various agencies of the national government, as well as, informally, by the local apparatus of the ruling party, the Parti Démocratique de la Côte d'Ivoire (P.D.C.I.). However, the Dyula have always been extremely loath to take any disputes – and particularly disputes within the *kabila* – to any outside party. The accepted procedure for settling any such dispute is to call a meeting of all parties concerned. All adult males of the group, whether it be *gba, lu* or *kabila*, will be summoned, and all are free to express their opinions. (In a large *kabila*, a meeting of the entire *kabila* is rare unless there is a particularly virulent dispute between two different segments, or unless the whole *kabila* is concerned with the issue.) In principle, the role of the head of the *kabila* or of the segment is to act as a mediator; in fact, this is not always possible, as he may well be a party to the dispute himself. Anyone is free to speak at these meetings, and, if the dispute is particularly bitter, it may drag on for a very long time. Such meetings differ quite radically from a court of law, or even a chief's court, in that their purpose is not so much to examine the evidence – this is usually common knowledge – as to determine the consensus of the group as a whole. The *kabila tigi* himself has virtually no power, except in so far as others will accept his authority. The consensus of the group may even be to ostracize the *kabila tigi* until he accepts their decision. Similarly, the group may ostracize any other member who refuses to comply with the general decision. The outcome is generally either a compromise solution or a situation in which one party finds itself in complete isolation from the rest of the group, and chooses to give in rather than face ostracism.

Ultimately, two features characterize Dyula descent groups. The first is functional diffuseness. This diffuseness is, as we have seen, often paralleled in structure. *Kabila*s may or may not have subdivisions. Moreover, whereas descent groups are, in principle, patrilineal, the genealogical ties between two members are often unimportant, and may well be unknown. The second feature is the sense of moral community, symbolized by life-cycle rituals. The nature and extent of this moral community is constantly being reasserted and indeed redefined during disputes and meetings of the whole group. The result of these features is that each Dyula *kabila* is, in some respects, different from all the others. The various *kabila*s themselves are conscious – often jealous – of their own individuality. These distinctions are often details in the performance of ritual, but they often underlie more deep-seated differences in structure and function. In a fundamental way, the flexibility of Dyula descent groups is the result of the fact that the Dyula are a minority community – in some ways a marginal one – in the Korhogo region. Such flexibility permits each descent group to adapt to its environment in its own particular way. To borrow an ecological metaphor, each *kabila* can adapt itself to fit the available niches in the social organization of the region.

The kinship network of the individual

Kabila membership is only one element of Dyula kinship. Any individual

Clansmen and kinsmen

Dyula is related by various ties of kinship and affinity to other groups and individuals, both inside and outside the *kabila*. The nature and extent of such ties varies widely among the Dyula, and is in turn related to such factors as the incidence of in-marriage within the *kabila*, the organization of productive activity and Moslem rules of inheritance. The Dyula themselves emphasize the particularistic nature of all bonds of kinship, at least those outside the nuclear family. Two kinsmen may be linked by mutual affection, by moral obligations stemming from services rendered by one to another or by joint participation in one or a series of undertakings. The mere fact that two individuals are related by kinship or by affinity does not tell us very much about their relationships with one another. In any case, the kinds of relationships that may exist between kinsmen do not vary significantly, whether the bond of kinship be patrilateral, matrilateral or often even affinal. This is, in part, due to the high rate of intermarriage within the *kabila*. As all members of one *kabila* are, in principle, patrilineal kin, this means that any two individuals in the *kabila* may be, at the same time, patrilateral, matrilateral *and* affinal kinsmen (see Barth 1973:12).

This is not to suggest that kinship among the Dyula is of little consequence. On the contrary, an individual is usually more likely to seek assistance from kinsmen than from outsiders. But the choice of which kinsmen on whom to rely is often left to the individual. The kinship bond, in itself, does not establish any necessary relationship of cooperation between two persons. Rather, cooperation between kin works differently from cooperation between non-kin. Kinsmen cooperate within a framework of more or less generalized reciprocity. Thus a Dyula is under the moral obligation to assist a kinsman who has already assisted him. But the nature of moral obligations between kinsmen sometimes discourages, rather than encourages, cooperation between them. For instance, one kinsman does not charge another for services rendered, though kinsmen can sell goods to one another. Under such conditions, rather than content themselves with the expectations of generalized reciprocity, kinsmen are sometimes unwilling to provide one another with services at all. Similarly, loans of money are rare between kinsmen; it is, at best, indelicate to insist on the repayment of such a loan. Much more often, transfers of money between kinsmen are in the nature of outright gifts. In general, loans of money are granted by friends unrelated by kinship ties. (Such loans are interest-free, in accordance with Moslem law.) We must not forget, however, that the Dyula are a trading people; their way of life necessitates that certain services, as well as goods, can be purchased relatively freely from individuals outside the kinship network of the individual. A kinsman, a friend or even a complete outsider may, in certain instances, all provide the same services; the difference lies, not so much in the services themselves, but in the expectations of the donor. These expectations are formed by the nature of the relationship between the

55

giver and the receiver: kinship, friendship or simply the dealings of a seller and his customer. At one extreme, the giver expects to be able to ask for other services as the need may arise; at the other extreme, immediate, or at least short-term, repayment is the set condition.

Before the colonial period, the day-to-day organization of production and consumption was in any case arranged largely along kinship lines. The major economic activities of the Dyula – warfare, scholarship, weaving and trade – required the cooperation of close kinsmen. Obviously, the nature and extent of such cooperation depended on the nature of the task at hand. Organized warfare required the participation of individuals outside the close kinship network; it was an affair that involved, at the very least, the whole *kabila*, and, more usually, an alliance of several *kabila*s. Slave raiding and the looting of caravans were much more individual affairs. Trading and scholarship, on the other hand, had to be pursued systematically if they were to be pursued at all. Normally, a senior kinsman controlled the labor of a number of junior kinsmen. Any junior kinsman would suffice: a son, a younger brother, a nephew (brother's or sister's son), a foster son or even a distant cousin, though this was rare. But, in fact, Moslem rules of inheritance imposed certain limitations on cooperation. Moslem law favors inheritance by lineal over all collateral relatives. A man working for his father was certain to inherit a portion of the wealth upon his father's death. This was not the case, however, if he were working for his older brother or his father's brother, much less for his mother's brother. Thus a junior relative did not have a lasting interest in the affairs of his senior relatives apart from those of his father. On the other hand, late marriage was standard practice among the Dyula, and it was quite common for a young man's father to be no longer alive. This goes a certain way in explaining the frequency of cooperation between non-lineal kinsmen.

To a certain extent, Moslem rules of inheritance could be modified to fit the circumstances. If his father died when he was young, a youth's portion of the inheritance might be entrusted to a father's brother or his own older brother. The youth would then work for his brother or his uncle until he married and had children, at which time he would reclaim his rightful portion of the inheritance. Similarly, if his brother or paternal uncle died while he was working under his orders, he retained a legitimate claim to his portion of what had been, in fact, his father's wealth. On the other hand, a youth could choose to work for a matrilateral kinsman, an affine or even a distant kinsman. Such a choice had both its advantages and disadvantages. In this case, the junior kinsman had much more freedom than if he worked for a father, brother or paternal uncle, as his senior kinsman had no prior claims to his services. He could leave to set up work on his own behalf without the fear of any sanctions. On the other hand, he had no claims on the wealth of his senior kinsman; he was entirely dependent on his generosity, and was left without resources if his senior kinsman died. Such a working relationship was only likely to occur if there was a particular bond of affection between the two kinsmen. In this way, a man without sons could still attract the labor of other kinsmen, and a wealthy or generous man the services of a wide variety of relatives (see Amselle 1971).

When such a relationship of cooperation existed between the two kinsmen, the junior kinsman was expected to turn over all of his earnings to his senior kinsman. (In fact, a rich kinsman might tolerate the fact that his junior kinsman held back a certain portion of his earnings. I was told that one rich trader in the nineteenth century used to tell his sons to count up his wealth from time to time, fully expecting them not to declare the entire amount, and to pocket the difference.) On the other hand, a man lodged, clothed and fed all kinsmen working on his behalf, as well as their families. He also arranged their marriages, defraying all the necessary expenses. Ultimately, he was expected to give them a sum of money to allow them to set up trade on their own behalf. But the system was not entirely free of contradictions; younger kinsmen were more eager for independence than were older kinsmen to accord it. Certain compromises were possible. A young man might set up trade or weaving in an outlying Senufo village and still send back his earnings to his senior kinsman, who would in turn provide his junior with the necessary capital. This way, a junior kinsman was gradually able to attain his independence, the exchanges between the two growing less and less substantial. Sometimes, such junior kinsmen settled permanently away from their home community; in other cases, they came back to assume the role of elder.

Units of consumption among the Dyula tended to be larger than units of production. Obviously, foster children, or the indigent elderly or sick relatives, had to be provided for. More importantly, women's earnings were kept separate from the men's. Though a man might have a claim to his sons', his brothers' or his nephews' earnings, he never had any claim to his wives' earnings. A successful woman trader was expected to make her independent contribution to the household budget, in particular to the purchase of foodstuffs. Within one productive unit might be found the heads of several domestic groups, while any domestic group might well have more than one separate budget. Yet all of these resources might be pooled for certain purposes.

More generally, certain kinsmen were said to 'eat together'. The concept of 'eating together' was, in fact, extremely vague, and could imply quite close as well as very occasional cooperation; the only safe generalization, if any, was that people who 'ate together' cooperated more closely than people who did not. The idea of 'eating together' was not entirely metaphorical. Minimally, it implied common participation in certain ritual meals, particularly meals offered from time to time in honor of the dead.

Responsibility for preparing the meal fell, in turn, to the head of each male productive unit within the group in order of seniority. Other groups might eat together during the month of Ramadan as well; still others regularly shared the midday meal. Some might even partake of all their meals together. The actual fact of the sharing of meals was, in a general way, an index of other forms of economic cooperation between two independent units of production. Such cooperation was occasional, and consisted of helping to finance trading ventures on the one hand, and helping to defray the costs of expensive rituals – principally the excision of girls, and marriages and funerals – on the other. Close cooperation was most common between all members of either a small descent group or a subdivision of a large descent group. The extent of such cooperation depended, of course, on the wealth of the group as a whole. In a relatively wealthy group, not only could the richer members help out the poorer ones, but they could also lend one another mutual assistance with a high expectation of reciprocity. In a poorer group, members were not in a position to provide each other substantial material help. The major exceptions to this rule were the few *kabila*s which were devoted in the main to scholarship; this common activity required the cooperation of the whole group. In any case, there was no set rule about cooperation between close kin. Each case was necessarily different, dictated in part by the circumstances and in part by the particular sentiments of the close kinsmen involved.

To conclude, the interaction of kin among the Dyula, whether in terms of established descent groups, units of production or the relations of the individual with his close and distant kinsmen, was subject to a great deal of variation. This was certainly due to the situation of the Dyula, first as traders, and second as a minority community. That is to say, they were very mobile, and they had to be able to adapt to a wide variety of local circumstances. Moreover, there was a high degree of specialization and differentiation among the Dyula themselves, and often within descent groups; in this respect, the Dyula were very different from populations where virtually the whole community was involved in farming or herding. As traders, corporate rights in property or land were of very little value to them as opposed to individual tenure. These factors combined to give Dyula kinship a bilateral – one might almost say an ad hoc – quality, despite the existence of descent groups with a patrilineal ideology; the Dyula attach a great deal of significance, at least emotionally, to descent group membership. All of the activities in which the Dyula specialized required the cooperation of kinsmen in most circumstances. In the vast majority of cases, these kinsmen did, in fact, belong to the same descent group; this was so in spite of the fact that kinsmen from outside the group were relatively easily incorporated into the unit of production. A very real notion of the solidarity of the descent group, even if it was often contradicted by actual behavior,

58

did check the bilateral tendencies of Dyula kinship. The contradictions of Dyula kinship were, to a certain extent, reflected in the organization of trade. Any trading venture required the cooperation of a number of kinsmen, under the authority of the senior member of the group. On the other hand, each of the junior members of the group aspired to be successful in his own right; in order to do this, he had sooner or later to secede from the group. On the other hand, the bilateral tendencies of Dyula kinship made it possible for a trader to recruit labor from outside the descent group. On the other hand, there had to be some means of keeping the unit of production together. Such an inducement was not provided by Moslem laws of succession, which excluded collateral kinsmen. The nucleus of such productive units was almost always, in fact, a group of close patrilineal kinsmen. The patrilineal bias of Dyula kinship and, more particularly, the sense of individual allegiance to the descent group gave a certain ideological support for the cohesion of the unit as a whole. Such contradictions between the patrilateral and the bilateral tendencies of the Dyula kinship system must be seen as an essential feature of the system as a whole. The ways in which such contradictions might be resolved account for the variety in Dyula kinship behavior, and for the difficulties in categorizing Dyula kinship in any simple schematic way. Both flexibility and cohesion were necessary to maintain the Dyula way of life.

5

The mechanics of marriage

The very flexibility of Dyula kinship makes the choice of a spouse all the more important. Any children born belong, of course, to the husband's *kabila*, but members of the wife's family are also considered an extremely important category of kin. Formerly, an adolescent or young man whose father was dead could choose to work for his maternal, rather than his paternal, relatives. The choice remains much too crucial an affair to be left to the whims of young men and women. Marriages are arranged by the kin of the bride and groom; most often, neither partner is consulted beforehand. On the groom's side, the decision rests with his father, if he is still alive, or with the senior kinsman under whose authority he is working. On the bride's side, the decision is also in the hands of her father or of a foster parent. Normally, the heads of the descent groups concerned, the *kabila tigi*s – and, in large descent groups, the *lu* or *gba tigi*s as well – are also consulted, if only as a matter of form.

Islamic law does not exclude the possibility of marriage between close kin. Prohibitions apply, for the most part, to close kinswomen of ascending or descending generations, and to the wives of close kinsmen of ascending or descending generations. On the other hand, within one's own generation, there are relatively few prohibitions, the only ones being sister, 'milk sister' and wife's sister. Marriage is allowed between any categories of cousins and between a man and his brother's widow (al Qayrawani 1968:173–83). More importantly, Moslem law restricts the marriage of Moslems to adherents of other religions. Moslem men may only marry Moslem, Jewish or Christian women; Moslem women, on the other hand, are forbidden to any but Moslem men. The importance of such restrictions to the Dyula is quite obvious, given that they live as a minority among the Senufo whom they regard as godless pagans. But these restrictions are applied quite differently as regards the marriage of Dyula men to Senufo women compared with that of Senufo men to Dyula women. For all practical purposes, the Dyula assume that a wife automatically adopts the religion of her husband. For this reason, the marriage of Dyula men to Senufo women

60

is quite permissible. On the other hand, it is out of the question that a Moslem Dyula women be given in marriage to a Senufo 'idolater'. In short, Dyula men, but not Dyula women, are allowed to marry out of the ethnic group. Thus the Dyula differ quite radically from Moslems in Gonja where a system of open conubium is in practice, and where Moslem women can be given in marriage to men from other estates (see E. Goody 1973).

The Dyula also have a few prohibitions against certain forms of marriage which can in no way be deduced or abstracted from the corpus of Moslem law. But these prohibitions tend to be purely local and apply to a very restricted number of cases. For example, in Kadioha certain joking partners (members of the Cisse and Keita *kabilas*) are forbidden to marry one another. The Dyula population in the Korhogo region is dense enough to provide an abundance of eligible candidates and, in principle, a very wide range of choice. If this range of choice is not reflected in actual practice, we must look for an answer not in any prohibitions, but in a system of stated preferences. We must ask not only what preferences exist, but why, if at all, they have an important effect on the actual choices made in Dyula society.

Marriage within the descent group

Marriage within the *kabila* was and remains by far the most favored form of marriage. As members of the *kabila* are, in principle, agnatic kin, such marriages amount to classificatory, if not actual, patrilateral parallel-cousin marriages. This is a typically Middle Eastern form of marriage; not surprisingly, most of the African peoples who practice it – for instance, the Peuls of Futa Jallon (Cantrelle and Dupire 1964) – are Moslems, like the Dyula.[1] The practice was conceivably diffused to the Dyula along with Islam from the Middle East via the Maghreb. Manding-speaking peoples such as the Malinke of Kita (Cisse 1970:77), the Bambara (Luneau 1974:312, 316) and even the Mandinko of Pakao (Schaffer 1980:88) – despite a long history of Islam – do not allow such marriages. Thus the practice is almost certainly not indigenous to Manding-speaking peoples.

Among the Dyula, unlike the peoples of the Middle East (Barth 1954; Patai 1955; Khuri 1970), a man has no positive claim to his father's brother's daughter, or for that matter to any parallel cousin, real or classificatory. The decision as to whom a girl may marry is entirely in the hands of her senior kinsmen; a young man's senior kinsmen are ultimately responsible for finding him a wife, but she does not necessarily have to be from the same descent group. Indeed, marriage between first cousins – in particular between the children of full brothers – is viewed with a certain amount of disfavor among the Dyula. Such marriages are not forbidden, but the Dyula voice the fear that any marital disputes might lead to hostility between the fathers of the spouses. Marriage with a father's full brother's daughter most often occurs in a situation where an older brother attempts to use his authority over his younger brothers in order to pressure them into supplying suitable spouses for his own children. Should an older brother decide upon such a marriage it is virtually impossible for a younger brother to refuse openly unless he is prepared to accept a considerable rift in their relationship. This situation is most likely to arise where there already exists close cooperation between the full brothers, and where the younger brothers are not willing, for whatever reasons, to put an end to it. More generally, the real preference among the Dyula is not marriage with the father's brother's daughter, but rather marriage between close – but not too close – kinsmen within the descent group.

Oddly enough, the Dyula do not generally associate descent group in-marriage with Islam at all. Their silence in this regard is striking, for they are quite prepared to explain a variety of customs, many of which are not enjoined or even mentioned in the standard texts of Maliki Islam, by claiming that 'this is the Moslem way of doing things.' This is probably because their closest 'pagan' neighbors are matrilineal; the differences between the Dyula and Senufo kinship systems are already so pronounced that it is hardly necessary to stress the presence or absence of such marriage preferences to highlight the differences between 'Moslem' and 'pagan' kinship.[2] Of course, while Islam may explain the adoption of patrilateral parallel-cousin marriage among the Dyula, it cannot explain its persistence, much less its high rate of incidence, since certain other groups of West African Moslems, such as the Wolof (I. M. Lewis 1966:52) and the Gonja Moslems (E. Goody 1973:77), have low rates of patrilateral parallel-cousin marriage. The Dyula themselves have no ready-made explanation. Some point out that marriage prestations are much less expensive when both spouses come from the same descent group. This certainly enters into the calculations of those arranging (and paying for) a marriage. It is significant, though, that nowadays, when they are given the choice, some Dyula men will readily marry outside the descent group, in spite of the increased costs that this entails. In any case, such an explanation begs the question; there is no reason why marriages within the descent group should be less expensive than others, except as an incentive to keep rates of in-marriage high.

Whatever the causes of this preference, its effects on Dyula social organization before the colonial period were to reconcile the two apparently contradictory principles of Dyula kinship: the patrilineal bias associated with the *kabila*, and the bilateral bias associated with flexibility and choice. In principle, close cooperation was possible between all categories of kin – patrilateral, matrilateral and affinal. In practice, with high rates of in-marriage within the *kabila*, most close kinsmen were likely to be fellow *kabila* members; an individual's actual range of choice tended to be quite restricted. The ideology of *kabila* membership (and, in a large *kabila*, of its various subdivisions) stressed common agnatic descent. In fact, such 'descent' groups can just as well be described as marriage pools whose members are linked by a very high density of kinship ties of all sorts. Whether one chooses to characterize the *kabila* as a patrilineal descent group or as a relatively endogamous corporate kindred depends on which aspects of Dyula social organization one wishes to stress. The ideology of agnation implies that membership in the group confers certain rights to individual members. However, such rights among the Dyula tended to be few and unimportant. For example, descent groups controlled access to farming land, but since the Dyula tended to avoid farming, land was not a particularly scarce or valued commodity. Certain groups enjoyed exclusive or shared control of offices such as those of the *imam*, village chief, and even – in the case of Kadioha – chief of a chiefdom. However, the majority of *kabila*s possessed no such rights. *Tun tigi kabila*s controlled *poro* groves; again, such rights only concerned a minority of *kabila*s in the region. On the other hand, while certain *kabila*s specialized in one or another economic domain, none had a *de jure* monopoly over any form of activity. In short, agnatic descent, even though it was the idiom in which the Dyula preferred to express social relationships, accomplished little in and of itself in Dyula society.

However, the importance of kin groups was not limited to their role as jural communities defining the mutual rights and obligations of their members. Competition was a fundamental feature of Dyula society as might be expected amongst a people of traders. Competition could be political, as well as economic. Success in either enterprise rested on the individual's ability to recruit the assistance of others – followers in the political domain, labor in the economic domain. The beneficiaries, whether in terms of power, wealth or prestige, were ultimately individuals; members of the same kin group could and did compete with one another. But, at another level, kin groups as well as individuals were units of competition. The scarce resources in question were the members of the group itself, as followers or laborers. Thus the competitive advantage of the group as a whole depended on the extent to which it could retain the allegiance of its individual members. The members of each group were united by their common interest in the labor and allegiance of the junior members; this by no means precluded competition within the group itself.

Although politics and trade were both competitive activities, the modalities of competition were somewhat different for each domain. The premium on the solidarity of the *kabila* as a whole was most explicit in the political arena. Although every Dyula village had a chief, and the office was vested in one particular descent group, the power of the chief was not particularly great. Other descent groups could also bid for power, and the chief could find himself at the head of a faction rather than of the whole village. In most villages, no single descent group by itself was in a position to dominate the whole village. So if a descent group wanted to challenge the authority of the chief, it had to ally itself with other independent descent groups. Under such circumstances, the balance of power was unstable. Any given descent group could alter this balance of power by giving its allegiance to one faction or another. Even though the factions were led by relatively few descent groups, all descent groups were in a position to augment their power within the village by participating in the factional struggle. But only a descent group whose members were able to present a united front with respect to other descent groups in the village could exert a significant influence. The unity of the descent group was an absolute necessity if its members were to exert any political influence within the community. The importance of these factional struggles certainly varied from place to place, and depended on the political stakes to be won. In Kadioha, which was the seat of a chiefdom under Dyula control, political factions were a very important element of village life. Korhogo, on the other hand, was a chiefdom controlled by the Senufo. All in all, the Dyula of Korhogo preferred to get on with the business of trade rather than involve themselves to a great extent in the even riskier business of politics.

Politics was by no means the only field in which the Dyula competed amongst themselves. Far more importantly, the Dyula were traders, and wealth was the principal avenue to prestige in Dyula society. The key to accumulating personal wealth in Dyula society was to control labor – the labor of slaves and the labor of junior kinsmen. Slaves could be bought and sold, but junior kinsmen had to be won over. A young man stood to inherit from his father, and so would continue to work for him as long as his father was alive. If his father were dead, on the other hand, he had a certain freedom of choice. His share of the inheritance might be deferred, and placed in the keeping of a close senior kinsman within the descent group. But if his share of the inheritance did not amount to very much, he did not stand to lose if he were to work, say, for his maternal uncle, especially if that man happened to be rich. So senior kinsmen had a considerable interest in keeping the labor of their juniors within the descent group. Descent group in-marriage was one means of doing this. In other words, if a young man's mother was a member of his own descent group, so was his maternal uncle. To the extent that any individual's matrilateral and affinal kinsmen were also members of his descent group, he could not transfer his labor to senior kinsmen outside the group; the grounds for choice were severely restricted. The young man's kinsmen had yet another means of keeping his labor within the descent group: his own marriage. The young man's own marriage expenses were defrayed by the kinsman under whose authority he worked. To the extent that men married within their own descent group, they depended yet once more on their senior agnates, in order to obtain wives from among the girls within the group. Nor was it a foregone conclusion that they could find wives from other descent groups, apart from any consideration of the increased expenses involved in such marriages. For the elders of other groups were committed to marrying their own daughters to their own junior kinsmen in order to retain their services. The obstacles to marriage outside the descent group were indeed less likely to come from the young man's senior kinsmen than from the girl's parents, who often refused to consent to the marriage. But whether the opposition came from the boy's or the girl's parents, the result was the same; young men were forced back onto a dependence on their own agnates, and this dependence tended to keep their labor within the descent group.

Obviously, rates of in-marriage in any given *kabila* depend to a certain extent, as they did in the past, on the ratio of eligible husbands to eligible wives within the *kabila* at a given moment. Any *kabila* may find itself with a surplus of young men or young women who may consequently marry outside the descent group. A small *kabila* may find itself in the situation where most eligible spouses fall within the categories of kin prohibited by Moslem law. It is particularly embarrassing for a *kabila* to be faced with a surplus of marriageable men. In the past, this problem was largely offset by the possibility of taking slave women as wives. This is no longer a viable solution, and recently the chief of Kadioha himself was obliged to beg wives from other descent groups for the young men of his own *kabila*.

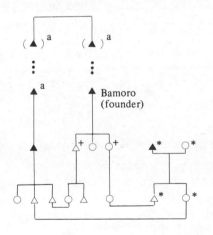

*   ... slaves
+   ... married to agnatic kin in Katia, near Korhogo
a   ... resident of Katia
▲   ... dead

Fig. 1. In-marriage in a very small *kabila* (Bamba-ra), Korhogo.

The legacy of the past

Figure 1 shows the pattern of in-marriage in one of Korhogo Koko's smaller *kabila*s. For obvious reasons, the sons of the founder were obliged to take wives from the parent community, in this case Katia, only a few miles away. By the third generation, the preference for in-marriage within the local *kabila* is already marked.[3] In very large *kabila*s, marriages are preferred not only within the *kabila* as a whole, but within each of its subdivisions (Figure 2).

Marriage with outsiders: slaves

Another form of marriage which was quite common, at least before the colonial period, was the marriage of freemen to slave wives. It is a rather banal occurrence to find slave women somewhere in the genealogies of freemen. This is all the more remarkable because such genealogies tend to have quite a short span, going back only three or four generations; moreover, because complementary filiation is not a mechanism for the segmentation of descent groups, the names and social origins of women tend to be forgotten even more rapidly than those of men. It is not very surprising that the Dyula should have married numbers of slave women. As traders, the Dyula had relatively easy access to the capital necessary to buy them. The origins of such wives were quite varied. Some came from ethnic groups

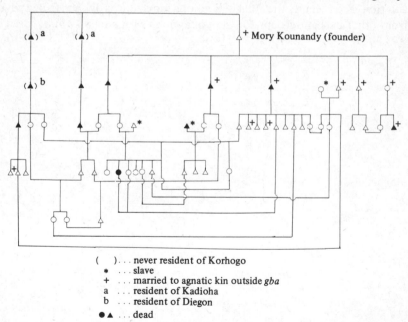

```
(   ) . . . never resident of Korhogo
 *    . . . slave
 +    . . . married to agnatic kin outside gba
 a    . . . resident of Kadioha
 b    . . . resident of Diegon
 ●▲   . . . dead
```

Fig. 2. In-marriage in one *gba* of Cisse *kabila*, Korhogo.

66

living on the fringes of the forest, particularly the Baoule and the Gouro; some were Senufo, particularly from the Tagbana subgroup, which suffered particularly heavily from slave raids; others came from the north, from what is now the Republic of Mali. On balance, the Dyula were increasing their population at the expense of other groups, not so much in the same region as further away.

A slave woman was not married until she had borne her master's child. If this occurred, she was freed, and the marriage ceremonies were performed exactly as for any other woman. Her children enjoyed the same status as the children of free wives, and they were neither particularly favored nor disfavored. In a sense, marriage to a slave women was a special case of marriage within the descent group, since slaves were, after all, incorporated into their master's descent groups. Usually, such marriage did not create any new kinship ties outside the descent group. I do know of a number of exceptions to this, however. In one case, the mother of a *worosso* (second generation slave) in Kadioha had been captured from a relatively nearby village. She remembered her village of origin, and her son still retains kinship ties with that village. In another case, two women (real or classificatory sisters) were taken as slaves from a Gouro village and both were sold to the Dyula, one in Korhogo and the other in the nearby village of Katia. The sister in Korhogo was married to a freeman and the woman in Katia to a slave, so that now most of the descendants of one sister are still of slave status while all the descendants of the other are free. Despite this difference in status, their grandchildren (now middle-aged) in both groups consider one another as kinsmen, and preserve close ties. These examples show that, at least in some cases, marriages to slave women could nevertheless result in the formation of kinship ties across descent group lines, even between Dyula and Senufo or between freemen and slaves. Still, such cases were exceptional.

The fact that a slave wife usually had no effective kinship ties outside her husband's descent group provided considerable advantages for her husband and his agnatic kin. First of all, of course, it made the wife completely dependent on her husband and on his close kin. Perhaps more importantly, her children were also completely dependent on the husband and his descent group. Normally, close kinsmen might compete for the labor of a young man for the purposes of trade, weaving or other enterprises. But the son of a freeman and a slave wife, having no matrilateral kin, had no choice but to work for his father or, if his father were dead, for other close agnatic kin. Paradoxically, a freeman had more control over the services of his own (free) son by a slave wife than over the sons of slave women whom he might have given as wives to his own slaves. Second generation slaves, in fact, although they enjoyed an inferior status, did not have to provide much work for their masters. Thus the marriage of a slave women to a freeman, even though it freed her from inferior status and, undoubtedly, from some of the more onerous tasks associated with that status, actually augmented her husband's control over the productive labor of others in the next generation.

Marriage with outsiders: Dyula

Most Dyula *kabila*s are too small to assure that every marriageable man and woman can find a spouse from within the group. To a certain extent, the problem is offset by the possibility of polygyny, and in the past it could also be offset by taking slave wives. Nonetheless, in spite of the strength of stated preferences, marriages with persons of free status from outside the *kabila* are by no means uncommon. It is absolutely necessary to distinguish between a woman's first marriage and her subsequent marriages. The elders of any descent group are generally reluctant to give an unmarried girl to an outsider. Nevertheless, pre-existing ties linking individuals and groups from different *kabila*s may well be reinforced by strategic marriages. For example, a scholar may give one of his real or classificatory daughters in marriage to a favored pupil. Similarly, a daughter may be given in marriage to a close friend or to his son. In the past such marriages were particularly likely if a man came to settle in his friend's home community, in order to attach the 'stranger' and his children as clients to the host's descent group.

The most common ties reinforced by inter-*kabila* marriages are in fact, pre-existing ties of kinship. If, as their first choice, the elders of any *kabila* prefer to marry their unmarried women to men within the group, their second choice unquestionably falls to kin from outside the group. Such kinsmen may be agnates who have left to found a nearby *kabila* (Figure 1). Once the new *kabila* has grown to reasonable proportions, it no longer needs to rely systematically on the home town for wives; as far as marriages are concerned, it becomes increasingly independent. Nonetheless, from time to time, women are exchanged between the new *kabila* and the descent group from which they have issued. Such marriages tend to represent a negligible proportion of the total marriages of either the old or the new *kabila*. During the ceremonies that are performed on such occasions, the Dyula themselves express a certain ambivalence as to whether they are to be treated as marriages within the descent group or as marriages between two descent groups.

The Dyula also have a stated preference for marriage with the mother's brother's daughter, real or classificatory.[4] I was told that a woman or her husband can claim one of her brother's daughters as a wife for one of her sons. This principle applies mainly for marriages between two descent groups, for obvious reasons; however, it is sometimes observed for marriages between distant agnates within the same descent group. Even as concerns marriage between descent groups, it would be a grave mistake to take this rule as a description of actual behavior. It is not consistently applied as such; rather, it is treated as something of a paradigm. Any close kinship link can serve as a pretext for a marriage between two different descent groups. Marriage between cross-cousins is the most common, but by no means the only, form.

This preference for marriage with kin from outside the descent group has some rather important implications. Because of preferential in-marriage, there is no complex web of matrilateral and affinal relationships linking various descent groups to one another. Each descent group has a few links with some other descent group, but not with very many of them. Marriage with kin from outside the descent group, in preference to marriage with outsiders, tends to reinforce the pre-existing kinship links, rather than to create new ones. Perhaps because there are relatively few such crosscutting links, the Dyula attach considerable importance to them. Often, enduring bonds are formed, not only between the kinsmen involved, but between two entire descent groups, or a least between substantial portions of both of them. What eventually happens is that each descent group develops a few special bonds of attachment with a few other independent descent groups, either within the village or outside. Such special ties are couched, in the idiom of kinship, as matrilateral or affinal ties. In fact, the nature of the original bond which links the two groups is of very little importance. Not all extra-group marriages evolve these kinds of enduring links; clearly, the more children born of such a marriage, the more kin are likely to be involved in subsequent generations. A great deal depends on ties of personal affection that may develop between individual members of both groups. In a small descent group, the whole group is very rapidly involved in such relationships. In a large descent group, on the other hand, each subdivision tends to have its own network of special ties with other groups, and these networks do not tend to overlap very much. But, in either case, matrilateral and affinal relationships are not seen as an ego-centered network of kin, but rather as a network linking separate whole groups.

Interestingly enough, the various *kabila*s of Korhogo and Kadioha preferred before the colonial period to develop matrilateral and affinal networks linking them to groups in different communities, rather than within each village. There were, of course, important exceptions, especially within certain *makafo*s, associations between several descent groups where one is the 'host' of the others. Although *kabila*s in both Kadioha and Korhogo Koko maintained important kinds of kinship outside each community, the pattern of such ties was slightly different in each case. These differences corresponded quite closely to the nature of the trade in each community. Trade in Koko was overwhelmingly devoted to supplying the neighboring Senufo with goods of Dyula manufacture, particularly cloths. The Dyula of Kadioha, situated nearer to the forest, were more systematically concerned with procuring cola from other Dyula communities lying further to the southwest. Consequently, the Dyula of Koko maintained close kinship ties with nearby Dyula communities. They could then use these ties to establish links with neighboring Senufo villagers; conversely, they were useful intermediaries between their Dyula kin in nearby villages and Senufo chiefs living in Korhogo. On the other hand, the Dyula of Kadioha expressed a preference for marriage links with communities to the southwest. Travel in this direction was potentially hazardous. Passing caravans, particularly if they were small and not too well armed, were easily plundered. One did not, however, plunder one's kinsmen or the kinsmen of one's neighbors. Kinship was the best, and certainly most convenient, passport. Moreover, such kinsmen could readily help incoming traders from Kadioha to procure the cola they were seeking, as well as to sell any goods they were bringing in exchange, and might even offer favorable terms of trade into the bargain. In short, for any *kabila*, maintaining kinship links within the village might procure political advantages, and the benefits of ties outside the village were primarily commercial. Not surprisingly, the Dyula, traders as they were, overwhelmingly preferred the latter.

This is not to say that kinship ties between *kabila*s in any one village were entirely neglected. Dyula elders exercised a very tight control over the marriages of unmarried adolescent girls. However, girls were married very young, between the ages of fourteen and sixteen. Men married much later, often after the age of thirty; after all, the later they married, the longer they remained dependents of senior kinsmen. This difference in age at marriage meant more women were much more likely than men to be widowed at least once in their marital careers. As the Dyula were Moslems, divorce was also possible; however, if the spouses were kin, they were subjected to considerable pressures to patch up their differences.

The Dyula, in accordance with Moslem law (al Qayrawani 1968:175), have always allowed a great deal of freedom of choice to widows and divorcees. The one freedom which the Dyula refuse to accord such a woman is to remain unmarried. For the Dyula, an adult woman is a married woman. Exception is made only for the recently widowed or divorced, but it is immoral to wait too long to find oneself a new husband. I was told that if such an unmarried woman dies, she is not accorded the normal funeral for an adult. Age is no refuge. A woman too old to find herself a husband is married to a real or classificatory grandson. Such marriages are, in fact, a 'joke'. Grandparents and grandchildren are joking partners, and this aspect of their relationship is manifested at funerals of grandparents. Such marriages are also legal fictions; they are never consummated, though the necessary ceremonies are summarily performed. When I was systematically inquiring about marriages in different *kabila*s, these were never mentioned. Indeed, though I was living in the same house as one of these grandson-husbands, I only found out about his marriage quite by chance, after a year and a half in the field. Such marriages, rare as they are, are merely the extreme expression of the general principle that a good woman is a married woman, decrepit grandmother though she may be.

Most women, even those long past their primes, need hardly go to such lengths to find themselves husbands. In principle, Dyula men favor the remarriage of the widow with a brother of her deceased husband (preferably a younger brother, but remarriage with an older brother is not prohibited, and occasionally occurs) or, failing that, with another close agnate of the same generation. Though she may be subjected to mild pressures from her own or her husband's agnatic kin to marry one man or another, she is in fact fairly free to marry anyone she chooses. If she has young children, or even grown children, her husband's kin will probably ask her to stay in the village. This does not prevent her from marrying anyone else she chooses within the village, or even a 'visiting husband' from outside the village. Clearly, the older a woman is, the less likely is she to be subjected to any pressures to marry anybody in particular. A woman past the age of child-bearing is still expected to remarry, though she usually lives with her brothers, or, if she has any children, with her first husband's kin. The Dyula rather uncharitably call such a woman a *lemburu forogo*, an 'orange peel', that is to say, what is left once all the juice is squeezed out. (The juice, of course, is a metaphor for the woman's fertility.) This is not to say that 'orange peel' marriages are only a matter of form. Such a wife may provide essential domestic services for her husband: cooking his food, washing his clothes, tidying up his house and so forth. Some husbands feel a great deal of affection for their 'orange peel' wives, although others tend to regard such marriages as a matter of mutual convenience, an exchange of financial support on the one hand for domestic service on the other. Such marriages do establish a relationship between the husband and his wife's kin, but these relationships only last during the husband's lifetime, and rarely, if ever, involve the other members of the husband's descent group to any great extent. In general, widows, whether they are 'orange peels' or not, are far less likely to bear children to their subsequent husbands than are young girls who are being married for the first time, or even than divorcees (see Table 2). Since it is primarily the existence of children born to a marriage which provides a basis for ongoing ties of kinship between two descent groups, the remarriage of widows, especially of 'orange peels', is of correspondingly less concern to either descent group. Of course, widows do sometimes bear children. Nonetheless, descent group in-marriage accounts for a higher proportion of fertile marriages – which are, after all, the marriages that count most in Dyula society – than of total marriages. Remarriages do, however, establish crosscutting links between members of different *kabilas* in a single village. Individually, these links are transitory, usually dissolving

71

The legacy of the past

Table 2. *Mean number of children borne by wife to present husband by wife's age and past marital history. (Sample from Koko and Kadioha: N = 487)*

| | Wife's age | | | |
Wife's marital history	Under 35 (244)	35–49 (137)	50–64 (94)	65 or over (12)
First marriage (366)	1.79 (212)	3.20 (93)	2.51 (55)	3.17 (6)
Widowed (88)	1.07 (14)	0.68 (31)	0.65 (37)	0.00 (6)
Divorced (33)	1.95 (18)	2.23 (13)	0.00 (2)	— (0)

with the death of one or other of the spouses, and lead to no stable patterns of alliances. But new links are constantly being formed to replace them. Together, they are a weak, but not negligible, factor integrating a Dyula village or quarter as a moral community.

Marriage with outsiders: Senufo

So far, we have only considered the possibilities of marriage within the Dyula ethnic group. The Dyula are only a minority, albeit a fairly substantial one, in the midst of their Senufo neighbors, and there existed a certain amount of intermarriage between the two groups. However, the Senufo have a system of matrilineal inheritance (Holas 1966; S.E.D.E.S. 1965, vol. 2), whereas the Dyula have a definite ideology of patrilineal descent. The problems involved in the intermarriage of patrilineal and matrilineal peoples have been discussed by J. Goody (1969). In brief, in a marriage between a 'matrilineal' man and a 'patrilineal' woman, the children do not stand to inherit through either line. This would certainly have reinforced any reluctance on the part of the Dyula to give their women in marriage to Senufo men. On the other hand, in a marriage between a 'patrilineal' man and a 'matrilineal' woman, the children might inherit through either line, and be incorporated into the descent group of either parent. In fact, such children were invariably brought up as Dyula, and were incorporated into the husband's descent group. Under such conditions, it is hardly surprising that Senufo men were reluctant to let their sisters marry Dyula men, as any children would be lost to their matrilineages.

As if this were not enough, there were even further obstacles to the

72

marriage of Dyula men to Senufo women. Senufo marriages were normally arranged according to a system of bride service. Once a Senufo man was engaged to be married, he worked on his prospective father-in-law's fields until the marriage actually took place. It is inconceivable that any Dyula would ever have consented to such an arrangement. Most Dyula were loath enough to work on their own fields, much less anybody else's, as long as there was the material possibility of engaging in some other form of profitable activity. Among the Dyula, only a slave worked on somebody else's fields. So, what a Senufo girl's brother stood to lose in terms of recruitment of members to the matrilineage her father stood to lose in the way of bride service in the event that she were to be married to a Dyula husband.

On the other hand, certain Senufo groups did acknowledge one form of marriage in which the husband or his kin pay a high bride-price, instead of bride service, in return for rights *in genetricem* as well as *in uxorem* over the wife (S.E.D.E.S. 1965, vol. 2:39–40). The one class of persons among the Senufo who stood to gain most from the marriage of Senufo girls to Dyula men were the Senufo chiefs. By giving a girl – whether she was a daughter or some other woman over whom he had a measure of control was irrelevant – to an important man in the local Dyula community, a chief stood to gain a useful political ally. The fields of Senufo chiefs were cultivated by their subjects anyway, so it was no hardship for a man in this position to forego his traditional right to bride service. The usefulness of such marriages obviously depended on local political circumstances. In Korhogo, which was under Senufo control but where the Dyula were very numerous within the chiefdom, such marriages could be of obvious advantage. In Kadioha, on the other hand, where the chiefdom was already in Dyula control, there was little point to such a marriage, unless it were to curry favor with the chief of Kadioha or his descent group. Consequently, marriages between Dyula men and Senufo women were more common in Korhogo than in Kadioha; in either community, however, such marriages formed a very negligible part of the total.

Economy and social organization: an overview

Warfare and politics, trade and scholarship were all legitimate enterprises among the Dyula. As the global division of Dyula society into 'warriors' and 'scholars' implied, the organizational requirements of these different activities were not strictly comparable. A successful leader in war or politics needed to be able to mobilize large numbers of able-bodied men under his command. A successful trader or scholar could manage with a relatively small group of kinsmen or slaves working on his behalf. The ideological importance of the *kabila* in Dyula society might appear to represent a compromise. Too small to constitute an independent political force, the *kabila* was nonetheless larger than the typical unit of production in Dyula trade and scholarship. Consequently, a systematic commitment to warfare and politics necessitated, at the very least, close cooperation between several *kabila*s; trade and scholarship, on the contrary, fostered competition between *kabila*s as well as economically independent units within *kabila*s. Different activities thus constituted different pushes and pulls on Dyula social organization; warfare and politics, trade and scholarship represented principles which were not only antithetical, but in a real sense competing.

Ultimately, the choice was not entirely up to the Dyula. Trade and Islamic scholarship were local Dyula monopolies. Warfare and politics, on the other hand, brought them directly into competition with their Senufo neighbors, with the Dyula at a clear numerical disadvantage. Dyula social organization reflected this fundamental fact; the dice were loaded in favor of solidarity within, at the expense of solidarity between, different *kabila*s, and in favor of trade and scholarship at the expense of warfare and politics. The clear and overwhelming preference for marriages within the *kabila* precluded the use of kinship as an idiom for integrating separate *kabila*s within any Dyula village. On the other hand, it made young men within the *kabila* doubly dependent on their elders for wives, reinforcing the elders' claims on the labor of their junior kinsmen for the purposes of trade. Similarly, when arranging marriages between *kabila*s, elders favored the development of links between the villages, which were useful for trade, at the expense of links within the village, which were more conducive to politics. Even the *poro* society, a 'warrior' institution *par excellence* among the Dyula, failed to foster inter-*kabila* cooperation on a significant scale; only a minority of Dyula in most villages participated in the *poro* at all.

Dyula communities were not, of course, entirely fragmentary. Remarriages of widows and divorcees served to maintain links between the different *kabila*s of any one village. Indeed, Kadioha successfully maintained its position as the capital of the Dyula chiefdom with Senufo subjects, a testimony to the real, if limited, success of the Dyula as warriors and political leaders in the region. But the history of Kadioha is one of factional rivalry between its different *kabila*s, a rivalry that was only periodically overcome by threats of invasion from outside or of Senufo rebellion from within. The *kabila*s of Kadioha were united enough to maintain their collective control over their subjects; they were not united enough to expand at the expense of their neighbors.

The small *kabila*, jealous of its identity and its independence, was a unit ideally suited to trade. Its very smallness meant that the demands of *kabila* solidarity did not impinge too much on the independence of individual units of production. On the contrary, the *kabila* operated in ways which fostered the viability of its component productive units, particularly by assuring the dependence of junior members on their seniors at the heads of such units. This was guaranteed by the preference for in-marriage; but the *kabila*, as an arena for resolving disputes among its members, also tended to reinforce the authority of the elders in the group over their sons, nephews and younger brothers. Although the *kabila* was too small to function as an independent political unit, its very cohesiveness allowed it to play a role in factional politics at the village level; a united *kabila* could ally itself with other such groups to constitute an effective faction. In any case, the Dyula *kabila* was a flexible enough social unit to function in a variety of ways and contexts, in the pursuit of political as well as commercial ends. Still, it was better adapted to the needs of trade and scholarship than to warfare and politics. This may explain why the Dyula, who arrived as conquerors in the region, rapidly assumed the status of subjects of Senufo chiefs in most chiefdoms. On the other hand, it is possible that, as a minority, they adapted their social organization to fit the requirements of activities complementary to those of their neighbors, rather than choosing to pursue warfare and politics in competition with the Senufo majority. But it does not really matter whether their social organization was the cause or the effect of the niche they came to occupy within the region. Until the arrival of the French, the Dyula never wholly abandoned warfare as an occupation. Nevertheless, the demands of politics always remained subsidiary to the demands of trade.

PART II

Responses to change

6

The seeds of change

Colonial rule came late to northern Ivory Coast. Indeed, with the sole exception of Rene Caillé, who passed from Odienne to Tingrela disguised as a Moor on his way to Timbuktu, it remained unvisited by Europeans until Binger's exploratory mission in 1888. Almost immediately afterwards, with the intensification of the campaign against Samory, French penetration began in earnest. In 1895, the French established a post on the Bandama River, not far from Korhogo. In 1898, Samory fled westwards with many of the Kadioha Dyula following in his wake. (The Kadioha Dyula had allied themselves quite closely with Samory in quelling a revolt among their own Senufo subjects as well as their neighbors; they were less afraid of the French than of bloody Senufo reprisals once their ally was in eclipse.) Samory was quickly defeated, captured and deported, and the French were left as undisputed masters of northern Ivory Coast. In 1903, the administrative post moved from the Bandama River to the village of Korhogo, and there it stayed. Within fifteen years, a whole region which had never before seen a white man became part of a French colony.

The early twentieth century saw bloody revolts against French authority. The 'pacification' of the Baoule, the Gouro and other peoples of southern Ivory Coast lasted almost twenty years. Throughout all this agitation, northern Ivory Coast stayed calm. The explanation for such pacifism lies perhaps in the widespread belief, reported by administrators, that the French would soon go away; after all, within less than two decades the local inhabitants had seen two African conquerors arrive and depart in rapid succession. Perhaps, having fought under or against these various conquerors, they were simply not prepared to go to war once more. This is hardly to say that the colonial regime was welcomed with open arms, but simply that resistance was rarely more than passive. The main bone of contention was forced labor.[1] Above all, the French needed porters. These were frequently sent to the coast, through Baoule territory, where 'northerners' such as the Dyula were always less than welcome, and where, in the frequent case of an insurrection, they were the first to be slaughtered. In any case, the Dyula

79

perceived this kind of work as appropriate for slaves rather than freemen. (An early report cites the cheeky rejoinder of a Dyula man to a French officer; that when the officer was prepared to act as a porter, only then would he, the Dyula, do likewise.) The authority of many of the chiefs in the region was weak; in despair, some chiefs offered to do the work themselves, having failed to recruit anyone else for the job! Not all the local chiefs were quite so lacking in authority; the French response was to bolster the power of those both capable and willing to cooperate. Foremost among these was Gbon Coulibaly, chief of Korhogo, who was quick to perceive all the advantages to be gained from having his own headquarters coincide with the seat of the local colonial administration. Within a few years, the French – and Gbon Coulibaly with them – were able to exercise a real authority over the region.

The first major reform instituted by the French authority was the abolition of slavery in 1908. This struck a considerable blow to Dyula trade, which had relied, at least in part, on slave labor. The wealthiest were, of course, hardest hit, seeing their resources fritter away overnight. Scholars, too, who had relied on slaves in order that they might devote their leisure to learning, found themselves thrown back on meager resources. Those slaves who had only recently been captured went back to their homes. Others who knew no other home, or who had married and had families, stayed on. They were now free to dispose entirely of their own labor, although they continued to retain slave status. The reform had a leveling effect on the Dyula community, temporarily reducing everyone to a comparable level of riches or poverty.

Local administrators, apprehensive that abolition would provoke the revolt they had so far managed to avert, were pleasantly surprised to find that calm still prevailed. Undoubtedly, the Dyula had already perceived that the blow struck to their economy by abolition was more than offset by the new horizons opened to trade by the *pax colonia*. Travel had by no means become safe overnight, but it was certainly much safer. To the north of Ivory Coast, where French authority had already been established for a considerable period of time, travel and trade had always been possible, but it was now made easier. Dyula traders could venture with little difficulty past Sikasso – where most of them had formerly limited their travels – to the markets of Bamako, Segou and Djenne, and as far north as Nioro. The situation was somewhat different to the south, the source of cola nuts. In the past, all access to the forest had been blocked, not only by the Baoule but also by Dyula communities along the Gouro frontier who jealously defended their monopoly (Launay 1978). Because of periodic revolts, the south continued to be dangerous until after World War I, but, for the first time in centuries, it was possible for the Dyula to venture there with the hope of coming back. At first, the markets on the fringe of the forest were opened up to the Dyula from Korhogo and Kadioha; formerly, these had only been accessible to Manding-speaking traders on the frontier. An old man in Kadioha described his first visit to Biba Logo, one of these markets on the Gouro fringe. The place was still full of terrors for the Dyula trader; he and his companions held on to their swords until they left the market. The Baoule were even more hostile than the Gouro, and the Dyula still hesitated to venture through their territory. However, during this period, Baoule traders apparently came north to Kadioha to buy cloths. To the east, the way was more secure, and traders from Kadioha sometimes carried their cloths as far as Kumasi, where they fetched a high price.

Slowly but surely, French 'pacification' opened up the southern frontier to Dyula traders. The old markets on the fringe of the forest fell into disuse as traders penetrated with impunity into the heart of the forest in search of cola. Towns began to spring up in the sparsely populated south, and Dyula began to settle there, most of them temporarily, but some on a more permanent basis, as agents of the cola trade.[2] Though the peoples of the south, unlike the Senufo, had a long tradition of weaving, they still bought cloths from the Dyula in exchange for cola. Dyula weavers could set up their looms in the southern towns, and even those who remained in the north found that the market for their cloths was expanding.

The growth of urbanization in southern Ivory Coast rapidly led to a rise in demand for cattle; the cattle trade supplanted in importance the old trade in rock salt. Cattle do not survive long at all in the forest, and so they had to be driven down from the north – mostly from Mali and Upper Volta – in order that they could be slaughtered for rapid consumption in the south. The cattle trade had its repercussions in the Korhogo region, where cattle survive at least moderately well. Cattle could consequently serve as an appropriate substitute for slaves as a means of investing profits from trade. This shift in patterns of investment had both advantages and drawbacks. Cattle were a much more 'liquid' asset than slaves, easily convertible into cash when necessary; moreover, their offspring, unlike the children of slaves, were treated no differently from their parents. On the other hand, cattle, unlike slaves, did not contribute anything to the processes of production, and they were also prey to different epidemics than their masters. A symbiosis developed between the Dyula who stayed north and those who moved into the towns of the south. The Dyula in the north provided their kinsmen in the south with cloths which could be sold in exchange for cola nuts. The profits of the cola trade were in turn invested in cattle which could be stored in the north. In short, those who stayed in the Korhogo region provided both goods for exchange for their southern kinsmen and 'banking' facilities for their profits, when these were converted into cattle. On the other hand, the Dyula in the southern towns provided oportunities for their kinsmen up north to participate in more lucrative forms of trade, particularly in cola.

But the Dyula from the Korhogo region were by no means alone in profiting from the opening of the southern frontier. Manding-speaking traders from elsewhere in Ivory Coast (especially the northwest), from Mali and from Upper Volta were all very real competitors. Traders from the Korhogo region were by no means at a competitive advantage compared to some of their colleagues. For example, numbers of Kooroko, originally from the Wassulu region of Mali, based themselves in Bamako early in the colonial period. From there, they could easily exploit the demand for cola, not only in Mali, but even more crucially in Senegal, linked to Bamako by rail. Cattle were both cheaper and in more abundant supply in Mali than in northern Ivory Coast. Finally, Mopti, down the Niger River from Bamako, was the principal source of dried fish, another staple trading commodity (Amselle 1977:189–206). The rail link from Abidjan to Bobo-Dioulasso, and later to Ouagadougou, similarly benefited traders based in Upper Volta, who were also nearer large herds of cattle. In short, traders from Mali and Upper Volta were much closer both to the centers of demand for cola nuts and to the centers of supply for cattle and dried fish. As far as these commodities were concerned, Korhogo's location was no more strategic than it had been before the colonial period. Yet the patterns of trade which had kept the Dyula in business beforehand continued to provide them with a living. Cloths could be traded to their Senufo neighbors, as always, and now in increasing quantities to southerners. Successful cloth traders could still profitably invest their gains in small-scale ventures in cola and cattle.

The Dyula were to discover that this apparent, if modest, prosperity was extremely vulnerable. The first – though ultimately the least consequential – blow came in the form of a cattle epidemic in the 1930s which virtually obliterated the herds of the region, wiping away at a single blow the capital reserves of the traders much as had the abolition of slavery in the first decade of the century. (The same phenomenon was to occur again in the 1960s.) Kadioha, described in the reminiscences of old men – but also in early colonial reports – as rich in cattle can now only boast a handful of cows. This vulnerability of cattle in northern Ivory Coast reinforced the competitive advantage of traders from countries further north. Still, as long as the basis of trade remained the same, new fortunes could be made and old ones reconstituted.

The advent of modern mechanized transport, and in particular the lorry, was to have far more revolutionary consequences than cattle epidemics. Formerly, a man needed a full load on his head or, if he were lucky, his donkey, in order to make a trading venture worth his while. Overhead costs of transport were high, but the proportions did not diminish very substantially, if at all, whether the trader possessed one, or twenty, head loads. Once traders began using lorries it was again to their advantage to transport a full load; anything less increased the proportion of overhead costs on any single item, and reduced the margin of profit. Of course, there is an enormous disparity between what one full lorry and one, or even a few, heads can carry. A trader now has to accumulate a very sizable starting capital before engaging in any venture of consequence. The full impact of this revolution in transportation really began to make itself felt after World War II. For example, between 1926 and 1930, only 300–400 vehicles per year were registered in the country. There were 960 vehicles registered in 1947, 11 517 in 1954 and as many as 43 974 by 1964 (Lewis 1970:146). The effect of the lorry was to divide traders into two sharply distinct categories; on the one hand the large-scale entrepreneur, dealing in bulk; on the other hand, the petty retail trader whose profits became more and more marginal. The lorry had a much more radical effect on the cola trade than on the cattle trade. A lorry full of cattle did not amount to very much, and cattle were still largely driven down to the south on foot. But as profits from cola sold in the north were often invested in cattle for sale in the south, and vice versa, all traders were affected to one degree or another. Formerly, the rich man had been the slave owner; now he was the lorry owner, the 'transporteur'. Few Dyula from the Korhogo region had ever managed to include themselves among the aristocrats of the cola trade. Now, the moderately successful among them found that they were no longer any match for the big traders. The competivite advantage enjoyed by certain Manding-speaking traders from Mali and Upper Volta turned increasingly to the disadvantage of Dyula traders.

Another decisive blow was to afflict Dyula traders during the same period. The cloth trade had always been crucial to the Dyula economy, its mainstay and its last resort, as well as the source of the capital necessary for investing in the more speculative long-distance trade. Once cheap, machine-produced textiles reached African markets – and particularly the markets of the north – the value of hand-woven textiles was bound to plummet. At the outset, these cheaper textiles were imported, but the situation was aggravated by the establishment of the textile industry within Ivory Coast itself, at Gonfreville in the south.

This competition has not yet spelled the end of the local Dyula tradition of weaving. Fortunately for the Dyula weavers, there still exists a certain demand for hand-woven as opposed to machine-produced cloths. The most important source of such demand remains Senufo funerals. The cloths buried on such occasions are never of the machine-produced variety; this fact alone has protected many local Dyula from the onerous burden of farming for their own food. But Dyula dependence on Senufo ritual conservatism is not without its risks. Senufo converts to Christianity and Islam have, in some cases, modified their burial practice in accordance with the tenets of their new religions, abandoning the use of cloths in funeral ceremonies. Even the more lukewarm converts, who adhere to traditional funeral ceremonies in response to pressure from neighbors or kin, are likely to restrict the number of cloths involved to a bare minimum. The tourist trade has also generated a very limited demand for hand-woven Dyula cloth. In particular, the village of Waraniene on the outskirts of Korhogo has become a local tourist attraction and has even specialized in the production of tablecloths! Its success, however, defies emulation, and elsewhere the tourist trade has had a negligible impact on the Dyula economy.

The output of the local Dyula weavers still exceeds the demands of those two sectors – Senufo funerals and tourist 'art' – where hand looms need not compete with machines. Consequently, a certain proportion of Dyula cloths must compete directly with machine-produced textiles in the local market. Local African women sometimes choose to wrap themselves in multicolored hand-woven cotton cloths which can also be tailored to make shirts for men. Yet even the Dyula weavers and their families tend overwhelmingly to prefer machine-produced cloth for clothing themselves. Dyula weavers in Korhogo town have even taken to weaving mono-colored synthetic fabrics, primarily used in making tailored robes for men, again competing, in an even more direct way, with the mass-produced item. Prices for Dyula cloths used as clothing need to be at least as low as those for industrially-produced fabrics. The fact that Dyula weavers are obliged to compete directly in at least some sectors of the cloth trade has tended to bring down the price of cloth even in those sectors where hand-woven cloth has no substitute.

Other items which the Dyula formerly produced for exchange have suffered even more than cloth. Formerly, Dyula weavers relied exclusively on their womenfolk for both spinning and dyeing. The tradition of dyeing had disappeared entirely by the time I was in the field; weavers now use machine-spun colored thread. Women still frequently spin white cotton thread in their spare time to sell to weavers, but the machine-spun variety can be purchased just as easily. I suspect that Dyula weavers continue to purchase homespun cotton from their wives as a cheap way of providing them with 'pin money' which they would otherwise need to dole out in any case! The fact remains that the days when women could amass real fortunes through spinning and dyeing are now but a distant memory. The tobacco trade has met with a similar fate. Machine-made cigarettes, now manufactured in Ivory Coast, are increasingly popular, especially with younger generations; only old men still tend to prefer locally-made snuff. Poorer Dyula men, even in town, still grow small plots of tobacco near their houses, though only in the rainy season. This has virtually become the male equivalent of spinning cotton; it can provide the household with a little extra cash without too much effort, if one has nothing more lucrative to do.

These economic changes have affected the Dyula of Korhogo and Kadioha in much the same way. However, at the same time, other changes were taking place which were to pose radically different problems for the two communities. In part because of the astute politics of its chief, Korhogo was to become the principal administrative center, not only of the immediate region, but of all of northern Ivory Coast. I was told that, at one time, the French administrators had also considered making Kadioha a minor administrative center, a *sous-préfecture*. This idea was unenthusi-astically received in Kadioha, and the eventual site chosen was Dikodougou, capital of another small chiefdom a few miles down the road. As a result, Kadioha's periodic market ceased to have any reason for existing, and the local Dyula have since been obliged to shuttle themselves and their goods to and from Dikodougou market every Monday for a fee. The story is perhaps apocryphal; the residents of Kadioha may never have been faced with the choice. In any case, while the benefits which might have accrued to Kadioha are not entirely negligible, the establishment of a *sous-préfecture* in Kadioha would not have made so very great a difference; compared with Korhogo, Dikodougou is a very small and insignificant place indeed.

Korhogo is the largest and fastest growing town in the north of Ivory Coast (Cotten 1969:63). This growth is all the more spectacular in that the town is off the major road and rail networks leading either to the capital or out of the country to Mali and Upper Volta; both the railroad and the major roads pass through Ferkessédougou, some 55 km to the east. The explanation undoubtedly lies in Korhogo's importance as an administrative center. Neither the early French administrators nor the African residents at the time could have predicted the consequences of the choice of Korhogo as the seat of colonial rule. Indeed, the effects were quite long in the coming. In 1931, a census of Korhogo listed only 4350 inhabitants. The numbers had risen to 11 450 by 1958 and to 23 766 by 1963 (S.E.D.E.S. 1965, vol. 1:87). In large measure, the rapid growth of the town coincided with the collapse of Dyula patterns of trade.

A casual observer might easily conclude that Koko has been engulfed by its growing surroundings. The community is bisected by a paved road (a rarity in Korhogo in 1973) and is further crosscut by a number of wide dirt arteries which are more or less (frequently less) amenable to motor transportation. Most houses are built of cement bricks and have corrugated aluminum roofs; the homes of wealthier residents are painted in various shades of pastel and boast porches where the inhabitants of more modest structures tend to congregate during the daytime. Here and there, isolated pockets of traditional mud huts with thatched roofs belie the impression of total 'modernity'. The layout of Koko is definitely a product of administrative decree; the neighborhood, like the rest of town, has been parceled out into privately-owned plots. The cement architecture also accords well with the aims of the postcolonial national government, though the Dyula eagerly build such homes on their own initiative when they can afford them as they are a sign of prestige and prosperity. The surprising fact is rather that, in spite of these trappings of modern urban life, the residents of Koko have been able to maintain their community relatively intact as such. Clan wards still exist as real entities in space, much as in Kadioha, though from time to time, for lack of an appropriate parcel, an individual may build his home in the 'wrong' part of the community. In appearance, Koko is just another part of the modern town, albeit situated along its edge; but, at least in certain respects, it has kept something of the essence of a typical Dyula village.

The Dyula of Koko have certainly profited to the best of their ability from the services which a moderately large town can offer: schools, dispensaries, a hospital, shops, a large daily market, etc. Almost all of these are 'across the stream', but this is only a short journey, even on foot. Even more importantly, from the point of view of the commercially-minded Dyula, any administrative center of importance necessarily implies a market for goods and services. Large numbers of African civil servants, mostly from the south, are posted in Korhogo (often to their dismay, if they have been accustomed to the more cosmopolitan life of the capital). The town even boasts a sizable expatriate (mostly French) community; in 1973, the Africanization of the staffs of the three public secondary schools had not proceeded very far.

The growth of the Ivoirian economy as a whole was to herald yet another development. Aside from its function as a regional administrative center, Korhogo at long last became a center of long-distance trade. Apart from Korhogo, major urban growth was concentrated in the southern half of the country. Compared with Abidjan, the capital, or for that matter to Bouake, the second-largest town in Ivory Coast, Korhogo is both tiny and provincial. The south boasts many towns which, if smaller in most cases than Korhogo, have few equivalents at all elsewhere in the north. Moreover, the countryside in the south is relatively sparsely populated and – more importantly – is heavily involved in the production of cash crops, mostly coffee and cocoa, on small plantations. The southern farmers may grow enough food to feed themselves, but otherwise they grow coffee and cocoa, rather than food for the migrants to the towns. In the north of Ivory Coast, the only cash crop of any consequence is cotton, far less lucrative than cocoa or coffee. On the other hand, any surplus of staple foods in the north can easily find a market in the towns of the south; the 'underdeveloped' north is frequently labeled the 'granary' or the 'breadbasket' of the country as a whole. Korhogo has become the capital of this trade, partly because the infrastructure required by the administration can serve the trade equally well, partly because the surrounding countryside is densely populated indeed by local standards; even if the average farmer is left with only a small surplus for sale, a large number of such farmers within easy reach of traders generally provide an ample supply.

The seeds of change

As one might imagine, the Dyula of Koko were well aware of these changing patterns of trade. When I asked about the cola trade, I was almost invariably told that it was a thing of the past as far as they were concerned; the risks far outweighed the profits. There was a clear consensus that, given the necessary capital, one could do no better than invest in the food trade. The goods are far less perishable, there is always a demand and all in all it is a much less risky affair. Yet, in spite of these convictions, very few Dyula in Koko were involved in the food trade in 1972–73, when I was in the field. It was not unusual for informants to state that they had participated in such ventures in the past. The prospect of engaging in such trade in the future seemed equally attractive, though few if any made concrete efforts to participate actively. It became increasingly apparent that the Dyula of Koko were simply not the principal agents of the trade. Dyula from neighboring villages such as Kadioha were even less likely to be involved. In other words, the Dyula communities native to the region, the very communities who had thrived in large measure before the advent of colonial rule on their monopoly of local trade, had lost this monopoly in the course of the twentieth century.

Many of their competitors were, in fact, people quite similar to themselves: Manding-speaking Moslems from other parts of northern Ivory Coast, from Mali, from Guinea and from Upper Volta. It is hardly surprising that Korhogo, the largest and fastest-growing town in northern Ivory Coast, attracted migrants from all over the north of the country, especially those whose cultural ethos, like that of the local Dyula placed a high value on commercial success. The relative prosperity of Ivory Coast has attracted migrants from all over West Africa, though particularly from neighboring francophone countries, all of which are conspicuously poor by any standards. Most of these migrants were attracted to the richer towns of the south, but Korhogo nonetheless managed to attract its share. Of course, many of these immigrants to Korhogo fared no better (though perhaps no worse) than the Dyula of Koko or those from nearby villages who also chose to settle in town. Yet some of them did manage to make their mark in the local food trade. There is no doubt that the failure of the local Dyula to corner the trade was the result of the collapse of the cloth trade. Cloth had always been the major source of capital in the regional Dyula economy; other trading ventures were largely financed by profits from the sale of cloth. With the decline in value of hand-woven cloth, such profits became increasingly unrealizable. In the meantime, migrants from Mali and Upper Volta were able to capitalize on the strategic locations of their home communities in order to dominate the trade in cola, cattle and dried fish. It may well be that some of the profits from other forms of long-distance trade were invested in Korhogo's burgeoning food trade. Such reinvestments would undoubtedly have been a wise move; the Kooroko, for example, who have involved themselves heavily in the cola trade, are acutely aware of the decline in profits in that sector (Amselle 1977:229–35). On the other hand, the explanation may lie in the very dependability of the cloth trade until relatively recently; the local Dyula may have waited too late to seek to diversify the source of their profits.

In any case, competition has come from yet another – and for the Dyula a more unexpected – source. Many of the immigrants to Korhogo have been Senufo from the numerous villages in the region. The first step in this urbanization has frequently been the adoption of many of the ways of their more cosmopolitan neighbors of long standing, the Dyula.[3] As usual, the pace was set by Gbon Coulibaly, the chief of Korhogo, who allied himself successively with each of the region's conquerors; as early as 1922, Marty (1922:173) mentions that Gbon was tending towards a conversion to Islam. Gbon became one of the first – if not the very first – Senufo Moslems in Korhogo, a feat which in no way diminished his authority over his subjects, nor his control over the local initiation societies. By 1963, no less than 72% of the Senufo living in Korhogo town declared themselves to be Moslems in a survey (S.E.D.E.S. 1965, vol. 1:94). Senufo migrants who did not already speak Dyula learned it rapidly; they were also more likely than their rural counterparts to refer to themselves by the Dyula equivalents of their Senufo patronyms. Like other immigrants, they also, whenever possible, sought to establish themselves as traders. A Moslem Senufo trader – the very idea would have been unthinkable in precolonial Korhogo – was no longer a curiosity by 1973. While some of the Manding-speaking immigrants to Korhogo may have been able to draw on profits generated through other forms of trade to set themselves up in the food trade, Senufo immigrants profited from their local connections. Closest to the producers – in some cases their own kin – they capitalized on their double status as 'insiders' from the point of view of Senufo villagers and as Moslems *vis à vis* their competitors and colleagues in trade. Thus, as far as the food trade was concerned, the local Dyula were outflanked on both sides: Manding-speaking immigrants controlled more capital; Senufo traders enjoyed closer links with producers.

Throughout all these changes, the Dyula community of Koko has somehow managed to preserve its integrity. A man's patronym is still a fairly reliable index of where he happens to be living. A stranger arriving in Koko need only mention an individual's name to receive directions to his home from virtually anyone. The Friday mosque for the town as a whole is still situated in Koko, and the *imam*ship rotates in the traditional way between the two *kabila*s, the Cisse and the Fofana, which enjoy rights to the office. Yet Koko's relationship to the rest of the town 'across the stream' has altered fundamentally and irrevocably. In 1870, any native Manding-speaker, any Moslem, any trader in the whole of Korhogo was a member of

The seeds of change

Koko's Dyula community. In 1970, the majority of individuals in any one of these categories were to be found 'across the stream'. For its Dyula inhabitants, Koko represents more than just the place where they happen to live; it is a community in the fullest sense of the word. But, for most residents of Korhogo, Koko is only another part of town, just past the cinema on the paved road leading away from the marketplace; many may not even have noticed the brooklet where a little water trickles under the tiny bridge along the road and which, for certain of their fellow townsmen, separates 'home' from the rest of the world.

7

Occupation, migration and education

Rapid economic change, especially since World War II, has afflicted both the Dyula of Koko and those of neighboring villages such as Kadioha. The collapse in the value of hand-woven cloth, which led to their loss of the traditional monopoly over local trade, has had bitter consequences for a people whose very name means 'trader'. Precisely because their daily bread has always depended on what they could earn in the market, if not the marketplace, they have had no choice but to face the situation as squarely as possible. Unlike their neighbors, the Senufo subsistence farmers, who can always fall back on what they produce in order to eat, the Dyula are virtually married to the international, national and local markets for goods and services. In principle, of course, Dyula villagers, and even some townsmen, could always turn to tilling the soil for their own food; but whenever and however possible, most would prefer to avoid this last – and unpalatable – resort.

In the search for a viable way of earning a living, the Dyula of Koko have one distinct advantage over their relatives in the surrounding villages. A market for a whole range of goods and services exists, if not at their very doorstep, only a short way 'across the stream'. Of course, they can no longer expect to enjoy any sort of monopoly over whatever they may have to offer; each new immigrant to the town is as likely to be a competitor as a customer. In any case, the Dyula have always been a mobile people. The Dyula villagers of Kadioha can always move to Korhogo, where they can expect some assistance from relatives in getting themselves established. From the outset of colonial rule, the Dyula have been quick to take advantage of opportunities provided by the opening up of what used to be the southern frontier. Now that the development of the south has far outpaced that of the north of Ivory Coast, the towns of the south offer an additional promise for a better way of life, or at least a better chance of making a living in the open market. Independence, too, has held out another sort of promise. Positions which used to be reserved for the French are now open to Africans with the educational qualifications to fill them. If the twentieth century has seen the

90

decline, and in some instances the demise, of older ways of making a living, it has also offered a myriad of new ways. Of course, despite their attractiveness, these new opportunities have their perils; the Dyula can no longer count on a monopoly of any sort whatsoever. But the perils of competition do not ultimately make much difference; the Dyula must face the open market or starve. These options – new occupations, migration and education – have been opened to Dyula from both Koko and Kadioha. The choices that individuals have made have also had important repercussions for the social organization of each community. The responses of townsmen and villagers have, in many respects, been similar – but they have not been identical; a comparison of the Dyula of Koko and Kadioha is instructive.

Occupation

A glance at the occupations of married men in Kadioha and in Korhogo (Table 3) shows how differently the two communities have adapted to the decline of trade. Behind these differences, we can still pick out certain similarities. Five occupations alone – weaver, trader, modern artisan, chauffeur and Moslem scholar – account for the vast bulk of the total in almost exactly the same proportion in both samples (80.6% in Kadioha and 76.0% in Korhogo). The proportion of traders and scholars is only slightly higher in Kadioha than in Korhogo. On the other hand, weavers, who account for the single highest category in both samples, are almost twice as numerous in Kadioha as in Korhogo. At the same time, modern artisans and chauffeurs together account for 26.6% of the Korhogo sample, but only 5.2% of the Kadioha sample. The two communities alike have over-whelmingly rejected the two occupations at the very bottom of the social ladder: farmer and unskilled laborer. Together these account for only 8.4% of the Kadioha sample and 8.8% of the Korhogo sample. The Dyula in Kadioha, living as they do in the 'bush', clearly favor farming over unskilled labor. In Koko, situated as it is in the town, the numbers are exactly equivalent. Nevertheless, there can be no doubt that the Dyula shun both of these occupations, and, on the whole, have succeeded fairly well in finding alternative means of supporting themselves. On the other hand, neither the Dyula of Kadioha nor those of Korhogo have had much success in obtaining the most coveted jobs, which are, for the most part, in government service (skilled salaried, low-level clerical and high-level salaried). Not surprisingly, the Dyula in the town have fared rather better than their cousins in the village in this respect, but even in Korhogo Koko, such jobs are a rarity.

The one feature that best describes the way in which the Dyula of Korhogo have evolved differently from the Dyula in the villages of the region is undoubtedly the decline of weaving as an occupation, and the corresponding and dramatic rise in the numbers of artisans and chauffeurs.

91

Table 3. *Occupations of married men in Kadioha and Korhogo Koko in 1973*

	Kadioha %	Koko %
Farmer	7.7(12)	4.4(7)
Weaver	43.2(67)	22.2(35)
Unskilled laborer	0.7(1)	4.4(7)
Modern artisan (tailor, mechanic, mason, etc.)	4.5(7)	13.9(22)
Moslem scholar ('marabout')[a]	9.0(14)	7.6(12)
Trader	23.2(36)	19.6(31)
Chauffeur	0.7(1)	12.7(20)
Skilled salaried or low-level clerical worker	3.2(5)	4.4(7)
High-level salaried	0.0(0)	3.8(6)
Other[b]	2.6(4)	3.2(5)
Unemployed[c]	5.2(8)	3.8(6)
Total	100.0(155)	100.0(158)

[a] Some scholars also practiced other professions; there were 5 weavers, 2 traders, one farmer, and one artisan.
[b] Includes one *canton* chief, 2 political party secretaries, one technical student, 3 Arabic students and 2 muezzins.
[c] All of these were either too old or too ill to work.

Weaving, even more than trade, has always been the occupation most characteristic of the Dyula of the Korhogo region. Even now, most Dyula boys are taught to weave, and this is always considered an occupation on which they can fall back, for lack of better opportunities. In this respect, weaving among the Dyula is like farming among their Senufo neighbors. The decline of weaving among the Dyula of Koko quarter in Korhogo may be even more advanced than the figures in Table 3 suggest. Many of the men currently engaged in weaving are in fact old men. Only in a few small *kabila*s, like the Samagassi *kabila*, does a substantial proportion of the young men continue to weave. Nonetheless, young men in almost all *kabila*s who have been unable to find more profitable occupations have continued to weave. But the case of Bazumana, a young man of about twenty-five, shows how meager a weaver's profits have become. He gave up weaving in order to man a small mill erected near his house; the women brought maize, sorghum and millet to the mill to be ground into flour. The work was extremely tiring, even though he was assisted *gratis* by his nephew. (He did not even have to feed his nephew, whose father, Bazumana's older brother, was fairly well off.) His salary was a mere 5000 Frs. C.F.A. a month (about £8.00), still not enough to feed himself, his wife and his child; Bazumana managed only by relying extensively on the assistance of his brothers, several of whom were quite prosperous. Only when the mill proved unprofitable after a few months and ceased operation did he return to weaving. When I left Ivory Coast, his brothers were still trying to find him a better job. Bazumana's plight exemplifies the situation of most, if not all, of the weavers of Korhogo. Weavers in Kadioha are better off, for two reasons. First, they have a traditional monopoly of *koso*, a special type of pattern which yields a somewhat higher price. For a while, other Dyula villages imitated these patterns, but the market was so glutted that the price fell sharply and, for the most part, they ultimately abandoned production, restoring Kadioha's monopoly. Second, the cost of living is much lower in Kadioha, partly because its relative remoteness from urban centers means that the Dyula can obtain food fairly cheaply in neighboring Senufo villages. Nevertheless, the prosperity of the weavers in Kadioha has certainly suffered a considerable decline in the past twenty-five years.

It is not surprising that many Dyula in Korhogo, during this same period, have given up weaving for other professions. Foremost among these, and still one of the most popular, is the occupation of tailor, hardly a drastic change for a people who have so long relied on the cloth trade. The growing importance of the lorry obviously makes the profession of chauffeur attractive, not to mention that of mechanic (though in fact there are relatively few Dyula mechanics). The recent destruction (statutory in most big towns) of traditional African dwellings, replaced by 'modern' cement houses of doubtful comfort but high prestige, has been a boon for masons and house-painters. The Dyula have been quick to enter these, and similar, professions, and become, for example, carpenters. Except for chauffeurs, I have classed all of these persons together as 'modern artisans'; the salient features of this group are that they all own their own equipment and work on their own behalf, rather than as salaried laborers. Chauffeurs, on the other hand, receive some sort of a salary or commission; as such, they can be compared to skilled workers such as electricians and plumbers in government service. But insofar as there are so many chauffeurs, compared with other skilled, salaried laborers, their position is not unlike that of the modern artisan.

If I have dwelt so long on the decline of weaving and the rise of the modern artisan, this is because it has had important repercussions on Dyula social organization as a whole. Production among modern artisans is organized on entirely different lines from the pattern traditional to the weaving industry. Formerly, the unit of production in the weaving industry was typically a group of close kin, working under the direction of the senior member of the group. At the outset, this was also true of the Dyula tailors, the first of the modern artisans. The very earliest of the Dyula tailors in Korhogo passed on their occupation to some, though not all, of their sons. (Sewing machines, unlike Dyula looms, were a scarce resource indeed, and a tailor with a number of sons could not put them all to work sewing at the same time.) But the situation soon changed, and artisans, chauffeurs and even skilled laborers in government service exploited the labor, not of their kinsmen, but of apprentices who were usually not kinsmen at all. Indeed, such persons told me that they definitely preferred *not* to have close kinsmen as apprentices; but, sometimes, a close kinsman who was unable to find a place in the service of an outsider was taken on, albeit begrudgingly. There is indeed a very rational reason for this bias against taking on a kinsman as an apprentice. An apprentice who is an outsider, if his work is not satisfactory, can easily be dismissed, and someone else taken in his place. It is much more difficult to rid oneself of a kinsman, even if he is lazy; to do so would to run the serious risk of censure by other members of the descent group, and to endanger its solidarity. The situation is very different for weavers. Virtually all Dyula can weave, and it is not always easy for a man to entice others to work on his behalf. But tailors, chauffeurs and the like possess rare and valuable skills, and there has never been any lack of persons willing to work for their profit – at least temporarily – in return for the chance to acquire such skills themselves. All the successful artisans I knew were constantly turning down offers of apprentices.

Apprentices from out of town are often lodged, fed and even clothed by their masters. An apprentice from within the town, on the other hand, stays with his parents, and an apprentice from outside who has any kinsmen in town is more likely to lodge with them than with the master. Thus most masters are likely to have a certain number of their apprentices living with them, and the rest living elsewhere in town. One scholar I knew was an exception; he had about forty pupils in all, and lodged a large number of them. This man was also a tailor, and he combined Koranic school and workshop. His older pupils were also his apprentices, and after they had finished with their lessons he would set them to work sewing. The combination of these two activities was quite successful, and he was indeed a prosperous man who, although only in his forties, had already twice made the pilgrimage to Mecca. Nevertheless, this kind of arrangement was quite unusual, and I know of no other scholars who followed his example. The labor of the apprentice is entirely for the benefit of his master, although many masters let their apprentices take on small jobs from time to time for their own account. The ability of a master to make the most profit possible from the labor of his apprentices depends both on his reputation and on the amount of equipment he owns. The most successful artisans work mainly on specific demands from customers, often on commissions from market traders. On the whole, it is less profitable to produce an item in the hope of eventually finding a buyer; the artisan may find himself compelled to sell an item more cheaply than its actual cost of production. It is not in an artisan's interest to produce a large quantity of goods with the labor of many apprentices unless he is assured beforehand of a market – in other words, if his reputation assures him a steady, regular clientele. If his reputation is big enough, he still needs to make the capital investment in equipment – sewing machines for a tailor, for example. Tailors with a very good reputation and several machines can set up a workshop in town, with large numbers of apprentices producing quantities of clothes on demand. Despite the high turnover rate in apprentices, such artisans never lack the personnel to man such workshops. Such an enterprise can cease to be highly profitable, however, if the quality of the work declines, and the artisan loses his reputation. Outside such workshops, there are many artisans with smaller reputations, little equipment and only one or two apprentices, if any.

One major drawback of the apprentice system is that it has led to a very rapid and massive proliferation of artisans. After a few years, the successful apprentice leaves his master and tries to set up on his own: a master's apprentice one year will become his competitor the next. The price the master ultimately has to pay for the cheap labor of his apprentices is competition from an ever-growing number of other artisans. Sabati Cisse, the first tailor in Korhogo Koko to invest in a sewing machine, was quite a rich man, and for a long time he enjoyed a virtual monopoly. But, with competition among artisans now, it is extremely difficult for any one man to establish a really solid reputation – and very easy to lose a reputation acquired with great effort. Certain industries are still in great demand, and in relatively short supply; the recent spate of building in the towns has kept the masons well fed; tailors have probably suffered the most. Tailoring was one of the earliest 'modern' crafts to attract the Dyula and other Africans; the supply of tailors has been increasing over a longer period of time, and is now well in excess of the demand. This glut on the market has been offset to a certain degree by younger artisans moving into the small administrative towns, the *sous-préfectures*, where the supply of artisans is still short of even the relatively restricted demand. Such solutions can only stave off the crunch for a little while. Modern artisans enjoyed a brief, but very real, golden age, but now the market value of their skills is in rapid decline, and the Dyula will shortly find themselves driven once more to find other sectors of the economy to absorb their labor.

In the meantime, the apprentice system has sounded the death knell of the traditional, kin-based Dyula unit of production. This is even largely true in village communities like Kadioha, where weavers prefer to send their sons out as apprentices to someone in the towns, rather than keep them weaving at home and profiting from their labor. In the short term, this has made life even harder for the remaining weavers, who can no longer profit from the labor of close kin to establish themselves in the cloth trade. But, if the situation of the modern artisan is in rapid decline, that of the weaver is even more desperate. By making their sons apprentices rather than weavers, the fathers have a better chance of having someone to support them adequately in their old age.

The virtual disappearance of the old unit of production has not eliminated close economic cooperation between kin by any means. Formerly, a group of kinsmen worked together in a common enterprise, under the management of a single one among them. This system survived for a while even among modern artisans. I know of one of the first tailors, who used to turn over a part of his earnings to his younger brother, who would engage in long-distance trading ventures. The profits from these ventures were then returned to the elder brother, who was uniquely responsible for managing their joint budget. Such cooperation has completely disappeared from the Koko quarter of Korhogo, though not entirely from among the weavers and traders of Kadioha. In Korhogo, brother and brother, father and son all have different occupations and each manages his budget independently. This is true even among kinsmen who eat their meals in common, as did a group of seven brothers I knew very well. Each brother buys his own food separately, and gives it to his wives to cook. All the food is then taken to the house of the eldest brother where the brothers in one place, their wives and children in another, all share it together. But, though they keep their budgets strictly separate, close kinsmen may still give one another substantial amounts of money in certain circumstances. They will all contribute towards the expenses of marriages and funerals, though the largest share almost always falls on those directly concerned. A man's kinsmen may also contribute sums of money towards trading ventures, building a house, buying necessary equipment such as sewing machines and so forth – initial investments which, if successful, will make him financially independent in the future; indeed, his continued prosperity may benefit the group as a whole in the long term, for he may be in a situation to render the same services to others. Finally, close – and even sometimes relatively distant – kinsmen will provide the necessities of life for the aged, the ill and even those unfortunates who never quite manage, despite all their efforts, to make enough money to support themselves and their families.

The moral basis of cooperation has necessarily changed radically. Formerly, cooperation rested on the authority of senior kinsmen over the labor of their juniors, with the rights and duties of each relatively clearly defined. Much of the kinship system, including in-marriage within the *kabila*, reinforced the dependence of juniors on their seniors. Nowadays, the positions are reversed, and seniors are often heavily dependent on their sons and nephews. But the moral obligations of the prosperous towards their less fortunate kinsmen are diffuse; to a large degree it is a matter for the individual to decide. The parsimonious face the resentment of other members of the group; on the other hand, they may feel that there is more to be gained by keeping their earnings largely to themselves, rather than by distributing them left and right to kinsmen in need. Such dilemmas are by no means peculiar to the Dyula; it is a common predicament of civil servants in African towns.[1] But the fact that the Dyula are almost entirely dependent on monetary earnings as opposed to farming for subsistence makes them especially vulnerable to this sort of situation. The Dyula still stress the moral authority of seniors over juniors; few individuals reject the notion in principle. But the economic basis of this authority has been undermined by the decline of trade and weaving and the system of production associated with these activities.

Migration

Very early in the colonial period, the Dyula were attracted in large numbers to the south of Ivory Coast because of the cola trade. But even as the prospects for trade declined, the flow of migrants continued, for the south of the country was growing much more prosperous than the north; coffee, cocoa and wood, Ivory Coast's three principal exports, all come from the south. With the notable exception of Korhogo, all the larger towns are in the south, and even the more modest towns are growing much faster than their counterparts in the north (Duchemin and Trouchaud 1969). The towns of the south, rich as they are by African standards, seem to offer better prospects for Dyula in all walks of life, from weavers to modern artisans to civil servants.

Migration, of course, was never an unusual phenomenon for the Dyula, even in precolonial times. As traders, they were always prepared to move on to new markets, where the prospects were better. The Dyula communities of Kadioha and Korhogo were themselves founded by migrants in this way. But the scale on which such migration began to take place in the twentieth century was unheard of before. Modern communications – the road and rail network – meant that individuals could travel farther, faster and more safely than ever before. Formerly, migrants who moved a long way off from the home community lost all touch with the home community, just as the Cisse of Kadioha gave up all contacts with their relatives in Bakongo, in northern Guinea, whence they first came. Nowadays, this is no longer necessary, and buses link Korhogo daily with the capital, some 650 km away, quite as far from Korhogo than is Bakongo.

Table 4 gives an idea of the extent of this migration today. Out of a sample of 318 married men in Korhogo and Kadioha, nearly 40% of those from Kadioha are living outside their home town, and more than 30% of those from Korhogo. It might be assumed on this basis that migration has a more pronounced effect in Kadioha than in Korhogo, but this statement must be qualified somewhat. A relatively small percentage of men from Kadioha are

Table 4. *Current residence of husbands from Kadioha and Korhogo Koko*

	Kadioha	Korhogo	Other north Ivory Coast	South Ivory Coast	Other
Kadioha	60.5% (95)	3.2% (5)	13.4% (21)	22.9% (36)	0.0% (0)
Koko	0.0% (0)	68.9% (111)	6.2% (10)	24.2% (39)	0.6% (1)

living in Korhogo, but quite a large number are living elsewhere in the north. Some of these are actually living very close to Kadioha, particularly those in Dikodougou, only 16 km away on the road to Korhogo. Most Dyula from Kadioha and Korhogo living elsewhere in the north are not very far away from their home towns, and are in perpetual contact with their kinsmen back home. The proportion of men from Korhogo living away from home but still in the north of Ivory Coast is much smaller than that from Kadioha. On the other hand, in both communities, between one-fourth and one-fifth of all men are currently living in the south of the country.

If we consider the lengths of stay of migrants (both those who have returned and those who are still away) from Kadioha and Korhogo, we can see a further confirmation of the differences between the two communities (see Table 5). A considerably higher proportion of Dyula from Korhogo have never been abroad at all. On the other hand, a higher proportion of Dyula from Korhogo have been outside the region for more than ten years. Of those who have been away for fewer than ten years, more than half from Korhogo have been away for fewer than five, as compared with one-third from Kadioha. Finally, very few men from Koko have spent any length of time in the north of Ivory Coast outside Korhogo, but those who have have been away for a long time. On the other hand, it is quite common for men from Kadioha to spend either a short or a long time in the north outside their home town. In other words, Dyula from Korhogo, if they leave at all, go to the towns of the south of Ivory Coast. Either they stay for only a short while, or more or less for good. This pattern is not very hard to explain. The opportunities in the towns of the south for individual Dyula are, for the most part, of the same kind as in Korhogo. Only, because the southern region is richer, it is perhaps easier to attain success in the south. So the Dyula from Korhogo may go south to try his luck. If he succeeds in setting up a prosperous enterprise of one sort or another, as a trader or artisan or cleric, he stays in the south, comfortable in his position. On the other hand, if his enterprise meets with only limited success – or if he fails completely – he can do just as well for himself in Korhogo, and so he comes back home.

Table 5. *Past experience of migration by husbands from Kadioha and Korhogo Koko*

	Kadioha %	Koko %
Never abroad	30.6 (44)	48.1 (74)
Less than 5 years abroad	11.8 (17)	11.0 (17)
5–10 years abroad, less than 5 outside the north	12.5 (18)	0.0 (0)
5–10 years abroad, more than 5 outside the north	11.1 (16)	9.7 (15)
10 or more years abroad, less than 5 outside the north	14.6 (21)	6.5 (10)
10 or more years abroad, more than 5 outside the north[a]	19.4 (28)	24.7 (38)

[a] Only one of these persons in Kadioha, and none in Korhogo, spent between 5 and 10 years outside the north.
All the rest, without exception, had spent 10 years or more outside the region.

The situation is rather different for Dyula from Kadioha. The towns of the south offer a host of opportunities which they cannot find back home, much more so than for their counterparts from Korhogo. Even the least successful are likely to earn more in town than they can in the village. Many weavers from Kadioha set up looms in the southern towns, where their cloths fetch a higher price than up north. A weaver from Kadioha – but not a tailor from Korhogo – is almost sure to be better off in the towns of the south than he is at home. Nevertheless, unlike the really successful men, Dyula from Kadioha who only make a modest living for themselves in the south will, for the most part, eventually come home. As they grow older, they can assume the status and authority of an elder in Kadioha; most prefer to become poor elders in Kadioha than slightly richer, but relatively anonymous, denizens of the towns.

However, the most striking difference between the Dyula of Kadioha and Korhogo is the frequency with which those from Kadioha leave home to establish themselves elsewhere in the north. First of all, even the smallest towns of the north, like Dikodougou, offer better prospects than staying at home in Kadioha. Although perhaps not so true for the weaver, this is certainly so for the petty trader and the modern artisan. But there are also real advantages in setting oneself up in another village (particularly a Senufo village) – quite apart from escaping the sometimes burdensome authority of one's elders. In a Senufo village, the Dyula weaver, trader or scholar enjoys much more of a monopoly than in either the towns, however small, or a Dyula village like Kadioha, all too full of other Dyula traders, weavers and scholars like himself. The security which such a situation offers is hardly enough, however, to tempt many Dyula from Korhogo nowadays. Even the small towns of the north offer few attractions to the Korhogo Dyula; the modern artisans who set up shop there are more likely to be young men from the villages like Kadioha who have finished their apprenticeship in Korhogo. Some traders, especially those in the grain trade, may find an advantage in basing themselves closer to the Senufo producers. Occasionally, a special opportunity in one of the small northern towns may present itself to a given individual; the *imam* of Dikodougou, for example, is a Dyula from Koko. But, for the Dyula of Korhogo as compared to those of Kadioha, migration within the northern regions is, for obvious reasons, very marginal indeed.

What have been the effects of this migration on Dyula social organization? It is difficult to arrive at any very general conclusions, because it has often had quite different effects on different *kabila*s. The proportion of men who actually go off varies greatly from *kabila* to *kabila* in both Korhogo and Kadioha. Small *kabila*s specializing in scholarship often have very low rates of migration. Part of the answer lies in the fact that they may have rights to the office of *imam* in the local mosque. Also, these *kabila*s enjoy a good local reputation, owing to their long tradition of learning, despite the fact that their scholars are by no means necessarily the most learned. Once such scholars leave their home town, they are often eclipsed by more brilliant rivals. In other *kabila*s, a migrant who achieves a notable success in one town is virtually sure to attract a cluster of kinsmen in his wake: the success of any individual in a given *kabila* is likely to affect the rate of migration of the *kabila* as a whole.

But even in *kabila*s with relatively high rates of migration, there is a wide range of variation in the possible relations that may develop between those who go off and those who are still at home. Examples from the Dambele, Keita and Kamagate *kabila*s of Kadioha can give some idea of this range of variation. On one extreme, there is the case of a number of individuals who left the Dambele *kabila* a relatively long time ago for the towns of the south. They broke off all contact with their kinsmen in the north, opting in the most definitive way to become, and to stay, citizens of the new towns. To all intents and purposes, they are no longer members of the original *kabila* in Kadioha, and their kinsmen up north do not know (or affect to ignore) who they are, what they are doing, etc. (Other members of the same *kabila* have left for the south and yet maintained strong bonds with the home community.) The Keita, the second largest *kabila* in Kadioha, has a large number of migrants in the towns. It is thought to be richer than other *kabila*s and it is said that this is because its migrants pay more attention to their affairs in the towns than to matters at home. On ritual occasions like marriages and funerals, rather than visiting home *en masse*, the Keita migrants send a delegation of only a few members. Dyula from other *kabila*s in Kadioha have mixed feelings about such an attitude. On the one hand, they attach a great deal of value to active displays of solidarity within the *kabila*, particularly on ritual occasions. On the other hand, the Dyula, as a trading people, have always respected success, even at the price of violating certain group norms. A third, and also extreme, example of what may happen in a *kabila* because of migration is that of the Kamagate. They have an extraordinarily high rate of migration: of seventeen married men from the *kabila* in the sample, only two – the two oldest – were living in Kadioha at the time. The rest were mainly concentrated in three or four towns, though a few were off on their own. Yet, when a newly-constructed *bron*, the ritual house belonging to the *kabila*, was recently consecrated, the majority of these migrants came back to Kadioha for the ceremony. The fact that such a house was constructed at all is ample proof that the migrants were still sending money back home and maintaining a lively interest in affairs in Kadioha. Ultimately, the relationships that persist between the migrants and those back home vary both from individual to individual within the *kabila*, and from *kabila* to *kabila* within the community as a whole.

Education

Western education came very late to the Dyula. As Moslems, they were hardly likely to be attracted to mission schools, which, in any case, were never very widespread in northern Ivory Coast. Furthermore, the whole of northern Ivory Coast was the region most remote from the capital, nor did it produce raw materials for export. Under these circumstances, it quickly became the most 'backward' region of the country, the last to receive roads, schools, hospitals and other fruits of Western technology exported to Africa. Even in a town like Korhogo, Western education made very slow progress. No Dyula from Koko quarter were enrolled at primary school until after World War II. At the time, Dyula fathers did not willingly surrender their boys to the influence of French schoolmasters; the first candidates had to be recruited by force. For almost a decade, education continued to be virtually confined to the towns. Kadioha, a large village indeed, with a population of about 2000 according to the official estimates, did not have a school until the mid-1950s. A survey of the Korhogo region shows that, in 1963, the Korhogo region still lagged way behind the rest of the country. The survey estimated that only 17% of school-age children in the region were actually enrolled in primary school. This compared with 24% for the region of Katiola and 34% for the region of Bondoukou, both in central Ivory Coast, and with 82% in the region of Abengourou, 77% in the region of Dimbokro and 97% in the region of Agboville, all in southern Ivory Coast. (For Ivory Coast as a whole, the rate of primary school enrollment was estimated at 45%.) (S.E.D.E.S. 1965, vol.1:60)[2] By and large, the level of education in any region varied in inverse proportion to its distance from the capital. Primary school education was very widespread in the south, only moderately so in the center and hardly at all in the north. Since independence, government policy has called for a very rapid expansion of education at all levels throughout the country; both the number of schools and the rate of primary school enrollment have increased significantly in the Korhogo region within the last ten years. Nevertheless, the gap in education between the north and the south in Ivory Coast remains very great indeed, and is not likely to close for a long time.

Thus French education among the Dyula of the Korhogo region is virtually restricted to men under the age of forty in 1973. A few men who have had no formal schooling have taught themselves to read and write for particular reasons. (For example, in Ivory Coast, candidates for the driving license are required to pass a test to prove that they are literate; this means that anyone who wants to become a chauffeur has to learn to read and write, and the driving schools in Korhogo actually provide courses – at a high price – to teach these skills as well as driving lessons.) In my sample of married men in Korhogo and Kadioha, I found that only 6.4% in Kadioha and 9.3% in Korhogo had ever been to school. For those between the ages of thirty-five and fifty, 4.0% in Kadioha and 10.5% in Korhogo had some formal schooling; as for those under thirty-five, 19.5% in Kadioha and 21.1% in Korhogo had been to school. It might appear that the gap between Korhogo and Kadioha, very apparent for those over thirty-five, has tended to narrow. However, for those married men under thirty-five, only 9.7% completed primary school in Kadioha as compared to 18.4% in Korhogo; moreover, none at all in the Kadioha sample had completed four or more years of secondary school as compared to 7.9% in Korhogo. Thus, if equivalent numbers enrolled in primary school in Kadioha and Korhogo, those in Korhogo, for the most part, pursued their studies to a significantly higher level than those in Kadioha.

The number of children being sent to school has continued to rise in both Korhogo and Kadioha (Table 6). A recent and most important development has been the education of girls. Here, the difference between Korhogo and Kadioha is most apparent. In Kadioha, the vast majority of girls still stay away from school; in Korhogo, there are still more boys than girls going to school, but the gap has become significantly narrower. In both communities, though, not only do fewer girls than boys go to school, but they also tend to stay in school for a shorter period of time. Statistics for children above the age of twelve are inadequate, but they show a striking difference between boys and girls. In Kadioha, no girl in the sample has actually completed primary school as compared to about 15% of the boys above the age of twelve. In Korhogo, about 21% of the boys over twelve, and a few twelve-

Table 6. *Percentages of children between the ages of nine and twelve with some formal schooling in Kadioha and Korhogo Koko*

	Kadioha %	Koko %
Males	39.4	55.2
	(N = 33)	(N = 29)
Females	12.5	41.9
	(N = 24)	(N = 31)

year-olds as well, have completed primary school, but only about 11% of the girls have done so, and very few of these have gone on to secondary school.

The Dyula themselves, as Moslems, also have their own system of education, in Arabic. As far as the married men in the sample are concerned, 86.4% in Kadioha and 92.5% in Korhogo have had at least some Arabic education, the vast majority having gone through the Koran at least once. In other words, most adult males are totally illiterate in French but are at least partly literate in Arabic. The normal age for entering Koranic school is seven or eight – the same age as for primary school – and so it is possible to compare the Arabic education of boys between the ages of nine and twelve with that of adult males. Of the boys in Kadioha, 67.9% have had some Arabic education; of those in Korhogo, 73.3%. Though these rates are still high, they do tend to suggest that, as more and more boys are entering primary school, fewer and fewer are getting an Arabic education. This suggestion is borne out quite unequivocally by Table 7. Those boys who have had no formal schooling in French have rates of education in Arabic quite comparable to those of adult men; but those boys who have gone to primary school are less than half as likely to have any education in Arabic at all.

One reason that schoolchildren are unlikely to have much education, if any, in Arabic, is that primary school in Ivory Coast is conducted entirely in French, and not in any African language. Primary school pupils are struggling hard enough with French, without the additional burden of grappling with Arabic. But whatever the reason, Dyula parents tend to believe that an education in French and an education in Arabic are antithetical, and the statistics bear this out. This antithesis does not apply throughout West Africa, and there are some governments which established primary schools for Moslems where Arabic is a part of the curriculum. Such

Responses to change

Table 7. *Percentages of boys between the ages of seven and twenty-four in Kadioha and Koko with some Arabic education*

	Kadioha %	Koko %
No formal schooling	85.1 (N = 87)	88.0 (N = 75)
Some formal schooling	40.9 (N = 22)	33.3 (N = 48)

schools do exist in Ivory Coast – there is even one in Korhogo – but they have no government recognition. As a result, Dyula parents who are anxious that their children receive a formal education prefer to send them to state-run schools, whereas those who want to give their children a religious education are much more likely to send them to a local scholar, either someone in the *kabila* or a man whose reputation they know well. Not surprisingly, those *kabila*s which show the greatest opposition to Western education tend to be those in which a high proportion of adult males have traditionally become scholars. Thus, as late as 1973, not a single child from the Diane *kabila* in Korhogo had ever gone to primary school. (In 1974, a young man from the *kabila* finally persuaded the elders, after a long struggle, to let him send his little girl to school.)

In deciding whether or not to send a child to school, each Dyula parent is faced with the dilemma of choosing between conflicting sets of values. On the one hand, education is the only means of obtaining a civil service job (or a high-ranking job in a private European-run firm). Such jobs bring high salaries (and often opportunities for additional and illegitimate sources of income), high status and fringe benefits such as paid vacations and family allowances. The Dyula, who have traditionally respected those who earn a large amount of money and can conspicuously consume luxury goods, are not insensible to these attractions. They are also well aware that such jobs are more secure than either trading or the crafts such as tailoring or automobile repairing, not to mention weaving. On the other hand, they are not always unreasonably afraid that the values inculcated by Western education will undermine the moral values of the Dyula community. They worry that the educated few are becoming more and more lax in their religious practices, especially as many have not benefited from a strict religious education. The relative security of government jobs, too, is a source of anxiety, insofar as it decreases the dependence of educated Dyula on their kinfolk, and may lead to a reluctance on the part of Dyula civil servants to fulfill what others consider their obligations toward their kin.[3] Finally, Western education, even more than the system of apprenticeship, erodes the authority of the elders: both the means of learning the necessary skills (i.e. formal schooling) and the source of revenue for civil servants are totally outside the control of the Dyula community. These fears are compounded by the fact that Dyula civil servants, when they have the opportunity, prefer to be posted outside their home region, precisely in order to gain a measure of freedom from the demands of their kinsmen at home. The fact that these coveted jobs are still so scarce among the Dyula (see Table 3) means that the lucky few are subjected to even more pressures from their kinsmen than might be the case if such jobs were more common.

Anxiety about the consequences of the spread of Western education can be found in both Kadioha and Korhogo, but, on the whole, parents in Korhogo tend to respond more favorably than their village counterparts to the attractions of education for their children. First of all, Korhogo is itself an administrative center, and most Dyula have regular contacts with civil servants, both from the region and from outside. Perhaps more importantly, townsmen are also more conscious of the decline in the security of the position of the modern artisan, and they wish to seek something better for their children. So, while weavers in the villages are sending their sons to the towns as apprentices in order that they may become modern artisans, the artisans in the towns are sending their own children to school in the hope that they may become civil servants. But the civil service, like the new occupations, is hardly a panacea for the predicament of the Dyula. With the rapid expansion of education in Ivory Coast, more and more people are becoming qualified for jobs in government work. This is not to say that there is no room for expansion; the secondary school system, for example, is still largely staffed by expatriates, most of them French. But within the last fifteen years, the educational level required of candidates for government posts has risen very rapidly. The primary school certificate, which not so long ago assured its holder a good job, is now almost worthless by itself. In the race for diplomas, the Korhogo region, despite the recent expansion of education, is still at a severe disadvantage compared to other regions within the country, not to mention neighboring countries whose educated elites are often attracted by the relative riches of Ivory Coast. Because Ivory Coast lagged behind its neighbors for a long time, as far as education is concerned, and because of its real, if fragile, relative prosperity, school leavers have only recently begun to feel the pinch, and their situation is still far from critical. The avenues to success are not yet blocked to educated Dyula, and they have not yet begun to worry about a future whose prospects, unfortunately, may well be bleak even for the educated.

105

8

Being Dyula in the twentieth century

What does it mean in Ivory Coast nowadays to call oneself, or someone else, 'Dyula'? In the first place, the original meaning of the term – 'trader' – has not lapsed. Nevertheless, the use of the term as an ethnic category label has spread far beyond the confines of the area where Manding-speakers lived as minorities before the colonial period. Precisely because of its newfound currency, the label has taken on somewhat different meanings for different people in different places. The shades of meaning which the term 'Dyula' can assume are not the same in Korhogo, in Kadioha or in the towns of the south.

Only in Kadioha has usage remained fairly straightforward. Almost the entire population of the village calls itself 'Dyula'. Aside from the families of one forest ranger, a few primary school teachers and – for a while – an anthropologist, everyone in the village descends from those Manding-speakers who came to settle there in the nineteenth century and, in many cases, before. This situation is by no means unique to Kadioha; numbers of nearby Dyula villages are virtual replicas of Kadioha on a smaller scale. But the fact that the term 'Dyula' in Kadioha seems so unambiguous is also a product of the cultural conservatism of Kadioha's non-Dyula neighbors, the Senufo. The basic distinctions between 'Dyula' and 'Senufo', the very cornerstones of the Dyula sense of identity in the region before the colonial period, still hold true today in the villages near Kadioha, and indeed throughout much of Korhogo's hinterland. 'Dyula' are Manding-speaking Moslems, practicing the time-honored occupations of weaver, trader or scholar for the most part. Senufo villagers living near Kadioha have tended to remain equally true to their old stereotype. They are still farmers, and most have chosen to remain faithful to their traditional religious ways. For the resident of Kadioha, the vast majority of individuals whose paths he might cross in the course of an ordinary day are either unequivocally 'Dyula' or unequivocally 'Senufo'. Of course, those who leave Kadioha to settle in Korhogo or, more likely, in the towns of the south have to leave this comfortably neat division of the world into 'Dyula' and 'Senufo' behind at

106

least until, as elders, they come back to Kadioha to finish their days at home.

The towns of southern Ivory Coast are largely peopled by 'strangers'. Very many of these migrants are from northern Ivory Coast. In 1965, an estimated 265 000 'Malinke' – no less than 40% of their total numbers in Ivory Coast! – were living outside their region of origin, as were 245 000 'Voltaics' – 34% of their total population – of whom 240 000 were Senufo and only 5000 were Lobi.[1] None of the other ethnic clusters in Ivory Coast showed comparable tendencies to emigrate, either in terms of absolute numbers or of proportions. Furthermore, immigrants from other African countries were, in overwhelming numbers, likely to be close cultural cousins of the inhabitants of northern Ivory Coast: these include an estimated 220 000 Malians, 200 000 Voltaics and 150 000 'other Africans', among whom are included many Manding-speaking Guineans (Roussel 1967:27; cited in B. Lewis 1970:41–2). In short, the towns of the south are hosts to 'northerners', either from inside or from outside the country, in very large numbers indeed.

Under the circumstances, it is hardly surprising that the term 'Dyula' has become a 'supertribal' ethnic label (see Rouch 1956), a global category lumping together peoples who heretofore, or in their home regions, considered themselves distinct, but who, as immigrant strangers, are seen – and may well see themselves – as relatively similar both culturally and socially. Yet, even as used most broadly by the peoples of the south, the term 'Dyula' contains fundamental ambiguities, depending on the different criteria used for ascription (B. Lewis 1971:273). On the one hand, any 'northerner', on the other hand, any Moslem (particularly if he is dressed in conspicuously 'Moslem' attire), may be labeled 'Dyula'. As it happens, these two criteria are not by any means entirely consistent. In the first place, not all Moslems are 'northerners'. Certain 'southerners' have converted to Islam, gone into trade and in other ways adopted at least some of the cultural mores of the Manding-speaking 'strangers'. Such individuals may in certain circumstances be labeled 'Dyula', but they have not relinquished their 'southern' identities; they are still Baoule, Bete, etc. (B. Lewis 1970:306–7). Admittedly, Moslem 'southerners' remain somewhat exceptional, if not absolutely isolated, cases. The majority of 'southerners' are at least nominally Christian. Islam is perceived, not entirely without reason, as the religion of 'northerners'. However, by no means all 'northerners' are Moslems. For example, the Senufo who move to the towns of the south are far more likely to convert to Islam than to Christianity, but a Senufo Christian is not really a rarity, and many of the Senufo 'converts' to Islam are lukewarm believers at best. While it may be true that the vast majority of Moslems are 'northerners', and even that most 'northerners' are Moslems, any given individual may well be one without being the other.

Responses to change

In another sense, it is still possible for an individual to be a 'Moslem northerner' without necessarily being labeled a 'Dyula'. A more precise meaning of 'Dyula' is a 'native Manding-speaker'; these are the people who are most likely to refer to themselves as 'Dyula', as well as being so labeled by their 'southern' neighbors. This sense of the term excludes Voltaics such as the Senufo as well as peoples such as the Hausa and Wolof from more distant African countries. Native Manding-speakers are automatically considered 'northerners' in the south, even if they were born in the south and have lived there all their lives. Moreover, the vast majority of native Manding-speakers in the south are Moslems, although many have only adopted Islam since the advent of colonial rule. Recent converts or not, they are all much more likely to conform to stricter patterns of Islamic observance than, for instance, many of the even more recent Senufo converts to Islam. While it is definitely false that all Moslem 'northerners' are native Manding-speakers (though the vast majority do speak Manding, if only as a second language, in the towns of the south), native Manding-speakers undoubtedly constitute the largest single category of northern Moslems in Ivory Coast. Socially, as well as culturally, they are in a dominant position among immigrants from the north, and it is for this reason that many southerners consider the categories of 'Moslem', 'northerner', and 'native Manding-speaker' as virtually equivalent – in a word, 'Dyula'.

These 'Dyula' communities of the south are by no means socially homogeneous.[2] In the first place, 'Dyula' immigrants from within Ivory Coast (such as the Dyula from Koko and Kadioha, but also Malinke from northwestern Ivory Coast), are distinguished from 'Dyula' whose homelands lie outside the national boundaries, in Mali, Guinea and Upper Volta. 'Dyula' from outside Ivory Coast have enjoyed something of a competitive advantage in long-distance trade. Not surprisingly, this has aroused the jealousy of Ivoirian 'Dyula', who feel that outsiders have deprived them of some of the benefits of citizenship. Such xenophobia has hardly been the monopoly of Ivoirian Dyula. For example, in October, 1958, the capital was the scene of three days of violent riots directed against immigrant Togolese and Dahomeans. Though the number of such immigrants was relatively small, these countries had benefited from a longer history of Western education, allowing Togolese and Dahomeans to occupy a disproportionately large number of coveted white-collar jobs in Ivory Coast (Zolberg 1969:245ff). The principal participants in these riots were undoubtedly 'southerners' who, better educated by far than most of their 'northern' compatriots, had a far greater vested interest in restricting clerical jobs to Ivoirian citizens. However, in 1956, Bouake – the second largest town in Ivory Coast – had been the site of skirmishes between Ivoirian and 'foreign' 'Dyula' (Zolberg 1969:202). Ivoirian 'Dyula' were sometimes the victims, rather than the instigators, of such riots; southerners, especially in the southwest, were prone to consider all 'northern' immigrants as 'foreigners', no matter how long their history of settlement within the modern borders of the country. This happened in Gagnoa, in 1955, where Bete indigenous to the region rioted against all immigrant 'Dyula', Ivoirian or otherwise (Zolberg 1969:203; B. Lewis 1970:289–90). This tendency among southerners to lump Ivoirian 'Dyula' willy-nilly with their 'foreign' colleagues has certainly inhibited any attempts on the part of Ivoirian 'Dyula' to align themselves with their southern compatriots against nationals of other African countries. In any case, relations between Ivoirian 'Dyula' and their 'foreign' counterparts can be quite cordial. The idiom of common culture binds them in opposition to the southerners. But national divisions between immigrant 'Dyula', corresponding as they do to divergences of material interests, always imply the potential for conflict, usually peaceful but conceivably violent.

The Ivoirian 'Dyula' communities in the south are in turn characterized by significant social distinctions corresponding to regions of origin. These are denoted by the Manding suffix *-ka*, meaning 'the people of', which can be tacked onto virtually any place name to designate groups or categories of widely differing sizes. At the large end of the spectrum, it can be added to the name of the whole country: Ivoirians can be called '*Côte d'Ivoire-ka*' and Guineans, '*Lajine-ka*' (for 'La Guinée'), etc. On the other hand, a clan ward, as a geographical entity, can be designated by the addition of the suffix *-ra* to a patronym; for example, the Cisse clan ward of Kadioha is called Cissera. The inhabitants, that is to say, the members of any particular clan ward, are also normally designated as a category by the *-ka* suffix, e.g. *Cisseraka*. Even a segment of a clan ward, if it corresponds to a place name in any way, will be accorded the *-ka* suffix. Ivoirian 'Dyula' (and, for that matter, 'Dyula' from neighboring countries) quite frequently refer to themselves in this way in terms of their home towns, as the 'people of Odienne', or Seguela, or Mankono, or Touba, etc. In principle, any village or town can serve as such a reference of origin; Dyula from Kadioha could style themselves *Kadioha-ka*, as indeed they frequently do in Kadioha and even in Korhogo. But in any particular southern town, there are not likely to be enough Kadioha Dyula for such a label to be very useful; moreover, most Ivoirian 'Dyula' not to mention the 'foreign' ones, are unlikely to have heard of Kadioha in the first place. Consequently, the *-ka* suffix among immigrant 'Dyula' is most frequently appended to the names of larger towns to designate both the town itself and its hinterland. Thus the Kadioha Dyula in the south are effectively *Korhogo-ka*.

Needless to say, Korhogo qualifies as a large enough place to serve as a reference of origin for immigrants in the south. For example, in Gagnoa, Ivoirian 'Dyula' have grouped themselves into spatially and socially distinct residential quarters according to their region of origin. Korhogo is one of six place names (along with Odienne, Mankono, Touba, Boundiali and Seguela) designating such a quarter. Although in Abidjan the *Korhogo-ka* are residentially dispersed, there are certain locations within the capital which serve as social foci for them. In 1972, a non-stop daily bus service was successfully inaugurated between Korhogo and the capital. As with all motor transport traveling north from the capital, the terminus was situated in Adjame, one of the northernmost quarters of town as well as a relatively favored place of residence for the *Korhogo-ka*. However, this terminus was situated most atypically at a petrol station some distance away from Adjame's *gare routière*, the hub of most passenger transportation leading in and out of the capital. I was told that the spot had been chosen precisely in a location where *Korhogo-ka* tended to gather; in any case, the bus terminal itself automatically made it a crucial meeting place, no doubt the most important one in Abidjan. I was also informed that the warehouse where staples exported from Korhogo for sale in the capital were stored was only a short distance away; this warehouse, known as *le magasin de Korhogo*, was apparently another focal point holding together the network of *Korhogo-ka* in the capital.

In one crucial respect, the category *Korhogo-ka* is not equivalent to most other such categories among Ivoirian Dyula, such as *Odienne-ka* or *Mankono-ka*. The northwestern part of Ivory Coast, the homeland of the majority of Ivoirian immigrant Dyula, is almost exclusively Manding-speaking. In the Korhogo region, on the other hand, Manding-speakers are a minority, both among the indigenous population and among the migrants. Depending on the speaker's criteria of ascription, Senufo migrants in the south may or may not be included in the general 'Dyula' rubric. On the other hand, Senufo from the Korhogo region are unambiguously included in the category *Korhogo-ka*, even by a native Manding-speaker. Indeed, the proprietor of the warehouse mentioned above as one of the central meeting places of *Korhogo-ka* in Abidjan is a Senufo – though as a northern Moslem trader, he is also in many respects a 'Dyula'! In short, the label *Korhogo-ka* includes large numbers of individuals who are not *necessarily* considered 'Dyula'.

Despite a very real sense of common identity as *Korhogo-ka*, Manding-speakers from the region are likely to have closer links with other Manding-speakers, and Senufo with other Senufo. In a similar vein, migrants from the same community – Koko or Kadioha, for example – are often bound by even closer ties. Indeed, the Dyula system of in-marriage within the clan ward, by inhibiting the development of kinship ties which crosscut local *kabila* affiliation, has tended to preserve the relevance of *kabila* membership even among migrants in the south; fellow *kabila* members are likely to constitute the majority of any individual Dyula's kinsmen, even within the broader immigrant community, not to mention the *Korhogo-ka*. Within (but only

110

within) the community of *Korhogo-ka* in any of the southern towns, labels like *Koko-ka* or *Kadioha-ka* can still designate effective subcategories. Indeed, within these subcategories, sub-subcategories such as *Cissera-ka* – members of the Cisse *kabila* of Kadioha or Korhogo – are by no means necessarily irrelevant.

Within this maze of category labels designating groups of various sizes and, in some instances, inconsistently applied, Dyula immigrants from Koko or Kadioha undoubtedly acknowledge two 'primary identities': 'Dyula' (in the specific sense of 'native Manding-speaker') and *Korhogo-ka*. However, each of these identities necessarily implies membership in broader categories. A Manding-speaker is necessarily a 'northerner' and almost certainly a Moslem; *Korhogo-ka* are by definition 'northerners' and Ivoirians. These various identities, rather than forming a segmentary hierarchy of greater or lesser exclusiveness, tend to crosscut one another. Consequently – in principle, at least – Dyula from Koko or Kadioha, by choosing to stress one identity rather than another, can align themselves with almost any segment of the local population in the southern towns in opposition to some other segment. It might seem that Dyula from the Korhogo region, by choosing to stress common ties of either nationality, religion, language and culture or region of origin, are in an optimal position of flexibility and able to manipulate their identity to fit any given situation. In fact, the tendency among southerners to treat all 'northerners' as quintessential 'foreigners' seriously restricts their options. Still, the ambiguities of Dyula 'ethnicity' due to these crosscutting ties are very real, and the Dyula can seek to use these to their advantage.

Ultimately, the sense of identity among Dyula in the south who are from Koko or Kadioha embodies something of a paradox. On the one hand, any of a number of these broad, crosscutting category labels link them to large numbers of their neighbors, particularly to other immigrants, but sometimes to 'southerners' as well. On the other hand, these broad categories have not superseded very particular and indeed exclusive identities; their affiliation to Koko or to Kadioha, and even to specific clan wards within these communities of origin, continues to have meaning in the towns of the south.

The notion of 'Dyula' identity is thus infinitely more complex in the towns of the south than in the villages of the north. In the north, the situation in Korhogo, and particularly in Koko, is, in a sense, the most complex of all. Like any of the towns of the south, Korhogo's population consists mainly of recent immigrants of very diverse origins. Yet, unlike the towns of the south, Korhogo is part of a region where the 'Dyula' – at least some of them – are at home.

The Dyula of Koko who live in Korhogo sometimes use the term 'Dyula' in the same ways that it is used in the south. Numbers of individuals within the community have lived in the south, and many close kinsmen are still living there now. But, in this respect, Koko is no different from Kadioha. Two crucial factors differentiate the two communities. In the first place, no recent Manding-speaking immigrants have come to settle in Kadioha. The Dyula of Kadioha, with the exception of a few wives, are all *Kadioha-ka*, full members of the community rather than just resident in it. As we have seen, Korhogo on the contrary, has attracted numbers of Manding-speaking immigrants in the recent past; some of these have come from relatively nearby villages, but most have far more distant origins. By and large, they have settled 'across the stream'; yet even Dyula residents of Koko will often label such immigrants 'Dyula'. The second phenomenon which characterizes Korhogo, but not Kadioha, is the presence of large numbers of Senufo Moslems. Some of these adhere only nominally to the tenets of Islam; such individuals may call themselves Moslem and yet not be recognized as such by the Dyula of Koko. But the Dyula have had to admit, if grudgingly, that some Senufo meet all the standards of piety which the Dyula set for themselves, and cannot rightfully be excluded from the community of Islam. The Dyula of Koko have, in some cases, been their teachers; this was certainly so for the former chief of Korhogo, Gbon Coulibaly, first and most conspicuous among the Senufo converts. Such Senufo have also adopted many of the mores traditionally associated only with Dyula: Moslem attire, 'proper' funeral practices, wedding rituals and, of course, trade. In the words of one of my informants, '*a kera Dyula ye*' – 'they have become Dyula'.

In spite of this, the Dyula of Koko have not entirely abandoned their traditional world view, their division of the social universe into the two categories of 'Dyula' and 'Senufo'. They sometimes talk as if Korhogo were still largely populated by Moslem Dyula traders on the one hand and pagan Senufo farmers on the other. Partly, this orientation reflects their maintenance of close ties with the villages nearby, where the traditional stereotypes are largely accurate descriptions. But it is also true that 'pagan' practices, and particularly the activities of the Senufo *poro* initiation societies, are an everyday sight in Korhogo town. A number of sacred – and still active – *poro* groves are situated in Koko itself, easily visible from within the Dyula community; after all, the Dyula were never the sole occupants of Koko, even before the colonial period. To the delight of tourists, Senufo funerals are periodically heralded by masked dancers in the streets of town, both in Koko and 'across the stream'. Indeed, the Dyula of Koko still frequently use the (somewhat disparaging) term *banmana* – 'pagan' – to refer to their Senufo neighbors, whether they are Moslem or not.

The persistent use of these traditional labels, 'Dyula' and *banmana*, would seem to imply that the Koko Dyula still define themselves with reference to other groups in town as 'Moslem traders'. In fact, these criteria of ascription are increasingly anachronistic. Before the colonial period, all

112

Being Dyula in the twentieth century

Moslems and all traders in Korhogo were to be found in Koko; until the end of World War II, I suspect this was still largely, if no longer absolutely, the case. But by now, that majority of either Moslems or traders lives 'across the stream'. While it is true that all Koko Dyula are Moslems, fewer and fewer can reasonably be called traders, and Koko has lost its position as the hub of trading activity in Korhogo. In fact, two criteria of ascription other than Islam and trade now differentiate the Koko Dyula community much more successfully from the rest of town. In the first place, they are 'native Manding-speakers', 'Dyula' in the sense of the word as it is used in the towns of the south; as such, they remain different from their Senufo neighbors, even the Moslems. In the second place, they are indigenous to the region, as are the Senufo, but unlike most of the 'Dyula' living 'across the stream'. Applied together, these two ascriptive criteria define 'Dyula' in quite another sense than 'Moslem traders' as 'native Manding-speakers indigenous to the region' (or, more precisely, indigenous to regions of Ivory Coast where Manding-speakers lived before the colonial period as an ethnic minority, primarily among Senufo). Consequently, a particular individual may be labeled 'Dyula' in one context, using one of the broader senses of the term ('Manding-speaker' or 'Moslem'), yet, in another context, it may be said that he is *not* 'Dyula', in the most restrictive sense of the word. Even in this restricted sense, the Koko Dyula are not the only 'Dyula' in Korhogo, but they are quite definitely in the majority.

The Dyula of Koko can thus claim to be the 'real' Dyula of Korhogo town, but they cannot claim to be the 'only' Dyula. This ambiguity, the polysemy inherent in the word 'Dyula' even in Koko, is largely a result of new patterns in the incorporation of immigrants in Korhogo town. Before the colonial period, all Manding-speakers, all Moslems, all traders settling in Korhogo would incorporate themselves as *lunans*, 'strangers', in Koko. For example, two small clan wards in Koko are said to be of Hausa origin, but their members have been fully assimilated into the Koko Dyula community. In other words, all 'Dyula' lived in Koko, whatever ascriptive criteria one might have chosen to define them. In the twentieth century, this ceased to be the case. In the first place, the colonial and later the African administration did not officially recognize Koko's status as *the* Moslem quarter, as had the Senufo chiefs of Korhogo. In any case, 'Dyula' immigrants had flocked to Korhogo in such numbers that there was no question of their assimiliation into the Koko community; on the contrary, the burden was on the shoulders of the Koko Dyula to differentiate themselves from the newcomers! It is not, strictly speaking, true to say that the Koko Dyula community is no longer assimilating outsiders. The status of *lunan*, of a 'stranger' incorporating himself into the Koko community by becoming a dependent of a particular clan ward, still exists. This was in fact my own claim to membership in the Koko community, but I was not alone in this respect. For example, the Coulibaly *kabila* of nearby Dyendana was linked through a series of marriages to a segment of the Cisse *kabila* of Koko. One young Coulibaly man was a promising scholar who, for obvious reasons, chose to settle in Korhogo, where he might hope to establish a reputation for himself, rather than stay in his village. At the time I was in the field, he was living as a 'stranger' in the *kabila* of his cross-cousins, the Cisse. While his cousins claimed that he was one of the most learned Arabic scholars in Koko, he was still too young to take the turban, and was consequently not in a position to earn a great deal from his practice. In order that he might pursue his studies full-time, his cousins subsidized his living expenses – even to the point of underwriting a large part, if not the lion's share, of the expenses of his marriage! While there were other such recent 'strangers' in Koko, they all (myself excepted) met two particular conditions: they were Dyula from nearby villages, and they were linked by prior ties of kinship to members of one or another *kabila* of Koko. Whereas, in the past, the Koko Dyula community assimilated a wide variety of immigrants, it has recently incorporated only a very few under precise circumstances. This is even the case for the small minority of Manding-speakers who have chosen to settle in Koko rather than 'across the stream'. For example, certain migrants from Odienne settled right next to the Dyula in Koko. Character-istically, they were known as *Odienne-ka*, a name which explicitly stressed their affiliations to a community outside Korhogo. Nor did it follow that Dyula from nearby villages, even if they had kinship ties within Koko, assimilated themselves as 'strangers' to the community. For instance, one Dyula from Kadioha was a distant patrilateral parallel cousin of the entire Cisse clan ward, as well as work-mate and father-in-law to one particular member. His son-in-law was also foster father to another daughter of his, and the two men were generally very close in all respects. Had this man chosen to settle in Koko, he would have been assimilated very easily. Technically, he would not even have been a 'stranger', but could rightfully have claimed full membership in the Cisse clan ward. However, he chose to live 'across the stream' and was thus considered *Kadioha-ka* by residents of Koko, despite the intensity of the ties linking him to members of the community. Thus, not only was the category of potential 'strangers' incorporated into the Koko community redefined much more restrictively, but even those who might potentially have incorporated themselves in this way did not necessarily avail themselves of the opportunity. A community which formerly incorporated immigrants very easily is now restricted largely to the principle of ascription by birth.

These changing patterns of recruitment have, of course, altered the very identity of the community itself. Once *the* Dyula community of Korhogo, it is now essentially a community of the descendants of the town's nineteenth-century Dyula inhabitants. This very exclusiveness undoubtedly accounts for Koko's continuing identity as a community, in every sense of the word. Not surprisingly, this sense of identity finds its fullest expression in ritual – not the rituals of worship, which ideally stress the unity of all Moslems in Korhogo, both inside and outside Koko, but rather life-crisis rituals: weddings, funerals and naming ceremonies for infants. Both weddings and funerals involve a whole cycle of rituals; in both cases, certain key rituals in each cycle involve the large-scale distribution of prestations known as *saraka.*[3] These prestations express virtually the entire web of social relationships of the protagonists and their immediate families. Many of these relationships are internal to the clan wards performing the ritual. However, no such ritual can properly be performed without a representative from each clan ward in Koko, who must receive a token prestation for his ward as a whole, being present. In a similar vein, every Dyula village in the vicinity of Korhogo must also be represented and publicly granted its rightful prestation; conversely, rituals in these villages require a representative from Koko. For the recipient, the cash value of such prestations is negligible; 50 Frs. C.F.A. is not unusual. While each such gift represents only a fraction of the total expenses involved in the ceremony, the relatively large number of groups involved makes the total sum seem less trivial. Yet the significance lies, not in the actual sums that change hands, but rather in the public, indeed ostentatious, way in which they are transmitted. Each wedding or funeral stresses for all concerned the bride's, the groom's or the deceased's membership in a particular *kabila*, the *kabila*'s inclusion in the total community of Koko and the place of the Koko Dyula community itself in a wider community which also includes the Dyula villages of the region. For the duration of such rituals, more than at any other time, Koko transforms itself into a typical Dyula village.

It may seem peculiar that members of the Koko Dyula community are willing to go to such lengths to maintain their sense of a separate and distinct identity. Why haven't they simply merged with the larger category of 'Dyula' living in large numbers 'across the stream'? In the first place, this separate identity has allowed them to preserve strong links with Dyula in neighboring villages, those very links being expressed in major life-crisis rituals. From the villagers' point of view, the advantages of these links are obvious. They facilitate immigration into town; even villagers who do not choose to incorporate themselves as 'strangers' in Koko can often count on help from kinsmen in Koko when they settle in. Also, villagers often need temporary lodgings in Korhogo, for example if they have accompanied a hospitalized kinsman; they can easily find a temporary 'host' in Koko. They may have to deal for one reason or another with the local government administration; residents of Koko are far likelier to have both contacts and know-how to help them in their dealings with civil servants. But, if these ties seem equally important to residents of Koko, they cannot work entirely for the villagers' benefit. The villages represent a potential source of wives for Koko Dyula, though it is exceptional to find urban-born women married to villagers.[4] Moreover, Dyula villagers tend to have closer ties to the rural Senufo than do their counterparts in Koko. Such links constitute the only advantage, albeit a minor one, which Koko Dyula enjoy in the food trade. For more modest ends, these ties have borne more fruit, from time to time permitting Dyula in Koko to obtain food in relatively small quantities at a considerably lower price than its market value in town. In any case, those Dyula in Koko who have not abandoned all hope of engaging in the food trade count on these links to get themselves back in business.

The importance of regional origins in the sense of identity among 'Dyula' migrants to southern towns constitutes a second factor for the maintenance of Koko's separate sense of identity in Korhogo. Precisely through their continued affiliation to the Koko community, Dyula emigrants can claim to belong to the broader category of *Korhogo-ka*. Paradoxically, the very fact that large numbers of Dyula from Koko have chosen to emigrate contributes to the cohesion of Koko as a Dyula community. Unlike precolonial patterns of migration, modern immigrants in Ivory Coast have not, for the most part, been fully integrated into the communities to which they have moved, even if they have chosen to establish permanent residence. This is equally true for emigrants from Koko to the towns of the south and for 'Dyula' immigrants to Korhogo, especially those from outside the region. A 'Dyula' without any regional affiliation has few claims on any of his fellow immigrants. If he belongs nowhere, his situation as a 'stranger' anywhere is all the more precarious. By preserving their sense of separate identity, the Koko Dyula not only ameliorate their position elsewhere but also preserve themselves from becoming 'strangers' in their own home town.

This jealously guarded sense of their separate identity does not, however, imply that the Koko Dyula have isolated themselves from the rest of Korhogo, that the community constitutes a village island in the midst of the ocean of the town. The history of a recent voluntary association in Koko provides an excellent example of the willingness and ability of the Koko Dyula to extend ties in Korhogo outside their own community. Following turbulent political events in Ivory Coast in 1963 and 1964 (Zolberg 1969: 345–55), the government kept a very strict watch on voluntary associations, actively discouraging, if not disbanding, any associations with explicitly 'ethnic' bases of membership. This policy was relaxed in 1970, alongside the rehabilitation of persons arrested or stripped of office in 1963. The Koko Dyula lost no time in forming an association, called *Lamogoya*. The name itself is difficult to translate; it denotes a group of people who may be less than kin but are more than mere neighbors, who not only live together but also, more profoundly, belong together. Membership was entirely restricted to Koko Dyula. In principle, the association was exclusively for the benefit of young men and women, and virtually all unmarried youths among the Koko Dyula belonged. However, the leadership of the organization was comprised only of married, middle-aged and relatively prosperous men; these were still 'young men' by the standards of elders in Koko, but they provided an even sharper contrast to the adolescents who formed the bulk of the association's membership. The stated purposes of the organization were twofold: to organize *goumbe* dances for the unmarried youth, and to provide moral and financial assistance to members in time of crisis, particularly for funerals. The organization proved quite successful, at least as far as the dances were concerned; my wife and I witnessed several of them shortly after our arrival in the field. The other purpose of the organization – helping members in time of need – never, to my knowledge, became a reality. Undoubtedly, its philanthropic aims were unrealistic. Adolescents are rarely, if ever, faced with the responsibility of paying for funerals; the older leaders of the organization, on the other hand, were chosen precisely because they were relatively prosperous, and would have been able to pay for funeral costs without resorting to extraordinary aid. I suspect that the ostensible charitable goals of the association were never actually taken very seriously; they lent an aura of respectability to an organization which essentially provided acceptable recreation for local youth as well as a forum where wealthier members of the community might attempt to assert their leadership.

Lamogoya, when I arrived in Korhogo, was visibly a success, a seeming proof of the vitality of exclusiveness among the Koko Dyula. I was consequently surprised to hear, several months later, that the very leaders of the association had chosen to dissolve it in its present form. This was not an admission of failure, but, on the contrary, of success. It was to be renamed, expanded and directed to an entirely new set of goals. The association was to include all *Koko-ka*, not only Dyula but also Senufo and Dieli. The inclusion of the Dieli – traditionally, the local 'caste' of leatherworkers – on an equal footing with Dyula and Senufo may seem surprising. The Dieli language is still occasionally spoken in Koko, but it is well on its way to extinction; even before the colonial period, Dieli were frequently assimilated into local Dyula communities, a process which has been dramatically accelerated in the recent past. However, the Dieli enjoy the prerogatives of being the very first settlers of Koko. All other groups are ultimately their 'strangers', and they have undisputed rights over the office of chief of Koko. Whatever limited authority the office may have had before the colonial period, the title is now purely honorary. But given these claims, even honorific, the Dyula organizers of *Lamogoya* could hardly expect to count on Dieli support for its projected expansion without due deference to their senior status.

The first issue which needed to be decided in the formation of this new

117

organization was its name. The three ethnic groups from which members were to be drawn speak three different languages. The ideal was to find a name which meant the same thing in all three languages, so that no single group could claim moral priority. A French name would, of course, have been equally neutral; in fact, I suggested this way out of the dilemma to one of the organizers, but he – and apparently the others – felt that this would be inappropriate. Astonishingly, a 'neutral' African name was discovered: *Koko Ton*, 'the Koko Young Men's Association'. 'Koko', though originally a Dyula word, was accepted by everyone in Korhogo as the name of the neighborhood; similarly, the Senufo had borrowed the Manding word *ton* before the colonial period (S.E.D.E.S. 1965, vol.2:59).

The aims of *Koko Ton* were very different from those of *Lamogoya*. In practice, the older organization had been purely recreational. *Koko Ton* was not at all concerned with organizing recreational activities, and took its philanthropic mission much more seriously. Moreover, the nature of this mission was conceived in very different terms. In theory (if only in theory!), *Lamogoya* was supposed to help individuals as the need arose; the purpose of *Koko Ton* was to benefit the neighborhood as a whole. Feelings ran high in Koko that other neighborhoods 'across the stream' had been the primary beneficiaries of the rapid growth of the town as a whole. Koko had only one primary school and no medical facilities. The stated aim of *Koko Ton* was to collect enough money to build either a school or a maternity ward in the somewhat unrealistic hope that they could then pressure the national government into staffing the facility.

Naturally, the new aims of the organization appealed to a different constituency from that of *Lamogoya*. The 'young men' who were members of *Koko Ton* were not, for the most part, adolescents. Essentially, all married men in Koko from those in their twenties to those in their fifties were considered members; the oldest 'young men' in the association could more reasonably have been styled 'young elders'! Moreover, the nature of *Lamogoya*'s activities had effectively limited participation to persons living in Koko at the time; *Koko Ton*, on the contrary, could aspire to involving emigrants from Koko as well as current residents. The dispersal of emigrants throughout all the major towns of the south precluded the effective inclusion of all the *Koko-ka*. But the largest, and generally the most prosperous, single group of emigrants was situated in Abidjan, the capital. Ultimately, the organizers of *Koko Ton* established two separate branches of the organization, one in Koko and the other in Abidjan. They decided that no fewer than three separate sets of officers were to be elected by members of the organization: one set for the Koko branch, one for the Abidjan branch and one for the organization as a whole! This proliferation of leaders was motivated by political concerns rather than by any notions of organizational efficiency. With so many slots to fill, each constituent ethnic group was assured of adequate representation in the organization's hierarchy.

Given *Koko Ton*'s ultimate goals, its first primary concern was to organize the collection of dues from its constituent members. The very real differences in wealth among *Koko-ka* had to be taken into account. Weavers and farmers were naturally recognized to be the poorest members of the organization; they were asked to pay 500 Frs. C.F.A. as an entrance fee and 100 Frs. C.F.A. per month. All others (civil servants and tailors were the specific examples I was given) were asked to contribute 1000 Frs. C.F.A. to enter and 300 Frs. C.F.A. per month. The organization's leaders, strategically chosen to represent every section of Koko's population (this meant taking into account differences within as well as between the constituent ethnic groups!), were assigned the task of explaining *Koko Ton*'s goals to the population at large, and of course of collecting the money. In this respect, the Abidjan branch has been very successful; I was told that they rapidly managed to collect as much as 75 000 Frs. C.F.A. The Korhogo branch met with considerably more difficulty. In the first place, many of Koko's residents are relatively poor and have developed effective tactics of passive resistance against any claims on their purses. Secondly, in Abidjan, the *Koko-ka* form a relatively cohesive group of 'strangers'; at home in Koko, internal factional rivalries are far more likely to come to the forefront of attention and to impede the effective functioning of any organization.

Partly because its goals are so much more ambitious, *Koko Ton* has been beset by far more problems than was *Lamogoya*. *Lamogoya*, while it lasted, was a success; realistically, *Koko Ton* is likely to be a failure. Nevertheless, the transformation of *Lamogoya* into *Koko Ton* was a highly significant event. Criteria for membership in *Lamogoya* stressed the ethnic exclusiveness of the Koko Dyula. *Koko Ton* did not deny their distinct identity. On the contrary, ethnic differences within Koko were very consciously reflected in nearly every aspect of the structure of the organization as a whole. But the very existence of *Koko Ton* implied that the Koko Dyula realized that, as such, they were part of a larger whole – the neighborhood of Koko – which transcended certain ethnic boundaries. Indeed, it was recognized that *Koko Ton* was the offspring of *Lamogoya*. If the Koko Dyula had incorporated themselves into the wider framework, this was hardly a matter of passive acquiescence. On the contrary, the Koko Dyula themselves, particularly the leaders of *Lamogoya*, had taken the leading role in broadening the scope of their own association to include outsiders.

This is hardly to say that internal rivalry did not plague the organization. The very choice of the name demonstrated that ethnic sensibilities were a delicate issue. The collection of dues was even more likely to lead to factional bickering. On the one hand, the honor of every constituent group was at stake; it was a matter of pride, at least for the leaders, that their own group paid more (or rather defaulted less chronically) than others. On the other hand, any group which paid relatively regularly had good reason to resent others who stood to benefit equally without their proportional sacrifice to the community weal. Obviously, the choice of leaders was also a potentially explosive issue. More than pride was at stake here. Leaders of *Koko Ton*, especially if the organization met with some success, could lay a real claim to leadership within the neighborhood as a whole. Officers in the organization could reasonably hope to use their position as a springboard for entry into the more rewarding world of town politics. The organizers of *Koko Ton* were remarkably astute in forestalling factional rivalry along ethnic lines; they took care to allocate positions of leadership to members of each ethnic group. Moreover, they chose Dieli candidates as the presidents of two of the three organizational hierarchies – the Abidjan branch and the 'Bureau National', the organization as a whole. It was explained to me that, as the most educated men in Koko (one was a pharmacist trained in France, the other an engineer), these were logical choices. However, as members of the smallest ethnic group by far, they were in no position to assert their own constituency's domination over the organization as a whole. By favoring Dieli, the organizers (consciously or not) diminished the far more serious threat of rivalry between Dyula and Senufo. However, this very success in averting inter-ethnic rivalry favored the emergence of factions *within* each ethnic group. This was the case, at least, among the Koko Dyula, where such factions, running at least partially along clan ward lines, already existed. Despite all these problems, the establishment of *Koko Ton* firmly demonstrated that the Koko Dyula were seriously prepared to consider themselves as part of a wider unit within Korhogo, the *Koko-ka*.

Through their participation in *Koko Ton*, the Koko Dyula linked their community *as a whole* to other communities in Korhogo. It was equally true that Dyula as individuals had ties to other individuals outside the community and living in town, not only in Koko but 'across the stream'. The Koko Dyula still preferred marriages within the clan ward. Nevertheless, I witnessed several marriages and engagements between Dyula residents of Koko, both men and women, and persons 'across the stream', almost invariably 'Dyula' – Manding-speaking Moslems. Far more frequently, the professions of individuals necessitate the development of outside ties. 'Across the stream', tailors, for example, are likely to find customers, apprentices (including ex-apprentices, for the affective link is usually enduring) and retail traders who order clothing on credit. Given the cutthroat competition among tailors in Korhogo, these latter deals are increasingly inevitable. Unless a tailor's reputation is so solid that he is assured a steady supply of individual customers, he has every advantage in

120

recruiting a clientele of traders, who invariably expect (and if they are reasonably trustworthy, receive) credit. Because of the risks involved, such relationships involve a considerable measure of trust on the tailor's part. This trust, if not betrayed, can blossom into a friendship which extends beyond the realm of business. Dyula from Koko who are fortunate enough to hold a salaried job form ties, sometimes very close, with work-mates. In any case, Korhogo is still a fairly small town, and social barriers between the Dyula of Koko and other Moslems, particularly Manding-speakers, are hardly formidable. Enduring friendships with 'Dyula' 'across the stream' are the rule, rather than the exception. While major life-crisis rituals *require* the presence of representatives from all of Koko's Dyula clan wards, they invariably attract others invited from 'across the stream'. For that matter, my host, whose personal network both within and outside Koko was very extensive, was constantly attending rituals 'across the stream'. Most Dyula men in Koko have neither the time nor the inclination to attend such rituals so assiduously, but virtually everyone is certain to do so from time to time.

Whether or not their personal networks outside Koko are extensive, all Koko Dyula are linked to others in town through national and local politics. Before independence, certain members of the community had been active in the Rassemblement Démocratique Africain (R.D.A.), which was to become the P.D.C.I., the ruling party of Ivory Coast. This was true even in the earliest days of the party, when it had been actively, and sometimes violently, repressed by the French colonial administration. However, political involvement became inevitable after independence when two rival factions emerged in Korhogo's local party hierarchy. When I was in the field, each of these factions was led by a member of the family of the chief of Korhogo. The 'ruling' family's policy of cooperation with the French had been extended to the postcolonial government to the point that it even controlled both rival factions in the local party bureaucracy! The political events of 1963 had allowed one faction to gain the upper hand. In 1970, the rehabilitation of the victims of 1963 was accompanied in Korhogo by a change in the balance of power which left the other faction in control. All Dyula in Koko had allegiances to one faction or the other. Many were content with expressing support for the winning faction, whichever one it happened to be at the time, taking care not to burn all their bridges behind them in case they had to switch back. However, certain individuals had strong ties to one faction or the other. This was a definite advantage if one's faction came to power; the most loyal supporters received the amplest rewards. But such allegiances involved real risks. Strong supporters of a losing faction could be harassed and even punished. But anyone who took an active role in local politics, or who aspired to do so, had to take sides publicly and unambiguously; such a decision automatically implicated their kinsmen as well. Ultimately, while allegiance to local party factions linked everyone among the Koko Dyula to outsiders, it also split the community in two along factional lines.

Through *Koko Ton*, work ties, personal friendship networks and party factional allegiances, the Koko Dyula community is connected in a variety of ways to the rest of town. Only in the case of *Koko Ton* do these ties presuppose the community's identity as such. Indeed, in the case of local politics, the community tends to be split rather than united. Yet the community remains a tangible reality, and not a sentimental memory, in the everyday lives of its members. Its nature, however, has changed radically, if imperceptibly. The tendency on the part of Koko Dyula to lapse into a vocabulary which divides their social universe into 'Dyula' and 'pagans' betrays this change. Such terms are becoming increasingly inadequate descriptions of social life in Korhogo. It is in many ways a comfortable view of the world, for it implies that a person's membership in the Koko Dyula community defines his place in society, and even, more generally, in life. This has simply ceased to be true. Koko now includes individuals in many different walks of life; in each case, similar individuals can be found just 'across the stream'. For the moment, Koko survives as a community because its occupationally and financially heterogeneous members still feel that they are, in fundamental ways, bound to one another, that they are, as it were, *lamogoya*. But these ties of solidarity necessarily place the greatest burden on the shoulders of the most prosperous, the most successful. They are the ones with the means to prove that this solidarity is effective, and not merely a show of words. They are also the only ones faced with the temptations of keeping the fruits of their success to themselves by preferring the less onerous company of their peers. Before the colonial period, 'class interests', however one might want to define this nebulous term, were firmly embedded within the community. Now such interests crosscut community membership and threaten the community's very existence as a meaningful reality.

9

Dyula Islam: the new orthodoxy

While I was in Koko, my opinion was solicited several times about the following matter: ought one to pray *Allahu Akbar*! with arms outstretched or with arms crossed? Proclaiming that I was not a Moslem, and consequently not a competent authority, I adamantly refused to answer. Leaving such a decision to me was, in any case, something of a joke. Yet normally, this was no joking matter, nor was any Dyula in a position to follow my example and remain neutral. The passions aroused in such discussions might seem – as they seemed to me at the time – out of all proportion to the nature of the issue. Actually, far more fundamental matters were at stake, though these were rarely made explicit. I was thus left to witness curiously heated arguments about whether or not crossing arms in prayer was the surest way to eternal damnation. Astonishingly enough, few Dyula in Koko were partisans of crossing arms in the first place; those who invoked the torments of hellfire were preaching largely to the convinced!

In fact, the arm-crossers, known as 'Wahhabi' or simply as *bras croisés*, were critical in a number of crucial ways of the typical Dyula practice of Islam. One question, though it usually went unasked, loomed behind the argument: which group, the 'Wahhabis' or the 'traditionalists' (for want of a better term), was truly faithful to the original practice of Islam? The Sunni interpretation of the nature of Koranic revelation makes this an explosive question. The Koran is not the inspired creation of Mohammed; it is, word for word, a dictation from God. One does not trifle with God's literal and definitive message. The accusation of 'innovation' is extremely grave in Sunni Islam; worse than blameworthy, it is heresy. In this context, 'innovation' does not only refer to invention; backsliding, the incorporation of extra- or pre-Islamic practices which violate the tenets of Moslem law, is also a form of 'innovation'. The 'Wahhabis' claim that the 'traditionalists' are guilty of precisely such backsliding; the 'traditionalists' accuse the 'Wahhabis' of inventing a heretical sect. Each side claims to follow the straight and narrow path of revealed 'tradition'; each damns the other as 'innovators'.

In fact the issue of backsliding has a longer history than the quarrel with the 'Wahhabis'. Only after considering this history can we understand the full impact of the 'Wahhabi' critique and the 'traditionalist' response. Before the colonial period, the question of backsliding had not haunted the Dyula of Koko. The Dyula were the only Moslems in the region. Within its boundaries, their religious practices were Moslem virtually by definition. True, long-distance trade, even on a very modest scale, kept this practice within certain bounds. The *mory*, or 'scholars', at least had every reason to be considered Moslems outside as well as inside their home territory. This was not nearly so true of the *tun tigi*, the 'warriors', who drank beer, prayed irregularly and, worst of all, participated in initiation society rituals. Yet comparable groups of 'lax' Dyula Moslems could be found in the much more cosmopolitan centers of Kong (Binger 1892:298) and Bondoukou (Bravmann 1974). Despite these distinctly unorthodox practices, such 'warriors', as Dyula, were without doubt considered Moslems.

In the twentieth century, particularly since World War II, this rather comfortable state of affairs came to an end. The increasing numbers of Dyula who emigrated from the region to the towns of the south found themselves part of a much larger Moslem community. Regional idiosyncrasies like beer drinking and initiation societies had to be abandoned if Dyula from Koko or Kadioha were to be counted among the ranks of the faithful by their co-religionists. Even the Dyula who stayed back home could not fail to be aware that such practices branded one immediately as a 'pagan' – or, worse, as an apostate – among most fellow African Moslems. In this respect, the Dyula of Kadioha and other villages enjoyed a distinct advantage. If, as migrants, they had to behave 'correctly', they were much freer in their home village to do as they pleased. Most nearby villages were peopled by staunchly 'pagan' Senufo who can only have provided a most comforting contrast. The Dyula in Koko were not nearly so lucky. 'Across the stream', scores of Moslem immigrants, many of them Mandingspeakers, were settling in growing numbers. What is more, many Senufo living in town adopted Islam. Admittedly, some of these were converts in name only, but Dyula in Koko rather grudgingly admitted that others were now better Moslems than they. Koko was surrounded, not only by Moslem 'Dyula', but even by Moslem 'pagans'! Not even at home could the Koko Dyula live by the assumption that their religious practices were, if not the most commendable, at least tolerated within the bounds of Islam.

The Dyula of Koko found themselves confronted with a dilemma. Islam had ceased to distinguish their own community from many – perhaps most – of their neighbors just 'across the stream'. On the other hand, Islam continued to constitute a fundamental aspect of their own sense of identity, not least because the Grand Mosque was still situated in their quarter and they supplied its *Imam*. The Koko Dyula were faced with no other choice but to bring their religious practices into line with those of their Moslem neighbors. First of all, the distinction between *mory* and *tun tigi* had to be abandoned. This was not necessarily a traumatic decision, as the *tun tigi* had always been a minority. In any case, the precolonial status of 'warriors' was connected in principle with the exercise of political power. With the establishment of colonial rule, warfare ceased to play a role in local politics, and any authority which village chiefs may previously have enjoyed lapsed to a bare minimum. This distinction between 'warriors' and 'scholars' was not only an embarrassment; it had also lost its former (and already restricted) utility. 'Warriors' unanimously adopted the code of conduct of 'scholars': regular prayers, no more alcohol, no more 'impure' meats and, of course, no more initiation societies. Younger 'warriors' were by no means regretful, escaping in this way the terrors of initiation. The elders who controlled the initiation groves were more nostalgic; this meant a considerable diminution of their authority. Typical Dyula pragmatists, they were willing to make the best of a bad situation, and sold rights over masks and initiation secrets to sister Senufo societies which were still operative. Dyula villagers followed suit. As migrants to southern towns, young village 'warriors' were also exposed to stricter notions of Islam. In any case, initiation societies and the 'warrior' ethos in general had outlived their utility in the villages, too. Dyula communities, in Koko as well as the villages, are still admittedly divided into 'scholar' and 'warrior' clan wards. But there is no longer any difference between the day-to-day religious conduct of ordinary Dyula in 'warrior' and 'scholar' wards.

Initiation societies were the most blatant examples of 'pagan' survivals in Dyula Islam. Nevertheless, the Koko Dyula were bent on eliminating any practices which might conceivably be labeled 'pagan', particularly excision ceremonies for adolescent girls. These were the only life-crisis rituals in which 'warriors' as such played a prominent role. The ceremonies required the services of a male 'counter-witch', invariably both a 'witch' and a 'warrior', to protect the girls from malevolent witchcraft at a moment when they were deemed especially vulnerable. Moreover, adolescent girls were excised collectively, publicly and very visibly. These rites, though common to both 'warriors' and 'scholars', were felt by some to be uncomfortably similar to 'pagan' initiations, especially since the local Senufo still have initiation societies for women as well as for men. The public ceremonies have been distinguished from the practice of excision itself, which is not considered objectionable. On the contrary, excision for girls has come increasingly to resemble circumcision for boys; the operation is performed individually rather than collectively, privately rather than publicly and preferably before adolescence rather than at its onset. Again, the villagers have followed suit. However, the reasons I was given for the abandonment of these rites were very different in Koko and Kadioha. In Koko, religious orthodoxy was invariably invoked. In Kadioha, the primary objection to the ceremonies was their expense for an increasingly impoverished community. Formerly, parents of adolescent girls had to defray the considerable costs, not only of excision, but, shortly afterwards, of the first marriages of their daughters. The elders felt that, for most members of the community, this double burden was too heavy.

By the 1950s, these 'pagan' elements had been purged from the practice of Dyula Islam both in Koko and in the villages. In communities such as Kadioha, abolition had been motivated largely, if not entirely, by consider-ations of expediency. But in Koko, orthodoxy had become a fundamental ideological issue. Naturally, the major protagonists in this quest for orthodoxy were the scholars. Only they had sufficient knowledge of the written texts to interpret their content for the mass of believers. They were the arbiters of right and wrong, of the pure and the impure, of orthodoxy and of 'innovation'. The rituals of Dyula Islam provided them with an ideal forum for disseminating their views.

On specified occasions – the evening of the fortieth day of funeral ceremonies, as well as during the whole month of Ramadan – scholars are obliged to give 'readings' (*kalans*) of passages of the Koran. The major part of such readings consists not of recitation but of an extemporized sermon on virtually any topic of the scholar's choosing; he may, but need not, refer to the Arabic text which has been recited for the occasions. Many individuals are effectively obliged to attend, particularly at funerals, but they tend in any case to draw a large audience. The kin of the deceased provide refreshments to all spectators. This is a social – and, in real respects, a recreational – occasion, but the scholar remains, the main focus of interest. Above all, the scholar is expected to be eloquent, delivering his sermon in short, measured, dramatic bursts, each burst being echoed by the response of an official 'speaker' (an office reserved for 'slaves'). It is by no means unusual for members of the audience to bring tape recorders to record the sermon. Criticism during the actual 'reading' is distinctly out of place, but individuals freely discuss the qualities and faults of individual sermons and speakers in private. Both the nature of the message and the way in which it is presented form an integral part of the sermon as a whole. 'Readings' thus constitute one of the principal ways in which scholars can attempt to impose their ideas on the community as a whole.

Any issues related to the general problem of orthodoxy can obviously form the subject of such a sermon. But not all sermons need allude to such issues. My impressions of sermons delivered in Kadioha by village scholars were that orthodoxy received little, if any, attention. The subjects of sermons seemed to concentrate on what one might call the traditional Dyula

126

Moslem view of the world: Islamic mythology (e.g. the Creation and Adam and Eve), the names and duties of the various angels, the nature of heaven and hell, etc. This corresponds to Kadioha's status as a Moslem island in a largely 'pagan' sea. The Dyula of Kadioha enjoy a relatively secure and unambiguous place in the local social universe; their sermons expand this universe to cosmic proportions. Similar sermons are by no means exceptional in Koko, whose Dyula residents are still reluctant to abandon their traditional division of the social world into 'Dyula' and 'Senufo'. But the growing inadequacy of such categories in describing the real situation of the Koko Dyula is reflected in many sermons given by 'younger' scholars in town – that is to say, scholars under the age of fifty. These are the men preoccupied with orthodoxy and reform; a real divide separates their outlook from that of the community's traditional Moslem leader, such as the *Imam.* This divide hardly implies hostility, much less conflict. The older scholars are content to leave the limelight to their younger colleagues provided that they receive the proper deference and respect due to their age and position. The younger scholars are more frequently invited to give 'readings', and only they will raise the issues of orthodoxy (though they, too, may give more traditional 'world-view' sermons). This concern can take different forms. On the one hand, sermons can focus on the behavioral ethics of the Koran. It can be pointed out, for example, that the polygynist who gives 200 Frs. C.F.A. to one wife and only 100 Frs. C.F.A. to his other wife will be severely punished in the hereafter, for the Koran states that a man must treat all his wives equally. However, such 'ethical' concerns are matched by a preoccupation with ritual detail. Thus, one scholar expostulated at length on the correct pronunciation of *Allahu Akbar*![1]: the ignorant garble the words in their prayers, uttering the nonsensical syllables *alla haki baru*!; conscientious Moslems ought not to settle for such approximations. Whether these sermons concern themselves with ethics, with ritual, or with both, the underlying message is the same: the Dyula of Koko have lost their exclusive claim to Islam in Korhogo. They can no longer content themselves with practicing Islam in any way they choose if they want to retain their credentials in the town as a whole as serious Moslems. Rather, they must conform to the same ethical and ritual norms as their co-religionists 'across the stream' within the confines of an internationally-accepted framework. The standards are laboriously set in the written classics. It is the task of scholars to interpret these texts for the mass of believers, and the task of the masses to conform.

Through their sermons, the younger scholars attempt to assume moral and spiritual leadership of the Koko Dyula community as a whole. At the same time, they judiciously avoid challenging the authority of their elder colleagues and thus dividing the community on generational lines. They have no such qualms towards one another. The very fact that each is bidding for leadership over the whole community makes other young scholars inevitable rivals. This contrasts sharply with the position of scholars in Kadioha. In the village, they are respected as a class for their learning, but individual scholars do not as such vie for prominence. If anything, the villages provide yet a further arena for competition among scholars from Koko. Town scholars are not infrequently invited to preach in villages, though I never witnessed a single instance of the reverse.[2] Here, town scholars may choose to voice their own preoccupations with orthodoxy, in the hope that villagers will follow suit, for whatever reasons, and thus add to their credibility as leaders in town. The younger scholars of Koko have also attempted to multiply the occasions for giving extended 'readings' in town, as further forums for their views. In particular, different holidays of the Moslem annual calendar have successfully become associated with 'readings'. Other pretexts may do, and sermons may even be delivered on occasions where a scholar feels he has something particularly important to say.

While I was in the field, three scholars were vying for the spiritual leadership of Koko: Dugubaka Toure, Benkoro Cisse and Mammadou-Labi Saganogo. Only the last was not a native of Koko. He was from Kong, a community to which Koko had close ties before the colonial period, and which was formerly the most important of the Dyula towns; he was, moreover, a member of the most prestigious of all the Dyula learned families, the Saganogo (Wilks 1966, 1968). There exists a Saganogo clan ward in Koko, recognized as an offshoot of his own clan ward in Kong, and so he was not without (relatively distant) kinsmen in Koko. However, his links were equally close, if not closer, with members of the Cisse clan ward, by far the largest and singly the most influential clan ward in Koko; he was the teacher (*karamoko-fa*, literally 'scholar-father') of important elders in the ward, and of the fathers of other, younger leaders. Unlike the others, he did not reside in Koko, but rather in Bouake, the second-largest town in Ivory Coast, and was certainly the only one to have a national, rather than a purely local, following. He visited Koko from time to time; more importantly, he had a permanent representative there, an advanced disciple, Laraseni Coulibaly. His disciple, though not a native of Koko, was from a nearby village and, in any case, incorporated as a 'stranger' and as a cross-cousin in the Cisse ward.

The rivalry between these scholars reflected factional rivalry within Koko itself. The disproportionate size and importance of the Cisse ward was counterbalanced by a tendency for other, smaller *kabila*s to unite in opposition. Mammadou-Labi Saganogo and his disciple, though not natives of the Cisse ward, were closely associated with it. Benkoro Cisse, as his name implies, was a *bona fide* member of the ward. Consequently, the various opponents of the Cisse tended to cluster around the third scholar, Dugubaka Toure. This rivalry came to a head on the occasion of Domba

(Arabic *mawlud*), the Prophet's birthday, which had relatively recently become another pretext for a public 'reading'. In 1972, two rival 'readings' were organized, one by Dugubaka Toure and the other by Benkoro Cisse. Each side strove to attract the largest audience, to provide the most lavish refreshments (the Cisse butchered an entire cow and purchased innumerable cases of soft drinks, in addition to the usual coffee) and to hold their 'reading' at the site of the Grand Mosque. The Cisse won this last battle, and installed loudspeakers with the express intention of drowning out their rivals. There was no effort to conceal the overtly political nature of the conflict, a fact which did not apparently disturb the scholars involved. Thus the hostility between Dugubaka Toure and his two colleagues received ample public attention. This was not the case for the rivalry between Mammadou-Labi Saganogo and his disciple on the one hand and Benkoro Cisse on the other. These three men were linked to the same individuals, men who, as leaders of the Cisse faction, had every interest in keeping the rivalry between 'their' scholars under control and out of the public eye. However, as a 'stranger' in the Cisse ward, I was occasionally privy to instances of private backbiting, sure signs that this rivalry was deeply felt by the scholars themselves and their closest followers, even if it was denied public expression. Despite their bitter rivalry, the younger scholars all preached similar versions of Islam (though they might engage in heated debate over particulars), and they were all firmly united against the 'Wahhabi' meance. Paradoxically, the younger scholars were ideologically closer in some respects to the 'Wahhabis' than to their older colleagues. Both they and the 'Wahhabis' were deeply committed to the process of 'reform' in Dyula Islam (though neither they nor the 'Wahhabis' would phrase the nature of their activities in these terms) – that is to say, the purging of extra-Islamic elements from religious practice.

The founders of the so-called 'Wahhabi' movement were graduates of Al-Azhar University in Cairo.[3] In the 1950s, Manding-speaking graduates of Al-Azhar clustered in Bamako, capital of modern Mali, where they founded an organization called *Subbanu-l-Muslimin*, the 'Young Moslems'. This organization successfully established branches elsewhere, not only in Mali but also in Guinea and, with considerable success, in towns of the south of Ivory Coast, particularly Bouake. Virtually from the outset, the French colonial administration took an extremely dim view of the organization; their experiences in North Africa made them suspicious of any pan-Islamic trends in African Islam. The very label 'Wahhabi' was the creation of French administrators, an attempt to stigmatize the movement as a coterie of dangerous radicals. This attempt fell dramatically flat. The adherents of the *Subbanu* themselves accepted the label proudly, capitalizing on the prestige of Saudi Arabia, the destination of the *hajj* which West African pilgrims were making in increasing numbers. In any case, Saudi Arabian

Wahhabism, like their own movement, was directed at purifying Islam of extraneous elements. Despite the very different historical and geographical roots of the two 'Wahhabi' movements, the name was not, after all, so very inappropriate. By the 1970s, the movement was known exclusively as 'Wahhabi' by both its adherents and its bitterest opponents.

If the scholars of Koko were so unanimously antagonistic to the 'Wahhabi' movement, this was not simply because, as fellow proponents of reform, the 'Wahhabis' were competitors. The 'Wahhabis' were not stigmatized as mere rivals, but rather as a real menace. In their public or private backbiting, scholarly rivals in Koko never questioned one another's orthodoxy, but merely the extent of their learning; the 'Wahhabis' were not accused of ignorance, but of heresy. The very violence of this hostility is not hard to understand. The 'Wahhabi' critique called into question the traditional role of scholars in Dyula Islam. Whatever other reforms they might wish to introduce, this was hardly a feature of Dyula Islam which the scholars themselves wished to alter!

Of course, the 'Wahhabi' critique was not directed against the idea of scholarship as such. Rather, they attacked practices which, while seemingly ancillary to scholarship, in fact ensured the scholars a livelihood. In the first place, the 'Wahhabis' inveighed against the practice of magic. This aversion to magic was justified to me by 'Wahhabis' or their sympathizers on two – logically contradictory – grounds. It was sometimes argued that magic was inefficacious, in other words, that its practitioners were frauds. On the other hand, if it worked, it was considered immoral. In fact, magic (not only the production of written charms but also divination and astrology) was not a particular specialty of the younger scholars; it was not even a monopoly of scholars as such. Even the rudiments of literacy allowed an individual to reproduce charms for his personal use. Most older and middle-aged Dyula men (including at least one 'Wahhabi' sympathizer!) possessed a sizable stock of them in their personal papers. Senufo 'pagan' customers not infrequently resorted to the services of Dyula charm-makers and diviners. (Diviners were not necessarily even literate; scholars, naturally, always resorted to books for such purposes, as did semi-literate Dyula with few, if any, claims to scholarship.) But the most active local specialists in magic were, without doubt, the older scholars. Younger scholars were by no means averse to making whatever money they could in this way, but their reputation lay elsewhere, and it remained a subsidiary, though not entirely negligible, source of revenue. Their defense of both the efficacy and propriety of magic was not, I suspect, motivated solely by personal financial considerations. By supporting the practice of magic, they were assured the crucial support of both the older scholars – who were most directly threatened – and those 'lay' individuals in the community whose occasional dabbling hardly assured them a livelihood but at least helped to improve their standard of living.

Saint worship was another target of 'Wahhabi' criticism. The worship of live saints has never, to my knowledge, been a part of Dyula Islam, as, for instance, in the Maghreb.[4] On the other hand, the tombs of saints are the objects of veneration, and even of pilgrimages. The most important tombs are those of scholars long dead, but even recently dead pious 'laymen' may achieve such posthumous distinction. An individual seeking to achieve a particular end may, after bestowing the saint's descendants with a token gift, beseech him at his grave to intercede with God on his behalf. Success is by no means automatically assured; the ultimate decision always rests squarely in God's hands. However, given the saint's favor in God's eyes, the process is considered to increase the suppliant's chances. While belief in the power of saints is quite common among the Dyula, the actual importance of pilgrimages to saints' tombs seems to have declined considerably in recent years. Boron, without doubt the site of the most important saints' tombs among the Dyula, was hardly a thriving community when I visited the village. This decline is not due to any loss of faith. Rather, the pilgrimage to Mecca, considered infinitely more efficacious, is now within relatively easy reach of many West African Moslems. Pilgrimages to saints' tombs in the region seem lackluster by comparison. Thus the scholars' defense of the efficacy of Dyula saints is hardly motivated by concern over profit. But, in another sense, the scholars are closely linked to the saints. The 'Wahhabi' leaders, educated at Al-Azhar, have attached themselves to a scholarly tradition with its roots outside West Africa. The Dyula scholars, on the other hand, legitimize their status through local 'chains of learning' (Wilks 1968:172–6) which include various local saints, and in particular Mohammad al-Mustafa Saganogo, buried at Boron, and indeed a lineal ancestor of one of the young scholars, Mammadou-Labi Saganogo. This is not to say that the 'Wahhabis' deny the learning or the piety of these 'saints'. But the belief in the mystical efficacy of their direct spiritual (if not genealogical) forebears clearly enhances the legitimacy of all Dyula scholars, older and younger alike. Paradoxically, while the scholars are largely unconcerned whether or not the saints are actually venerated in practice, they are adamant defenders of the principle that such veneration is praiseworthy and effective.

The secondary role of saint worship, at least in modern Dyula Islam, makes it a relatively minor issue. Not so the 'Wahhabi' attack on the Sufi orders, the Qadiriyya and especially the Tijaniyya. Most scholars belong to one of these two orders, as do many older and middle-aged men. There exists no rivalry between one order and the other in Koko, or between different branches of either order. One adheres to the order of one's teacher, whichever that might be. Whatever allegations younger scholars in Koko made about one another while I was in the field, brotherhood membership was never once at issue. For the 'Wahhabi', the veneration expressed in the brotherhood rituals for the founders of the orders (in particular, in the rituals of the Tijaniyya[5]) reflects, like saint worship, an improper belief in the existence of mediators between God and the believer. For the scholars in their role as teachers, the brotherhoods reinforce the moral dependence of their disciples whether scholars themselves or pious 'laymen'. Because brotherhood affiliation lays most stress on this personal link, it does not much matter whether one joins the Qadiriyya or the Tijaniyya. Here again, the 'Wahhabi' critique strikes at the very roots of the scholars' influence over the community at large.

Perhaps the most damaging of all the 'Wahhabi' attacks is their criticism of the Dyula practice of *saraka* (Arabic *sadaqa*) – 'a gift made with the object of obtaining merit in the eyes of God' (Fyzee 1964:259). Dyula translate the term into French as 'sacrifice', though 'alms' would be a more appropriate term, denoting a freely-given gift for ostensibly charitable purposes, as distinct from *zakat*, a charitable 'tithe' which, though one of the five pillars of the Faith, has never been collected in Dyula society. Although in principle *saraka* is a 'free' gift, there exist circumstances where it is absolutely obligatory. Many life-crisis rituals involve the distribution of *saraka* on a large scale. Indeed, at certain wedding ceremonies (*woro siri* and *furu*), every individual attending receives a small *saraka*; once this has been apportioned, additional such gifts are presented to a wide category of individuals or representatives of groups. Naming ceremonies and certain funeral rituals also involve the widespread distribution of *saraka*, although the precise content of the gift, its importance and the categories of individuals who must receive such gifts vary from ritual to ritual. For all such gifts the obligatory counterpart is a blessing (*duau*) on behalf of the newborn infant, the married couple or the deceased, as the case may be. The manifest purpose of the process is to obtain the blessing of the whole audience and, by implication, of the entire community. Aside from these public and obligatory prestations, *saraka* can in quite different contexts be bestowed privately and on a purely voluntary basis. Typically, an individual with a problem or particular wish will consult a scholar, who will frequently advise him to bestow *saraka*. Sometimes the precise nature and amounts of the gift(s) are specified; more often, this is left to the donor's discretion. Such *saraka* need by no means be granted to the scholar who prescribes it. Pious elders as well as scholars are appropriate recipients. Since the purpose of the gift is to obtain an effective blessing in return, scholars are likely to be favored candidates for the honor. Should the wish in question come to pass, the scholar consulted will inevitably be given further *saraka*. The extent of this remuneration is again left to the donor's discretion; the wealthier the client, the more he is expected to give. This system of voluntary *saraka* obviously benefits scholars more than anyone else; it probably accounts for a substantial part of their revenues. Elders are also beneficiaries, though much more marginally. The 'Wahhabi' objection to this practice is, not implausibly, that it does not constitute charity at all, as the very notion of *saraka* implies. Beneficiaries are in every instance chosen because of their status as scholars or elders in the community or because of their particular relationship to the donor, but not in any case according to financial need. A reform of the *saraka* system along such lines would deprive scholars of the resources they need in order to pursue learning as a full-time occupation.

The 'Wahhabi' critique attacks, directly or indirectly, the vested interests of scholars so their hostility to the movement is hardly puzzling. But Koko's 'lay' community also supports the 'traditionalist' scholars against the 'Wahhabi' enemy. There have, it is true, been a few defections from the ranks. Two very small *kabilas* have joined the movement. One relatively wealthy trader from Koko, settled in Bouake, has also converted to the Wahhabiyya along with some (but not all) of his co-resident kin. A close friend of this man, still living in Koko, made little effort in private to conceal his 'Wahhabi' sympathies; strong pressure from his younger brothers, among others, has prevented him from making any public commitment. It is true that the 'Wahhabi' critique of Dyula Islam threatens the interests of 'lay' individuals as well: occasional diviners, descendants of saints and elderly beneficiaries of *saraka*. But the abolition of magic, saint worship and the *saraka* system would not make a serious dent in the pocketbooks of any ordinary Dyula, whereas it would do irreparable damage to the finances and the moral authority of scholars. If the Dyula of Koko have overwhelmingly rallied behind their scholars, the key lies rather in the general public image of the 'Wahhabis'.[6] The typical 'Wahhabi' is supposed to be a wealthy trader. The movement as a whole is considered a sort of brotherhood of rich merchants. 'Charity' among 'Wahhabis', it is claimed, is largely internal to the membership. In other words, if a trader faces temporary setbacks, or has a sudden pressing need for liquid capital, fellow members will help him out. The implication of this allegation is that the practice of *saraka* among 'Wahhabis' is even further removed from the spirit of 'charity' than the traditional Dyula *saraka* system. Paradoxically, although membership in the Wahhabiyya clearly cuts across lines of community membership and even, to a lesser degree, ethnic boundaries, their opponents accuse them of 'exclusiveness'. In the first place, they consciously strive to appear different from others in the community (or so it is claimed), boasting long full beards and white robes. Precisely in this context, the full significance of the 'traditional' emphasis on the evils of crossing arms during prayer becomes clear. In this way, 'Wahhabis' distinguish themselves from the rest of the

Moslem community during the midday Friday prayer at the Grand Mosque. This is the occasion where the Moslem community as a whole gives ritual expression to its unity and solidarity, a unity which transcends (at least in principle, and only perhaps for the duration of the prayer) allegiances to community, to class, to linguistic or ethnic categories, to political factions and to Sufi brotherhood affiliations. By crossing their arms at the very moment that everyone else outstretches them, the 'Wahhabis' violate in the most visible manner this very demonstration of ideological unity. As if to make the point unambiguous they cry *Amina*! ('Amen!') out loudly, clearly, and – in their opponents' opinion – uncouthly at the end of each prayer, rather than whispering the word along with the rest of the congregation. By focusing explicitly on these seemingly (but only seemingly!) trivial points of ritual detail rather than on substantive issues raised by the 'Wahhabi' critique, the defenders of 'traditionalist' Dyula Islam stand on firm ground. The substantive critique tends to suggest that Dyula Islam, *in spite of* its efforts at 'reform', has not yet freed itself of extraneous 'innovations'; any such suggestion is extremely embarrassing to the 'traditionalists' of Koko. The 'traditionalists' have counterattacked by arguing that the real 'innovations' are embodied in the 'Wahhabi' manner of praying. The force of this objection does not lie in the fact that they have introduced 'new' elements into ritual practice; the younger scholars have done as much by organizing 'readings' for Moslem calendar holidays. But, unlike the introductions of the younger scholars, the 'Wahhabi' prayers distinguish adherents as a separate group within the community of Islam. Every Friday, they refuse to set aside their particularities to assert that, at heart, they are Moslems like everybody else.

For this very reason, ordinary residents of Koko as well as scholars are able to conceive of the Wahhabiyya as a 'menace'. If indeed the Wahhabiyya is a 'brotherhood of the rich', and if its members set themselves apart from the rest of the community, it would provide a most dangerous temptation for the wealthier traders and artisans of Koko. It would provide a convenient ideology for more prosperous individuals in Koko to assert their solidarity as a separate class. Individuals in Koko are thus confronted with two opposed models of solidarity. Allegiance to clan ward and community unites the relatively rich with the relatively poor. The prosperous are thus burdened with the moral responsibility of devoting at least some of their resources to the assistance of their poorer kin and neighbors. The Wahhabiyya not only transcends, but in a fundamental sense seems to deny, the importance of intra-community ties in favor of class solidarity. The rich could thus help one another to stay rich or get richer, leaving the poor to their own devices. Seen in this light, the 'Wahhabi' attack on the 'traditional' *saraka* system threatens not only the scholars but also the poor. Scholars are the primary beneficiaries of private and voluntary *saraka* prestations, but the 'Wahhabis' also condemn the public distribution of *saraka* as wasteful. From a purely financial standpoint, this is no doubt the case. But these public prestations, like Friday prayers at the Grand Mosque, are also expressions of higher moral norms and ideals. In the first place, they constitute the most dramatic expression of Koko's separate identity as a Dyula community; all component clan wards must be represented at life-crisis rituals and publicly awarded *saraka*, as must all Dyula communities in neighboring villages. But they also lay stress on the binding fabric of the community, on the public acknowledgment of ties between kin and between fellow members of individual clan wards. By denying that these prestations are appropriately Islamic, the 'Wahhabis' are implicitly denying religious sanctions for the ties of kinship and community without which Koko would lose its distinct identity apart from the rest of town. For the scholars, the struggle against the 'Wahhabis' represents an attempt to maintain their privileged position in the community. The others have followed their lead because this is also a struggle for the community's very existence as such, a struggle to maintain ideals of community solidarity in the face of incipient divisions along class lines.

The 'Wahhabis' are anathema because their ideology might persuade wealthier members of the community to secede. However, well-to-do merchants are not the only prosperous members of the community, nor is the Wahhabiyya the only ideology which favors solidarity along class rather than community lines. Those younger men in the community who have received enough Western education to procure salaried jobs – primarily in the civil service – constitute a very different social and financial elite. Unlike the 'Wahhabis', such men are far less likely to criticize 'traditionalist' Dyula Islam than to ignore it in favor of what might be called 'secularism'. It is virtually impossible to practice a 'secular' style of life in Koko, where remonstrances from kin and neighbors force one to conform to the outward manifestations of conventional Islamic piety. But middle- and higher-ranking civil servants from Koko, few as they are, are unlikely to be posted in Korhogo. Far more positions are open in the capital and in the numerous, more prosperous (though not necessarily larger) towns of the south. The tendency of such individuals to live elsewhere is not exclusively due to the exigencies of their careers. Those whom I met while they were visiting 'home' often stated in no uncertain terms that they had no desire whatsoever to be stationed in Korhogo. Because of their relative wealth, civil servants are repeatedly pressed by kinsmen and neighbors for financial assistance. These demands, by no means always refused, are often deeply resented. The social standing of civil servants depends on their maintaining a certain standard of living – in other words, a certain degree of conspicuous consumption.[7] They cannot simultaneously satisfy these demands as well as the seemingly ceaseless requests of their poorer brethren. The very social pressures which incite conspicuous consumption among civil servants also lead them to behave even more reprehensibly in the eyes of the pious: they may pray irregularly, disregard the annual fast at Ramadan and even drink liquor. Even in Moslem countries, such 'Western' patterns of behavior have proved attractive to the educated elite. In Ivory Coast, where Moslem civil servants are a small minority, standards of elite sociability are even less likely to take the moral norms of Islam into consideration. Civil servants from Koko are faced with the alternative of behaving in ways appropriate to their 'class' or to their home community. Those who live away from home can, while visiting Koko, behave as proper Moslems; in the towns of the south, under the cloak of anonymity, they can shed many of their ostensibly Moslem ways. This double standard has not escaped the attention of other members of the Koko community. Individual deviance is tacitly accepted as long as it is kept discreet; but without naming names, pious members of Koko are highly critical of the 'secular' ways of civil servants in general.

Unfortunately for the 'traditionalist' scholars, the ideology of 'secularism' is much more difficult to combat than 'Wahhabism'. The 'Wahhabis' publicly flaunt their differences, whereas civil servants simply ignore Moslem standards of conduct in private. The scholars can castigate deviance from Moslem norms in their sermons, threatening the impious with damnation. But even with public opinion behind them, they can at best enforce only public conformity. The strength of the 'secularists' lies precisely in the fact that they can avoid public confrontations. Ultimately, the scholars have only been able to attack 'secularism' indirectly. Perhaps the most outstanding example is that of a marrriage ceremony which one scholar has attempted to introduce in Koko.[8] This ceremony is, in many respects, reminiscent of a civil wedding as well as an attempt to introduce readings in a ritual context in which they are traditionally absent. In fact, civil servants are the most likely members of the community to seek civil weddings. This is simply because such weddings are required by individuals seeking to collect family allowances – a privilege enjoyed only by those who receive regular salaries, notably civil servants. The contents of the sermons delivered at these wedding readings stress the moral components of Moslem marriage, implicitly exhorting the couple to obey Moslem rather than 'civil' norms. But – unlike the campaign against the 'Wahhabis' – this ceremony has not met with a great deal of popular success.

Indeed, the only effective stance against 'secularism' is to oppose Western education. This was the point of view expressed to me by one 'Wahhabi', though I do not know how widely this view is shared in the movement. He claimed that he did not reject modern education as such, but only the inculcation of Western values at the expense of Moslem ones; he would, he said, accept a system of education which incorporated Arabic language instruction and Moslem religious values into the curriculum.

While such schools do exist, they have no official recognition. This hostility to Western education is by no means unique to the 'Wahhabis'. Yet Dyula parents are willing in increasing numbers to gamble on the schools. Even if the failure rate is distressingly high, and if the 'fortunate few' who succeed are all the more likely to succumb to the temptations of the 'secular' ideology, the schools still offer the hope that Dyula children may embark upon the most successful and safest of careers – and that perhaps, after all, they will not entirely neglect their parents.

Ultimately, the Koko community is caught in a paradox, a paradox reflected in their religious attitudes and preoccupations. Without its quota of relatively prosperous members, the community as such is unlikely to survive. Otherwise, norms of solidarity along community and kinship lines would lose all practical significance. Thus the resources of individual families are frequently deployed towards putting children, particularly boys, through school, or towards establishing individuals in trade or as craftsmen. If these individuals succeed, they are in a position to assist others in the community in turn. But the burdens of solidarity fall most heavily on the shoulders of the successful, and they are likely to be tempted to renege on what others perceive as their moral obligations. This very temptation is embodied in the ideologies of 'Wahhabism' and 'secularism'. Each of these ideologies promotes forms of solidarity which not only cut across community boundaries, but are ultimately at the community's expense, fostering links between wealthy traders or civil servants rather than between rich and poor in Koko. The 'Wahhabi' 'menace' is more direct. It has received more public attention, and the scholars of Koko have met with considerable success in curbing its possible appeal. Moreover, while the 'Wahhabis' may indeed be wealthy merchants, it is by no means difficult for a wealthy trader to repudiate 'Wahhabism'. The case is very different for civil servants, who are invariably expected by their colleagues to conform to 'secular' ways of life. Koko can repudiate 'Wahhabism' without rejecting trade or traders; it cannot eliminate 'secularism' without rejecting Western education. But Koko has lost its monopoly over the region's trade and cannot afford to renounce the hopes, as well as the fears, of gambling on education. Koko has largely succeeded in exorcising 'Wahhabism'; it will have to learn to live with 'secularism'.

10

Kinship in a changing world

The kinship system of the Dyula was very well adapted to their precolonial status as an ethnic minority enjoying a monopoly over trade. The basic units in the system were the joint family and the *kabila*, or clan ward; the preference for in-marriage within the *kabila* provided an integrating mechanism. For males particularly, the joint family was both a budgetary unit and a unit of production, headed by the senior male of the group. The association of several joint families within a single *kabila* reinforced this structure of authority. Accession to leadership within the *kabila* was ascribed according to strict principles of seniority determining a precise order of succession. Strong pressures to settle internal disputes within the framework of a *kabila* council further buttressed the moral authority of senior members over their junior dependents. On the other hand, the *kabila* was large enough to serve as a bridge between individual joint families on the one hand and the local community as a whole on the other. *Kabilas* were, on occasion, units of economic specialization, and they were inevitably a preponderant factor in local faction politics. High rates of in-marriage within the *kabila*, accentuating the relative independence rather than the interdependence of the constituent *kabilas* within any local community tended to impede political integration on a larger scale. On the other hand, such a pattern of marriage made junior members of the *kabila* doubly dependent on seniors in positions of authority in order to obtain wives. Ultimately, in-marriage reinforced the authority of elders both within the *kabila* as a whole and in the joint family. Thus a typical Dyula community included a number of fairly small and relatively independent groups whose members were linked to one another through multiple ties of kinship. In the absence of larger-scale mechanisms for integration, such units were fairly ineffectual actors in regional politics. On the other hand, such groups were extremely effective units in the domains of trade and weaving. In short, there existed a close 'fit' between Dyula social organization and their specialized roles within the Korhogo region in the social, political and economic domains. Yet, during the colonial period, and

138

particularly since World War II, the Dyula suffered not only the loss of their local trade monopoly but also a drastic decline in the value of hand-woven cloth, which essentially spelled the doom of the traditional Dyula economy. What, then, of social organization? Have the old forms survived as anachronisms, a relic of past glories? Have they dissolved along with the conditions for which they were so eminently suited? Or have they, under new conditions, acquired new reasons for being, and ultimately a new meaning?

The Civil Code of 1965

In Ivory Coast, these questions have acquired particular relevance in the light of postcolonial government policy. In 1965, the government put into effect a Civil Code (Ivory Coast, *Journal Officiel*, 27 October 1964) with the explicit aim of changing 'traditional' African family patterns. Many of the measures were aimed specifically at the institution of marriage. Polygyny was outlawed (though polygynous marriages contracted before 1965 could be legalized until 1970); bridewealth was abolished; forced marriages (and all marriages involving males under twenty and females under eighteen) were outlawed; and grounds for divorce were strictly specified, making divorce in general difficult to obtain. In addition, the Code opted unequivocally for lineal as opposed to collateral (including all forms of matrilineal) inheritance. Ivory Coast was only one among several postcolonial francophone African nations to codify its civil law. However, of all these, the Ivoirian code most closely resembles the French Civil Code, and makes the fewest concessions to any notion of African customary law. Indeed, in those domains where it does depart from the French code, it is intentionally in a direction even further removed from 'traditional' African practice (Hilaire 1968). The guiding rationale for these measures is that the Western-style nuclear family is a necessary condition for economic development.[1] Consequently, the Code seeks to undermine all 'traditional' forms of social organization – polygyny, matriliny, lineages, the 'extended family', etc. – that are presumed to constitute so many obstacles to development.

The Civil Code of 1965 bears in two different ways on the problem of changes in Dyula social organization. In the first place, the Code itself rests on the assumption that there is a fundamental 'fit' between a society's family system and its economic system. Precisely because of the specialization by the Dyula in trade, and their consequent reliance on the 'market', their economy has been disrupted more completely than that of subsistence farmers such as their Senufo neighbors. It follows that, if such an intrinsic 'fit' does in fact exist, the kinship system ought to have followed suit; it should be in an advanced state of dissolution if it has not by now entirely

139

disappeared. In the second place, whatever the effects of economic change, the Code itself constitutes an additional factor promulgating change in family patterns. In other words, the Dyula system of social organization has been, and is being, subjected to pressures to change both from 'below', through the disruption of the Dyula economy, and from 'above', in the form of political and ideological pressures embodied in the Civil Code.

Not all the provisions of the Civil Code affect the Dyula family system equally directly and forcefully. The Civil Code's insistence on lineal inheritance, while differing in detail from the strictures of Islamic law, certainly remains much closer in spirit to Moslem practices than to most other African systems of inheritance. On the other hand, many of the rules concerning marriage directly contradict Dyula practice. For example, divorce is easily obtained in Dyula society, though rates of divorce are relatively low. The abolition of polygyny flies even more directly in the face of Dyula practice; in a sample of Dyula marriages, as many as 49% of husbands were polygynously married, and the incidence of polygyny was 169.2 wives per 100 husbands.[2] But by far the greatest threat to the traditional Dyula system is the provision that spouses must freely consent to the marriage. The Dyula practice of arranging marriages within the *kabila* can only work if parents and other elders, rather than the spouses themselves, make the final decisions.

However, the effects of the Civil Code cannot be gauged simply in terms of its strictures and their logical implications. The practical effects depend, not only on its contents, but in the way in which they are implemented. For the Dyula, the Code contains a loophole: only civil marriages, registered as such, have any legal standing. The traditional Dyula ceremonies, which legitimize a marriage in the eyes of the community, have no legal weight whatsoever. Consequently, a man may be legally married to a woman with whom, from the Dyula point of view, he is simply cohabiting; a Dyula elder may firmly believe he has four wives when, legally speaking, he is still a bachelor! This disparity between the official and the Dyula notions of what actually constitutes a marriage permits a certain, though sometimes uneasy, coexistence. A man may have as many wives as he pleases without violating the law, as long as he does not register the marriages. A Dyula elder may marry off his daughter as he sees fit since, from a strictly legal point of view, she remains unmarried after the completion of the traditional ceremonies. Conceivably, the Civil Code might have no effect whatsoever on Dyula practice. This would certainly be the case if no Dyula ever chose to register their marriages.

The fact remains that some Dyula marriages are registered. Government officials have, at times, compelled couples to register; but the government does not have the means, even if it has the inclination, to carry out such tactics systematically. There are also circumstances in which people willingly register their marriages. First, all salaried employees (civil servants, and also houseboys and chauffeurs, for example) have a right to government family allowances, but only for children of legal marriages. This was the case even before the promulgation of the Civil Code. Second, a girl married or promised by her kinsmen to one man can run off with another of her own choice. If she registers her marriage with the man she wants, her parents cannot force her to return home without violating the law. Her parents can still refuse to allow her to perform the traditional rituals, but often they give in to the inevitable after a few years. The stratagem is not quite as simple as it might seem. In practice, a girl can only run off in defiance of her parents if her lover's kinsmen are willing to take the couple in. Usually, this depends on whether the lover's own kinsmen have already planned to give him another bride. If they have other plans, they may refuse to consent to the elopement, and the couple will have nowhere to go. For the same reason, a girl may easily be married against her will if she has no lover at all, even though she could stop the proceedings by complaining to government officials. But, unless she has somewhere else to go, she would have to go back home and face the wrath of her parents. This kind of elopement did not come into being with the Civil Code; even before it, couples could and did go off to seek the interference of government officials and even that of the court of the chief of Korhogo, but in these cases the parents or the husband of the girl were awarded compensation. Under the provisions of the Civil Code, such compensation is no longer awarded as the parents have no right to marry the girl off without her consent – especially, as is often the case, if she is less than eighteen at the time. Thus the inducements to register a marriage are much the same under the Civil Code as they were before; the major difference is that now the rights and obligations of individual spouses who register their marriages are clearly defined – and are, in principle, enforceable – by law.

In fact, the Code has not had the same impact in Koko and Kadioha. Table 8 shows the numbers of marriages registered at the administrative headquarters of the *sous-préfecture* of Korhogo from 1960 to 1971. These figures are misleading: marriages in many of the neighboring *sous-préfectures* were in fact registered in Korhogo until after the Civil Code was passed. This explains the dramatic decrease in the registration of marriages in 1965. Unfortunately, it was quite impossible to isolate marriages in Koko quarter, or in the Dyula ethnic group as a whole. (The widespread Senufo practice of adopting Dyula patronyms means that it is futile to attempt to draw any conclusions from the names on the register.) At any rate, it is quite clear that, after 1965, only a small proportion of total marriages were registered. The Dyula of Koko quarter were no exception. Though I have no statistics, in every case I knew in Koko, not a single marriage was registered after 1965 except where registration would permit the couple to receive

Table 8. *Marriages registered at sous-préfecture of Korhogo (1960–71)*

1960	100
1961	70
1962	59
1963	91
1964	71
1965	45
1966	116
1967	97
1968	55
1969	66
1970	50
1971	66

821 marriages anterior to 1965 registered
1965–70.

family allowances or to elope against the wishes of the girl's parents. The effect of the Civil Code, even on those marriages which have been registered, has been negligible in most domains. The exchange of prestations in Dyula marriage rituals has been entirely unaffected. I know at least one case where a husband with a legally registered wife has recently taken a second wife (not registerable, of course). I know of no case where a legally registered couple have attempted to divorce. The one real change that has taken place so far is that some young men and women are becoming more adamant about their right to choose their own spouses, knowing that they can go to the administrative headquarters of the *sous-préfecture* if necessary to enforce that right. By no means all young Dyula from Koko are prepared to do this, and the attitude of the young man's parents is still very crucial. This is not a new phenomenon; I know of similar cases going back almost twenty years. But such marriages are becoming increasingly common in town, and the Civil Code cannot but give moral and ideological as well as legal support to the claims of Dyula youth in the towns.

The situation is quite different in Kadioha. I was at first astonished at the disproportionate numbers of marriages registered in Kadioha (see Table 9). Kadioha, with only about one-eleventh of the population of the *sous-préfecture* of Dikodougou, accounted for nearly a third of all registered marriages, and yet I could think of no reason at all why the Dyula of Kadioha should be more enthusiastic about registering their marriages than those in Korhogo. However, the answer is relatively simple. After passing the Civil Code, the government embarked on a vigorous campaign to put it into practice, and particularly to compel people to register their marriages.

Kinship in a changing world

Table 9. *Marriages registered at sous-*
préfecture of Dikodougou (December
1965–October 1973)

	Kadioha	Total
1965	0	2
1966	26	68
1967	26	54
1968	6	18
1969	0	2
1970	0	6
1971	6	26
1972	7	13
1973	5	7
	76	196

241 marriages anterior to 1965 registered
1965–70, of which 18 were from Kadioha.

This campaign was at its height in 1966 and 1967, as is apparent in the statistics for both the *sous-préfectures* of Dikodougou and Korhogo. It so happens that Senufo weddings are quiet and unobtrusive, while the festivities of any Dyula wedding last more than a week, full of constant and unmistakable drumming and dancing. Moreover, in the villages, all the marriages in one year very often take place at the same time. Kadioha, the biggest Dyula village in the region, was an obvious gold mine for government officials who wanted presentable statistics in the register; generally twenty-five to thirty couples get married at one time each year, and news of this travels for miles. The government officials simply needed to visit Kadioha once a year, during the celebrations, and round up all the couples, as clearly happened in 1966 and 1967. The same tactics were applied in large Dyula villages on the outskirts of Korhogo: Waraniene, Kapele and Katia. Paradoxically, this was not true in Koko quarter, within Korhogo itself. Because the town Dyula are more prosperous, marriages are planned with less precision: two or three at a time in one *kabila*, with no attempt at all to match up the dates from *kabila* to *kabila*. Unlike the villages, a once-yearly operation yields little fruit. The most convincing proof that the registration of marriages in Kadioha was not a matter of individual choice, but of official compulsion, is found in rates of registration of marriages in Kadioha anterior to 1965. It was obviously impracticable to enforce the registration of such marriages, and very few couples from Kadioha have ever bothered to register them. After 1967, when government officials ceased to compel couples to register, the fall in registration for Kadioha, and for the *sous-préfecture* as a whole, was dramatic.

143

Responses to change

There is less inducement in Kadioha to register marriages except under compulsion than there is in Korhogo. Few Dyula from Kadioha earn regular wages, and so they cannot seek family allowances; those few who earn salaries will, of course, register their marriages. Moreover, the uneasy tolerance of elopement in Korhogo is entirely absent in Kadioha. If a girl elopes, whether she registers her marriage or not, her parents almost invariably persist in refusing to let the traditional ceremonies take place. This is not to say that elopement never takes place; indeed, the one reason I was given in Kadioha for voluntarily registering a marriage was to provide the husband a legal recourse should his wife run away with another man. In such cases, I was told, a husband could ask officials to bring her back, though I never heard of any specific instances where this was ever attempted. But I was very struck in Kadioha, as opposed to Korhogo, by the total ignorance of most individuals about the Civil Code itself. Many Dyula in Kadioha were totally unaware that polygyny was prohibited under the Code, and expressed real surprise and not a little skepticism when I claimed that it was. Young brides, usually without education and generally younger than those in Korhogo, did not seem to be aware that they could contest arranged marriages at the nearby administrative headquarters of the *sous-préfecture*. Paradoxically, despite the high proportion of marriages in Kadioha registered since 1965, the Civil Code has had virtually no impact there; its provisions, generally unknown, are not taken into any account. This is not at all true in Korhogo, where most Dyula are at least vaguely aware of the contents of the Code, and some are very well informed. The Dyula of Korhogo often ignore the Code, but they do so quite consciously. On the contrary, many are willing to manipulate the Code to their own ends, not only young couples but the close kinsmen of the young man involved in an elopement. This manipulation is still very selective. The same persons who abet the elopement of one couple sometimes oppose the elopement of another couple, under different circumstances, though the two situations may appear identical under the terms of the law. Moreover, if use of the law to allow elopement is recognized by the community, use of the law in its other domains (for instance, by a wife who wants to prevent her husband from marrying another woman) is still considered absolutely unacceptable by almost everyone. Thus, in spite of the law, the Dyula of Korhogo and Kadioha have successfully maintained social controls over the way in which the Code is used by individuals. Changes have taken place, at least in Korhogo, but these had already begun before the Code went into effect. This is not to say that the Code is entirely insignificant; it is quite possible that younger Dyula, and especially women, will increasingly use the Code to further their own ends. But, in the final analysis, the long-term effects of the Code will depend, not so much on the planned objectives of the Code for furthering development and the conjugal family, but on the ways in which individuals are willing and able to manipulate sections of the Code to their own ends, whether these coincide with the original objectives or not.

The building blocks of kinship

If the Civil Code has not yet had any very direct impact on Dyula social organization, it hardly follows that other important changes have not taken place. Indeed, for such a commercially-minded people as the Dyula, one can only expect that the radical economic changes they have undergone would in certain ways be reflected in other institutions of Dyula society. Of all the features of the Dyula kinship system, the joint family was the most directly tied to the economic system. The joint family survived well into the colonial period; elders frequently remember turning over their earnings to their older brothers, middle-aged men similarly to their fathers. But the decline of the weaving industry spelled doom for the joint family. As more and more Dyula turned from weaving to crafts such as tailoring, they shifted from a dependence on the labor of junior kinsmen to a dependence on that of apprentices, preferably unrelated ones. The joint family as a unit of production is a thing of the past. Yet, in a sense, it survives as an ideal. For example, my host was the eldest of a group of nine brothers. One was still a young boy and another was a civil servant posted in the south. Every day, the remaining seven ate their midday and evening meals in common, on the porch of the eldest brother's house. In principle, one wife of each brother was responsible on any given day for the cooking, but the wives of the two poorest, monogamous brothers pooled their cooking with the wives of other brothers. Each brother was individually responsible for financing his contribution, though again richer brothers assisted the two poorer ones. The budgets of the brothers were strictly separate, yet they (and, in a separate area, their wives and children) ate in common. This communal meal coming from separate pots (both literally and metaphorically) is an appropriate symbol of the modern ideal. Kinsmen are expected to assist one another financially as well as in other ways. The extent of such cooperation ideally corresponds to a notion of 'closeness' determined partly by structural criteria (full brothers, for instance, are expected to be 'closer' than half brothers), partly by calculated reciprocity (one owes help to those who have provided it in the past) and partly by affection. For the poorest – often but not always the elderly – this assistance means contributing to their daily upkeep. For the relatively poor, it may mean helping to establish them independently in trade or as craftsmen. For example, one civil servant posted in the south bought a sewing machine for his younger full brother, a tailor. For all, it means assistance with important life-crisis rituals, weddings and funerals. However real this assistance may be, budgets are kept strictly separate – even, as we have seen, when brothers eat the fruits of their labors in common.

But if the joint family subsists only as an ideal, the *kabila* still exists as an almost palpable reality. Even the division of Koko into privately-owned lots has only slightly disturbed the arrangement of the community into spatially distinct clan wards. Neither in Koko nor in Kadioha, is any single member of the community not attached to a specific *kabila*. Yet, in subtle but important ways, the *kabila* too has changed as an entity. Before the colonial period, the *kabila* could incorporate new members as slaves or (though only provisionally) as 'strangers'. The incorporation of slaves has been a dead letter for a long time. The incorporation of strangers is equally a thing of the past in Kadioha, and even in Koko only a very occasional affair, despite the ever-increasing influx of immigrants to Korhogo. However, in precolonial Dyula society, a *kabila* could lose members as easily as it could incorporate them. When, for example, members of the Cisse *kabila* of Kadioha settled in Koko in the nineteenth century, they founded an independent *kabila*, despite the preservation of close ties between the two groups. The Cisse *kabila* of Kadioha itself maintained no ties whatsoever with its parent community in Bakongo (modern Guinea), remembered only as a place of origin. Individual Dyula might leave their communities of origin to seek a living elsewhere; those who chose not to return became potential founders of new *kabila*s. The advent of colonial rule paradoxically brought this process to a halt. Emigrants continued to leave their home communities in ever-increasing numbers. While many eventually returned, others made their permanent homes elsewhere. But this emigration did not lead to the formation of new, independent *kabila*s in the towns of the south. On the contrary, emigrants did not renounce *kabila* membership in their communities of origin. Of course, individual emigrants might always choose to sever ties completely with their home communities – on occasion, Dyula in Kadioha or Korhogo alluded to such instances – but this was the exception rather than the rule. In a sense, the *kabila* became a two-sided entity. On the one hand, it was tied to a particular locality, such as Koko or Kadioha. On the other hand, its effective membership transcended geographical boundaries.

The relationship of emigrants to their *kabila*s at home finds its most dramatic expression in two domains: life-crisis rituals and dispute settlement. Funeral ceremonies take place in the home *kabila*. Weddings are a somewhat more complicated affair, since they always take place at the home of the bride. Men do not necessarily come 'home' to be married unless their bride comes from their own *kabila*, but this is frequently the case. In such instances, weddings will invariably take place at 'home' even if both spouses happen to be residing elsewhere. Emigrants do not only return to

146

their 'home' *kabila*s for their own weddings and funerals or those of their close kin. The mass weddings which take place on a single occasion in Kadioha and other Dyula villages, as well as the funerals of important elders, invariably attract a large contingent of emigrants. The settlement of disputes between fellow *kabila* members living elsewhere also tends to bring them back 'home'. This is particularly true for marital disputes. Because of high rates of in-marriage, such disputes tend to involve other *kabila* members besides the spouses themselves. For example, in Kadioha, I assisted an elder in writing to his son, enjoining the latter to be understanding in his treatment of his wife; the parents of the two spouses were brothers, and there was concern that a rift in the marital relationship would have wider repercussions for the families concerned. When such disputes escalate, the couple is summoned back to the home community where the matter is thrashed out at a meeting of the *kabila* or *kabila* section. In these ways, the 'home' *kabila* continues to be the primary ritual and jural arena for migrants living abroad, even on a permanent basis.

In these ways, although the *kabila* is still anchored in space, residence is no longer a criterion for membership. The 'home' location serves as a hub, linking migrants abroad with those who have stayed behind or who have returned, but also those in different towns of the south to one another. The advantages are obvious for residents of the 'home' community, particularly in a village. Fathers in Kadioha who wish their sons to learn one of the modern trades must send them away, either to Korhogo or to one of the towns of the south. In most cases, they will be sent to live with an emigrant member of the *kabila*. Such a patron will not only be well placed to find a master to whom the young man can be apprenticed – not always the easiest of tasks, as the demand for apprenticeships exceeds the supply and successful craftsmen continually turn down requests – he will also generally lodge, feed and even clothe his charge *gratis*. Opportunities for learning a trade are far more numerous in Koko than in the villages; nevertheless, even in Koko, it is hardly unusual to send young men abroad to live with emigrant kin. Despite their declining participation in trade, the Dyula have chosen to enter sectors of the economy both heavily dependent on the market and subject to fluctuations in supply and demand, not only in Ivory Coast as a whole, but from town to town. In such sectors, mobility is crucial, not only for Dyula at home but also for the emigrants to the south, who will readily change their base of operations if their fortunes are slack and opportunities seem better elsewhere. A semi-dispersed *kabila* constitutes the core of a ready-made network of contacts throughout the country. This network extends beyond the strict confines of the *kabila* to include the affines and friends of fellow *kabila* members. These networks, essential to the emigrants as well as to the Dyula back 'home', cannot function in the absence of strong moral norms of reciprocity. The patron who takes in a young apprentice, finds him a master, feeds him and clothes him, does so out of a sense of obligation. *Kabila* membership is by no means the exclusive idiom in which these obligations are expressed. Kinship ties outside the *kabila*, as well as ties of friendship, perform similar functions. Nevertheless, *kabila* membership is unequivocally the tie with the widest ramifications. To put it another way, *kabila* membership provides each individual with a moral identity. In large measure, it defines what kind of assistance he can expect and from whom, and to whom he is expected to provide it in turn. *Kabila* membership has even wider repercussions for defining the identities of Dyula, either in the north or in the south. Dyula from Koko or Kadioha define themselves in the towns of the south as *Korhogo-ka*, natives of Korhogo and its hinterland. *Kabila* membership is an essential precondition for establishing a claim to such a broader identity. One can only belong to the whole by belonging to one of its precisely defined parts. In Korhogo, membership of *Lamogoya* and, later, *Koko Ton* were ascribed on similar lines; one's *kabila* affiliation automatically entailed – or excluded – one's participation. For the modern Dyula, the *kabila* stands between identity and anonymity.

The survival of the *kabila*, in spite of the demise of the joint family, implies that it both embodies and guarantees principles which are still essential to the modern Dyula. But the network of obligations which the *kabila* represents presupposes more than an abstract principle of reciprocity. Moral obligations, however binding in principle, can easily be violated. The Dyula are no more saintly than anyone else in this respect. The enforcement of norms presupposes a structure of authority. In the case of the *kabila*, this structure rests on the application of strict principles of seniority based on sex, age, generation and free or slave status. All of these distinctions are still in operation today. The notion that one *must* defer to one's seniors, especially in public, remains firmly rooted in Dyula practice. For example, in Kadioha, a middle-aged man struck his elder brother, who had borrowed a bicycle pump, returned it broken, and refused to have it repaired. A meeting of the appropriate *kabila* section was convened, and the man was roundly and unanimously condemned. Reprobation was not, by any means, confined to elders; an assistant of mine, a secondary-school student from Korhogo, was present at the meeting, and privately expressed his profound shock at the culprit's behavior. The attitude of second-generation slaves (*worossos*) is even more striking. By joking obscenely at the expense of freemen – both a privilege and a hallmark of *worosso* status – such individuals freely and publicly acknowledge their junior status, both in ritual contexts and in everyday social interaction (Launay 1977b). This deference accorded to elders is all the more striking because the real power of the elders has radically declined. In the past, a man's economic

148

independence marked the beginning of his accession to the status of elder. Nowadays, fathers no longer control the earnings of their sons. The wealthiest members of the community, and those who hold the most political influence outside it, are all middle-aged men rather than the most senior elders, most of whom tend to be relatively poor. These rich and powerful middle-aged men in fact make all the important decisions concerning the *kabila*'s policy towards outside groups and institutions. Yet, in spite of their real power, they invariably solicit the approval of their seniors. This divergence of power and authority rarely if ever leads to confrontation; both sides are committed to keeping up appearances. While the authority of the elders in determining the *kabila*'s external relations is largely a polite fiction, their voice carries far greater weight in the settlement of internal disputes. The resolution of such disputes through consensus, formally or informally, is essential to the maintenance of norms of reciprocal solidarity within the *kabila*. Public opinion militates very strongly against any resort to outside authorities in the handling of internal conflicts. When members of one *kabila* of Koko complained to the police about an incident with members of another *kabila*, the second group (in council) expressed unanimous outrage; they felt that a dispute internal to Koko ought to be settled as such, through consensus rather than through the threat of official sanctions. Paradoxically, the search for consensus, which is formally democratic (anyone can speak out at a meeting), and the strict protocol of seniority, which is not, go hand in hand. The hierarchy of seniority itself generates the procedures for resolving disputes. In any particular instance, one party will necessarily be 'senior' to the other. If the junior disputant feels that the senior has overstepped his authority, he ought properly to call a council in order that the senior be publicly rebuked, overruled or obliged to make reparations. Should he confront his senior directly (and, what is worse, violently), he will automatically place himself in the wrong. Similarly, the senior may call a council against his junior, ostracisim being the ultimate sanction against a refusal to acknowledge authority properly invoked. In general, this hierarchy of protocol works to discourage direct confrontation. It protects, not only the unity of the *kabila* as a whole, but ultimately the ideal, if not the reality, of the joint family, where the same principles apply.

In short, the modern kabila, despite its semi-dispersion, continues to function as a moral community, itself part of larger and more diffuse moral communities – the village of Kadioha, the Koko Dyula community, the *Korhogo-ka* in the southern towns. The moral principle on which it is based is reciprocity; the mechanism for enforcing reciprocity is consensus; and the procedure for obtaining consensus is implied in the hierarchy of seniority. The disruption of the Dyula economy has stripped the elders of their power; paradoxically, it has made their authority all the more necessary.

Responses to change

Marriage within the 'kabila'

Before the colonial period, the Dyula preference for in-marriage was a crucial factor in maintaining the integrity of the joint family. Until a man married, often as late as the age of thirty, he was financially dependent on the head of the joint family, who would ultimately find him a wife and defray the expenses of the marriage. Marriages of daughters were controlled even more strictly than those of sons. Since women were preferentially married to men of their own *kabila*, a young man depended on the goodwill of the head of his own joint family as well as on other elders in the *kabila*, in order to find a bride. But the joint family is a thing of the past. Fathers (much less uncles and elder brothers) no longer attempt to control the labor of their sons. Quite the contrary, elders are frequently dependent on the goodwill of their adult sons. In-marriage might seem to have outlived its function in Dyula society, and, like the joint family, be on the decline if not on the verge of extinction. The collapse of the Dyula economy, and with it the joint family, have afflicted Koko and Dyula villages alike; the system of in-marriage has been further threatened by political and ideological factors, particularly in Koko. The Western ideology of romantic love, the notion that spouses have the right to choose one another freely, is part of the 'package' that has been disseminated with Western education. For instance, secondary-school pupils present short skits in public in Korhogo each year. In one such skit, the young heroine, in love with a destitute but worthy young man, is promised by her avaricious father to an old lecher offering a high bride-price. The girl is held prisoner, and while the marriage ceremonies commence, the young man rushes to the local *sous-préfet* to apprise him of these dastardly goings-on. The administrator arrives with a contingent of policemen who break up the wedding, threaten the lecher and the father with jail and marry the young couple to the accompaniment of a chorus of praises of the Civil Code which permits young men and women to live happily ever after in each others' company. The scenario is overly melodramatic – the police are never involved and no one is ever threatened with jail – but it is not entirely unrealistic. Young couples in Koko can and do force the elders' hand by registering their marriages, either annulling or ruling out the marriages planned by the girls' families. Not only are many adolescents in Koko fully aware of this possibility; the stratagem can only succeed with the connivance of the husband's kinsmen. Even the elders accept the possibility of a love match, although they do their best to prevent their own kinswomen from contracting them.

Given the much more widespread acceptance of the principle of romantic love in Korhogo than in Kadioha, one would expect that rates of in-marriage would be significantly lower in Koko than in the village community. With this hypothesis in mind, I collected as complete a sample as possible of the marriages of all males in eight *kabila*s in Kadioha and nine in Koko (Table 10). Total rates of in-marriage for the Koko sample are indeed significantly smaller than for Kadioha (Table 11), but these figures are misleading. In each community, the Cisse *kabila* is disproportionately large – perhaps as much as a fourth of the total population – and also constitutes more than half of each sample. Discounting these two large *kabila*s, the rates are roughly comparable in the two communities. Roughly half of all marriages of men in other *kabila*s are with women of their own groups; the Cisse of Kadioha show considerably higher rates, and the Cisse of Koko significantly lower ones.

The inordinately high proportion of in-marriages among the Cisse of Kadioha is relatively easy to explain. The *kabila* is subdivided into three major *lu*s, or sections, and further subdivided into seven minor *lu*s (see Chapter 4). The populations of these minor *lu*s are, in fact, roughly comparable to those of other, entire, *kabila*s in the village. Consequently, there exists a hierarchy of marriage preferences impossible in the other, smaller *kabila*s: marriage is most favored within the minor *lu*s, then within the major *lu* and finally within the *kabila* as a whole. Indeed, the rates of in-marriage within the minor *lu*s among the Cisse are comparable to rates of in-marriage within other whole *kabila*s in Kadioha; first preferences in both instances operate with equal force. Higher rates of in-marriage among the Cisse can be explained in part by the operation of secondary preferences for marriages outside the minor *lu* but still within the *kabila* as a whole. Patterns of remarriage of widows also explain these higher rates among the Kadioha Cisse. Since widows are allowed to exercise their free choice in finding subsequent husbands, their remarriages are likely to approach a situation of random choice. The likelihood that any particular widow will remarry into any particular *kabila* is largely a function of its size. Since the Cisse *kabila* is so large, there is a reasonable chance that any widow will marry into it in the absence of any rule of choice; size again dictates that a large proportion of these widows will also be Cisse. In fact, 20.1% of all marriages within the Cisse *kabila* in Kadioha were remarriages; in the other *kabila*s in the Kadioha sample, not a single widow or divorcee remarried within her own *kabila*. All in all, the very size of the Cisse *kabila* in Kadioha explains its significantly higher rates of in-marriage.

Logically, the Cisse *kabila* of Koko ought to display similarly high rates. It, too, is subdivided into sections. Its widows, too, exhibit a significantly higher tendency to remarry within their own group, though somewhat less strikingly so than in Kadioha: remarriages account for 18.4% of all in-marriages within Koko's Cisse *kabila* as compared to 6.0% of in-marriages among other groups. Yet, contrary to expectations, rates of in-marriage are actually lower among the Cisse than among other *kabila*s of Koko, though in-marriage still accounts for about three-eighths of the total. Part of the

Responses to change

Table 10. *Sample of men's marriages by clan ward in Kadioha and Koko*

	Number of husbands	Number of marriages[a]
Kadioha		
Cisse	85	178
Haidara	6	13
Konate	6	11
Dambele	17	33
Dagnogo	9	12
Kamagate	16	26
Wattara	13	33
Samagassi	5	7
	157	313
Koko		
Cisse	87	195
Wattara	12	24
Fofana	7	16
Diane	18	31
Bamba	5	8
Saganogo	12	27
Samagassi	9	15
Milagaso (Fofana)	4	10
Dakurufeso (Coulibaly)	7	19
	161	345
Total	318	658

[a] Includes marriages terminated by divorce or death of wife.

Table 11. *Descent group in-marriage as a percentage of total marriages of men*

	%
Kadioha	
Cisse	80.3
Other *kabila*s	47.4
Total	66.1
Koko	
Cisse	37.4
Other *kabila*s	54.0
Total	44.6

152

answer undoubtedly lies in the *kabila*'s involvement in local politics. Since Korhogo is a large town by Ivoirian standards, local politics have repercussions on a national level, and local politicians in Korhogo can aspire to a measure of national influence unlikely for ordinary village leaders. The very size of the Cisse *kabila* enhances its chances in the local political arena, provided it can recruit additional clients and allies from outside the group. This is precisely what they have attempted to accomplish: the Cisse were among the first supporters of the R.D.A., the ruling party, in the Korhogo region – this at a time when it was an opposition party, sometimes violently repressed by the French. Since then, their position of leadership, especially in Koko itself, has often been contested by a coalition of other *kabila*s, but they remain the single most influential Dyula *kabila* in all Korhogo, and boast the region's only Dyula politician of any supralocal importance. This unique political role has led them to cultivate affinal ties outside the *kabila*, just as it makes them attractive potential affines for outsiders. But, in order to wield influence, the *kabila* must also be mindful of its own internal cohesion so that it can maintain a unified front, and marriages outside the group have to be balanced against marriages within. In this respect, the Cisse of Koko are absolutely unique among Dyula in the region; no other Dyula *kabila* combines the size and strategic location necessary to play a similar role in politics. For this reason, it is unlikely that they might constitute an example for other groups, either in Koko or in the villages.

With the partial exception of the Cisse of Koko, overall rates of in-marriage in Koko as well as in Kadioha suggest that the system of marital preferences has survived both the demise of the Dyula economy and the diffusion of the ideology of romantic love. However, both of these changes happened relatively recently: the decisive crisis in the Dyula economy came only after World War II; widespread education, responsible for instilling the notion of free choice of a spouse, only came in the 1960s. Thus overall rates would not be a sensitive measure of such changes, as they include marriages contracted before crucial changes had taken place. Table 12, which shows the relationship between husband's age and rates of in-marriage, demonstrates conclusively that high rates of in-marriage cannot be explained solely by the marriages of older men. On the contrary, rates of in-marriage vary consistently in inverse proportion to the ages of husbands. (The Cisse *kabila*s show rises in the rates for the higher age groups, due to the fact that widows are more likely to marry within the descent group.) It is not possible to infer, on the basis of these figures, that in recent times rates of descent group in-marriage have risen. Many young men take, as their first wife, a girl from their own group. Additional wives are often widows and divorced women from other *kabila*s. Such women are far more likely to marry older men, thus lowering the rates of in-marriage for husbands over

Responses to change

Table 12. *Descent group in-marriage as a percentage of total marriages, controlling for husband's age*

	Under 35	Husband's age 35–49	50–64	65+
	%	%	%	%
Kadioha				
Cisse	100.0(19)	78.4(40)	75.0(36)	87.0(42)
Other *kabila*s	55.2 (16)	54.8(23)	42.9(15)	29.6(8)
Total	72.9 (35)	67.7(63)	61.4(51)	61.7(50)
Koko				
Cisse	38.5 (10)	31.2(24)	43.1(25)	41.2(14)
Other *kabila*s	74.1 (20)	58.3(28)	48.3(14)	41.3(19)
Total	56.6 (30)	41.6(52)	44.8(39)	41.3(33)
Total	64.6 (65)	52.4(115)	52.9(90)	51.6(83)

thirty-five, and especially for husbands over fifty. At any rate, young men are still consistently taking their wives from within their own group.

Another group which might conceivably differ in its marriage habits from the rest of the Dyula population is that of the migrants. Two options are open to the migrants: either they can take women from within the communities in which they have settled or they can seek their wives back home within their descent group. In fact, 55.0% of the marriages of migrants living in northern Ivory Coast (outside Korhogo and Kadioha) and 52.3% of the marriages of those living in the south were with women from their own descent groups. Migrants still look for wives from their own descent groups, even if they also take wives from their new neighbors in the towns of the south. Nor does the length of time that people have stayed away seem to affect rates of descent group in-marriage very much (Table 13). Those who have lived in the south for the longest period of time do have a slightly reduced rate, but this difference may simply be due to the fact that these men are, for the most part, older and consequently more likely to have taken additional wives from outside the descent group.

It might appear from these rates that the system of preferential in-marriage has remained largely unaffected by the various economic and social changes which have beset the Dyula in town and in the villages. This is not absolutely the case in Koko. Table 14 compares divorce rates for marriages within and outside the *kabila* in Kadioha and Koko. In Kadioha, marriages within the *kabila* are strikingly stable and very rarely end in divorce, especially as compared with other marriages. In Koko, the reverse holds true: marriages within the *kabila* are *more* likely to end in divorce

154

Table 13. *Descent group in-marriage as a percentage of total marriages, according to length of stay abroad*

	%
Never abroad	54.6
	(N = 137)
Less than 5 years abroad	66.7
	(N = 44)
5–10 years abroad, less than 5 outside the north	63.2
	(N = 24)
5–10 years abroad, more than 5 outside the north	55.4
	(N = 31)
10 or more years abroad, more than 5 outside the north	47.6
	(N = 68)

Table 14. *Percentages of marriages ending in divorce*

	%	N
Kadioha		
Within the *kabila*	3.9	206
Outside the *kabila*	15.1	106
Total	7.7	312
Koko		
Within the *kabila*	16.2	154
Outside the *kabila*	11.5	191
Total	14.2	345

than other marriages. The divorce rates are still fairly low. One can certainly not infer that the system of preferential in-marriage is breaking down in Koko. But the ideology of romantic love appears to have gained considerable ground in town. Elders can still oblige individual young men and women to contract the marriages they choose for them, particularly uneducated girls married in early adolescence. The lovers of these girls are usually adolescents considered too young for marriage with whom they consequently cannot elope. But young wives may later run off with another man, or bring pressure on their husbands to divorce them by refusing to perform domestic or sexual services. In Koko, where there is widespread, if limited, acceptance of the principle of free choice of a spouse, such tactics, though publicly condemned, can be quite effective. In Kadioha, where attitudes remain more conservative, a recalcitrant wife married within her own *kabila* can rarely, if ever, expect to win the eventual acquiescence of her own kinsmen.

Even in Koko, despite the real inroads of the new ideology, the system of preferential in-marriage has shown remarkable resilience. Like the *kabila* itself, it has survived the demise of the joint family as an economic unit. Indeed, in-marriage, like the hierarchy of seniority, is one of the integrating devices which holds the *kabila* together. Unlike many other African descent groups, the *kabila* is not primarily associated with communal rights over valued scarce resources such as land or livestock. Its existence as a moral community is not in any way embodied in material terms; its perpetuation rests entirely on the sense of obligation pertaining to individual ties of kinship of various sorts. The system of preferential in-marriage generates a network of matrilateral and affinal as well as patrilateral ties within the group; bilateral links of kinship, rather than pulling the group apart, cement it together. The marital careers of emigrants are a case in point. Precolonial patterns of emigration, leading to the formation of new *kabila*s, tended to isolate daughter from parent communities as marital units. Modern emigrants to the south, on the other hand, still retain effective membership in their *kabila*s of origin. By coming 'home' to marry, and by giving and receiving brides, they not only symbolize but also perpetuate their affiliation. Marrying in counteracts the effects of moving out.

In-marriage also serves to buttress the keystone of the *kabila*, the hierarchy of seniority. Young men continue to depend on the goodwill of the elders in order to find brides. Within the region as a whole, young Dyula women are relinquished in marriage to outsiders only with great reluctance, unless other ties of kinship or strong bonds of friendship link the parents of the spouses. Moreover, the cost of an exogamous wedding is often more than twice as great as a wedding between members of the same group. Prestations are invariably more lavish, particularly for ceremonies which legitimize legalized elopements after the fact. I witnessed a number of such ceremonies where the bride's kinsmen insisted on their prerogatives, and where hard bargaining took place throughout the course of the occasion; such bargaining is distinctly out of place in a wedding which the bride's kinsmen have arranged themselves of their own free will. The cost of an exogamous marriage may deter a young man from attempting to marry outside the *kabila*; the very possibility of contracting such a marriage depends on the goodwill of his kinsmen, as few individuals are wealthy enough to bear such costs alone. Even an elopement presupposes the complicity of the groom's kin. Generally, young men are eager to marry, as this marks their passage into social adulthood. Consequently, unless their hearts are set on a particular young girl, they are unlikely to attempt to thwart the plans laid for them by their elders. If they do have a particular match in mind – by no means always the case – they have other reasons to solicit the support of their senior kinsmen. All in all, marriage is a domain where the elders of a *kabila* exercise real power as well as authority over their juniors.

However, even this power is mitigated by the relative economic independence of the young men who, if they cannot find an available bride and defray the expenses of the wedding on their own, nevertheless no longer rely on their seniors for their livelihood. Formerly, it was in the interest of the head of the joint family to delay the marriages of junior dependents, within acceptable limits, in order to maintain them in their dependent status. With the demise of the joint family as a unit of production, there is no longer any reason to impose a late age of marriage for men. On the contrary, fathers who depend on their sons for financial assistance are solicitous of their goodwill. Fathers may attempt to strengthen this link by arranging the son's marriage as early as possible. If the marriage takes place within the *kabila*, the elders of the bride's family have a similar interest; the marriage gives them a double claim, as close affines as well as fellow *kabila* members, on the groom's assistance. In the past, the labor of young dependents was a scarce resource, and preferential in-marriage helped to keep this resource within the *kabila*. Nowadays, the independent earnings of the young and middle-aged men have replaced their labor. This is a considerably less dependable means of assuring the elders' livelihood, but the system of in-marriage reinforces the elders' claims on their sons as well as their sons-in-law.

Marriage outside the *kabila*

No matter how strong the preference for in-marriage, most *kabila*s are far too small to achieve demographic autonomy. Dyula men very simply do marry women from outside their own *kabila*s, and by no means infrequently. The liberty with which Dyula widows and divorcees can choose subsequent spouses means that many of these wives are married as older, and sometimes infertile, women. Even so, a high proportion of the marriages of husbands in the sample with wives from outside the *kabila* – 53.5% in Kadioha and 61.7% in Koko[3] – were first marriages for the women concerned.

Next to in-marriage, the Dyula express a stated preference for marriages between kin from different *kabila*s. Similarly, marriages are likely to occur between different *kabila*s within the same community, whether or not they are related by previous ties of kinship. In the sample of marriages in Kadioha and Koko, nearly two-thirds of wives from *kabila*s other than their husbands' were either previously related by other kinship ties, or from the

157

same local community, or both.[4] Nevertheless, as Table 15 shows, there are substantial differences in patterns of out-marriage in Kadioha and Koko. As far as these 'closer' forms of out-marriage are concerned, men in Kadioha showed an overwhelming tendency to take wives from within the village, whether or not any previous ties of kinship existed. Men in Koko are somewhat less likely to marry women from other *kabila*s in their own local community than men in Kadioha.[5] The two communities contrast sharply in their preferences for taking kinswomen outside the *kabila* as wives. Kadioha men are far more likely to marry kinswomen within the village than kinswomen from elsewhere; on the contrary, Koko men are more likely to marry a kinswoman if she hails from outside the community. All in all, patterns of wife-selection in Kadioha suggest a strong preference for in-marriage within the village as a whole as well as within the *kabila*. Koko men are either more interested in acquiring, or more successful in attracting, wives from elsewhere.

Not surprisingly for such a mobile people as the Dyula, marriages also take place outside the local community and the individual's network of kin. The social distance between spouses may vary considerably among such instances. Marriages with Dyula or other Manding-speaking peoples are definitely 'closer' than marriages with other ethnic groups. Again, for both intra- and inter-ethnic marriages, spouses from the Korhogo region are 'closer' than those from outside. If social distance between spouses were an accurate indicator of rates of intermarriage, one would expect the highest proportion of such wives to be Dyula from within the region followed by Manding-speakers from outside followed by Senufo from the region and finally by members of other ethnic groups.[6] As Table 16 shows, the Dyula of Koko conform exactly to these predictions. On the other hand, while the Dyula of Kadioha do indeed prefer Manding-speaking wives to members of other ethnic categories, they also consistently prefer wives from other regions in both intra- and inter-ethnic marriages outside the village. Both communities exhibit similar patterns of preference for marrying wives from outside the region: marriages with Manding-speaking women are not uncommon, especially compared to marriages with women from other ethnic groups. This is hardly a surprise. Many Dyula from Koko and Kadioha have emigrated to the towns of the south where they have been incorporated to some extent into a larger 'Dyula' ethnic category. In a similar vein, Manding-speakers from elsewhere have immigrated to Korhogo; as a result, the Koko Dyula as a whole, despite their emphasis on their distinctiveness, are also part of a larger 'Dyula' community. This broader 'Dyula' ethnic identity is reflected in marriage preferences. Still, these rates of interregional marriages with 'Dyula' remain relatively low. Dyula men in both communities prefer to take wives from within the region if not from within the village and above all from within their own *kabila*s. As far as

Table 15. *Wives from outside the* kabila *(1): marriages with kin and within the local community*

	Kin (outside local community) %	Kin (within local community) %	Local community (except kin) %
Kadioha			
Cisse	3.9 (7)	1.7 (3)	7.9 (14)
Others	0.0 (0)	8.9 (12)	25.2 (34)
Total	2.2 (7)	4.8 (15)	15.3 (48)
Koko			
Cisse	8.8 (17)	1.0 (2)	14.9 (28)
Others	9.4 (14)[a]	0.7 (1)	18.7 (29)
Total	9.0 (31)[a]	0.9 (3)	16.5 (57)

[a] Includes one Senufo.

marriages are concerned, the incorporation of Dyula from Koko and Kadioha into a broader 'Dyula' category has not in any way eroded their own sense of distinctiveness.

The most striking difference between the two communities lies in their different preferences for wives from within or outside the region. Kadioha men are actually less likely to marry a Dyula woman from some other community in the region than to marry a Manding-speaker from some other region. Senufo wives are an even greater rarity in Kadioha; the only one in the sample was married to the chief of Kadioha whose authority extends over several nearby Senufo villages. Koko men, on the other hand, are more likely to take a wife from another community in the region than to marry someone from another *kabila* in Koko itself. Ultimately, marriages with kin outside the *kabila* reflect the overall structure of preferences in each community. Kadioha men tend overwhelmingly to take wives from within the village whether or not the spouses are previously related. Koko men, however, are more likely to take wives from other Dyula (and, to a lesser extent, Senufo) communities in the region, again whether or not there exist previous ties of kinship.

These figures suggest that the network of relationships between different communities within the region has changed in the recent past. Genealogies in Kadioha suggest that Dyula men there used to take wives from Manding-speaking communities some distance to the southwest, as far away as Sakhala. In other words, marriage alliances followed the major trade route leading away from Kadioha towards the source of cola. With the opening of

Table 16. *Wives from outside the* kabila *(2): marriages with non-kin outside the local community*

	Dyula (Korhogo region) %	Manding (outside the region)[a] %	Senufo %	Other ethnic groups[b] %
Kadioha				
Cisse	2.8 (5)	2.2 (4)	0.0 (0)	1.1 (2)
Others	5.2 (7)	10.3 (14)	0.7 (1)	2.2 (3)
Total	3.8 (12)	5.8 (18)	0.3 (1)	1.6 (5)
Koko				
Cisse	15.9 (31)	10.8 (21)	6.7 (13)	4.7 (9)
Others	11.3 (17)	3.3 (5)	2.7 (4)[c]	0.7 (1)
Total	13.9 (48)	7.6 (26)	4.8 (17)[c]	2.9 (10)

[a] Includes Dyula from other regions, Malinke, Bambara and Dafing.
[b] Includes Fulani, Songhai, Baoule, Agni and Gouro.
[c] Includes one marriage between kin (also included in Table 14).

the southern frontier and the diffusion of modern motor transportation, the trade route faded into obsolescence – and so, apparently, have the patterns of marriage alliances. At the same time, the growth of Korhogo as an administrative center has made it an obvious focus of interest for all villages of its hinterland. Villagers may move permanently to seek work, or simply visit in order to buy and sell various commodities, seek modern medical treatment or deal with the government bureaucracy. For any of these purposes, kinsmen or affines in town are an invaluable resource; they not only provide the food and lodging expected of 'hosts' in Dyula society but also serve as intermediaries with local traders or, even more commonly, with government officials with whom they are conceivably on familiar terms. It may well be worth a villager's while to grant a sister or daughter in marriage to a townsman in order to reap these benefits. The sense of community which Koko shares with neighboring Dyula villages makes Koko men particularly likely candidates for such alliances. If the marriage rates in Kadioha are in any way typical of other Dyula villages,[7] they suggest that the affinal network of alliances between different Dyula villages in the region has been supplanted by a network which links the different villages to town, but in which women 'flow' exclusively in one direction: townwards.

Clearly, villagers perceive themselves as the primary beneficiaries of such alliances with townsmen since they are willing to give up their sisters and daughters in marriage without much, if any, hope of return in kind. This

160

is not to say that townsmen regard Dyula villagers merely as suppliers of potential wives. Townsmen who entertain any considerations of entering or reentering the food trade see village affines as essential resources closer to sources of supply. More ordinarily (indeed more realistically), village affines sometimes provide foodstuffs at cheaper prices than in town. Not infrequently, village-born women use their connections with their home communities to engage in petty trade, selling yams, rice, fruits or vegetables in town. Even this practice benefits Dyula husbands in town indirectly; not only need they expend less pocket money on their wives, but they can also expect wives who engage in petty trade to contribute to the domestic budget. Such services are nonetheless of marginal importance to most townsmen, especially compared to the benefits the villager reaps by having 'connections' in town. Ultimately, Koko is gaining wives (and children!) at the expense of its Dyula hinterland.

Polygyny

Just as Koko and Kadioha differ in their patterns of selecting wives, particularly from outside the *kabila*, one would expect to find differences in rates of polygyny. On the one hand, Koko has been much more fully exposed to the Western ideology of the conjugal family, as embodied in the Civil Code. If this ideology has been at all pervasive, one would expect lower rates of polygyny in Koko, particularly among younger married men. On the other hand, Koko is without doubt a wealthier community than Kadioha. Unlike their counterparts in Kadioha, the men of Koko have succeeded in attracting wives from neighboring Dyula villages. The attractiveness of townsmen as husbands and affines should plausibly make them more successful polygynists. In fact, the overall incidence of polygyny is almost exactly the same in both communities: 163 wives per 100 husbands in Koko, as compared to 165 wives per 100 husbands in Kadioha. The real differences between the two communities only emerge when one takes the husband's age into consideration (Table 17). In Kadioha, the incidence of polygyny increases dramatically with husband's age; in Koko, age makes relatively little difference except for husbands under the age of thirty-five. The incidence of polygyny is considerably higher in Kadioha among men older than fifty, and particularly among those over sixty-five; in Koko, younger husbands, particularly those between the ages of thirty-five and forty-nine, are far more likely to be polygynists than in Kadioha. In the first place, these figures indicate that the ideology of the conjugal family has had little effect on behavior, at least as far as polygyny is concerned. True enough, younger men in Koko were not averse to expressing the opinion to me that one wife is better than two – but such opinions were frequently expressed by polygynists! More importantly, the figures indicate that the

Table 17. *Mean number of wives per hundred married men, by age of husband*

	Age of husband			
	Under 35	35–49	50–64	65 and over
Kadioha	107	156	197	227
	(N = 41)	(N = 50)	(N = 35)	(N = 26)
Koko	118	177	180	183
	(N = 38)	(N = 57)	(N = 36)	(N = 30)

relative importance of age and wealth as determinants of polygyny are not the same in both communities. Wealth has always been an important factor among the Dyula, given their commercial ethos. Nevertheless, the Kadioha pattern shows the clear preponderance of age there. This pattern is not simply a reflection of the hierarchy of seniority. Formerly, women married much earlier than men, and were thus likely to be widowed at least once in their marital careers. Such widows accounted for most of the second, if not third and even fourth, wives of elders in the Kadioha sample. With the demise of the joint family as a unit of production, there is little to be gained in delaying the marriages of younger men in order to keep them as dependents. The age differential between men and women at first marriage has decreased, and the incidence of polygyny, particularly among elders in Kadioha, is likely to decline dramatically in future generations.

The situation in Koko is quite different. Elders are far less likely to acquire additional wives. Older widows are under less pressure to remarry, particularly if their sons are wealthy enough to assure their upkeep and consequently less eager than their Kadioha counterparts to shift the burden of responsibility onto subsequent husbands. Moreover, the poverty of elders in Koko is far more conspicuous, and makes them less attractive as spouses. Unlike those in Koko, middle-aged men in Kadioha are often little wealthier than elders, especially as they face the added burden of caring for their dependent children. In Koko, many of the wealthiest men are between the ages of thirty-five and fifty. Not surprisingly, such men are far more likely to be polygynists in Koko than in Kadioha. Wealth is clearly supplanting age as the major determinant of polygyny in Koko. Moreover, additional wives of the wealthy in Koko are frequently young girls marrying for the first time, or at least young divorcees.

In short, patterns of polygyny and of exogamous marriages suggest that the relatively wealthy husbands of Koko are attracting wives at the expense of the relatively poor, not only from Koko but also from the surrounding

162

villages. These trends are not yet marked enough to allow us to speak of class differences between townsmen and villagers, and between successful traders and civil servants and their less fortunate fellows. Yet the threat that such class differences will emerge in Koko's Dyula community is very real. The hierarchy of seniority, one of the pillars of the *kabila*'s integrity, is no longer expressed in Koko, as it is in Kadioha, by patterns of polygyny. The virulent reaction of Koko's majority against the superficially antithetical ideologies of 'Wahhabism' and 'secularism' testify to their anxieties that the relatively rich might succumb to the temptation to renege their perceived obligations. The gulf between the rich and the poor, while not yet unbridgeable, really exists. Rates of polygyny in Koko demonstrate that its effects have already begun to alter the kinship system in ways that may undermine the solidarity of the *kabila* and ultimately of Koko itself as a community.

11

Conclusions: Heraclitus' paradox

You cannot step twice into the same river, for other waters are continually flowing on.

Heraclitus (Wheelwright 1964:29)

A Dyula community existed in Koko before the twentieth century. Modern Dyula residents of Koko are convinced that, in a fundamental sense, they belong to that same community. They are, after all, descendants of earlier settlers. Any one of them can provide a genealogical pedigree to attest to the fact. More than anything else, this consciousness differentiates them from the multitudes 'across the stream' who resemble them in so many other aspects.

This deeply-felt sense of continuity belies the obvious fact that modern Koko is a very different place than it was a hundred, or even fifty, years ago. What was once a large village has now become one of the largest small towns in the country. Whereas all 'Dyula', however defined, used to be members of the Koko community, many, if not most of Korhogo's modern 'Dyula' residents would scarcely think of themselves as *Koko-ka*. Korhogo's trade with the outside world, once a monopoly of the Koko Dyula, has largely passed into the hands of all sorts of individuals 'across the stream'. Sometimes, Dyula in Koko speak as if these changes had never taken place, dividing their social universe into the neat categories of 'Dyula' and 'Senufo' (or, even more anachronistically, *banmana*, 'pagan'). Yet they are hardly in a position to ignore these changes.

Undoubtedly the most obvious way to assess, and ultimately to explain, change in Koko would be to compare the community as I observed it in 1973 with a plausible reconstruction of Koko in 1873. The most striking, and certainly the most fundamental, change became obvious to me from the very onset of fieldwork. Expecting to find a community of specialized traders, I found myself living in a place where most of the old men were impoverished weavers and where relatively prosperous younger men were more likely to be craftsmen, chauffeurs, skilled laborers or civil servants than traders. This shift has been less traumatic to the Dyula than one might imagine. The traditional opposition between 'Dyula' and 'Senufo' rested largely on the distinction between those who produced primarily for their own subsistence needs and those who relied largely on the market to make a

164

living. For the most part, Dyula in Koko have managed to avoid both farming for their own food and the pitfalls of mass urban unemployment. The new walks of life which many have chosen – at least those which do not imply regular salaries – are not after all so very far removed from traditional notions of 'traders'. The difference lies rather in the fact that, whatever their occupations, the Dyula of Koko no longer enjoy any monopoly. The goods and services offered in Koko are found just as easily 'across the stream', even in the hands of Senufo who have 'become Dyula'. One need hardly be an economic determinist to predict that, among a people who call themselves 'traders', such changes have affected other domains of everyday life. In particular, the decline of trade has spelled the disappearance of the joint family as a budgetary unit and a unit of production. Among the Kooroko of modern Mali who have fared more successfully as long-distance traders, the joint family unit has shown considerably more resilience (Amselle 1971).

On the other hand, real changes have taken place in Koko, and for that matter in neighboring village communities like Kadioha, which cannot be explained in strictly economic terms. Most striking is the disappearance of Dyula initiation societies. Although the Dyula have not ceased to speak anachronistically and each *kabila* can still be labeled *mory* or *tun tigi*, 'scholars' or 'warriors', this distinction has lost virtually all practical significance. Similarly, excision ceremonies for adolescent girls have been discontinued. These changes also result from the loss of a monopoly, in this case a religious rather than an economic one. Formerly the only Moslems in the region, the indigenous Dyula have witnessed an influx of Manding-speaking Moslem immigrants, as well as growing numbers of Senufo converts to Islam, particularly in town. The Moslem world of Koko is increasingly supra-regional and indeed international, leaving little if any latitude for the Dyula to set their own standards of conventional piety.

In short, a preliminary comparison of Koko today with the Koko of the past yields a list of things which were, but are no more: no more monopoly of trade, no more joint family, no more initiation societies and no more excision ceremonies. A comparable list of 'new' features of Koko would include: widespread emigration to urban centers in the south, Western education, the adoption of new occupations, the incorporation of the community into a modern nation-state and (alas) ugly and rather uncomfortable cement houses. These new features are not peculiar to the Dyula, but rather typical of modern Africa as a whole. The conclusions which seem to leap out from such a description of change in Koko are that the Dyula are rapidly losing those characteristics which used to distinguish them from other African peoples under the pressure of vast homogenizing processes of change exported from the West.

But viewing change as a series of radical discontinuities, of deletions and accretions, is fundamentally misleading. One simply cannot assume that those features of Dyula society which have persisted over time – and there are many – have not altered in fundamental respects. Perhaps the best example is the *kabila*. The *kabila* has remained the core unit of Dyula kinship. The principle that members be recruited by patrilineal descent has remained unchanged, and even, in a sense, been reinforced; after all, slaves can no longer be incorporated into the group through capture or purchase. On the surface the *kabila* of 1973 is quite the same sort of unit as the *kabila* of 1873; certainly most Dyula consider this to be the case. Yet the *kabila* has changed in at least one very fundamental way; before the colonial period, membership of a particular *kabila* entailed residence in a particular locality. Emigrants from any community typically founded new units in the villages or towns where they happened to settle. The settlement histories of Dyula communities throughout the region show that *kabila* formation through out-migration was an ongoing process until the onset of the colonial period. The modern situation is entirely different. In spite of high rates of emigration, new *kabila*s are no longer being formed. Even those emigrants who settle permanently away from home maintain full effective membership of their 'home' *kabila*. The modern *kabila*, though anchored in a particular locality, also serves as the hub of a network of members dispersed throughout Ivory Coast. The Dyula communities of Kadioha and Koko, like their constituent *kabila*s, now include emigrants as well as residents as full members. What is more, they have largely ceased to assimilate new members as 'strangers'. Communities which before the colonial period were 'open', regularly recruiting and losing members through in- and out-migration, have now become 'closed', their memberships ascribed on a purely hereditary basis.

Dyula Islam is no longer the same, particularly in Koko. The essential doctrines are unchanged and, in principle, unchangeable. Yet in town, the whole tone of Islam, especially the increasing preoccupation with ritual and ethical orthodoxy and the accompanying changes in the role of scholars, contrasts sharply with the more reassuring world-view of village Islam. Rural Dyula remain unambiguously Moslem and the Senufo equally unambiguously 'pagan'.

The paradox remains: the Dyula's own image of themselves embodies a sense of continuity, the notion that their present way of life can and should be justified in terms of the past. Yet the very features which seem loudest to proclaim this continuity turn out, on closer inspection, to exhibit subtle but hardly inconsequential differences with the way things were. The Dyula have managed to combine deep-seated ideological conservatism with a hard core of pragmatism which allows them to accept and indeed initiate changes in their own society in the face of inevitable changes in the world outside. One might be tempted to conclude that this sense of continuity is nothing but an illusion, blinding the Dyula to the real changes taking place in their own world. But the Dyula are definitely not insensitive to change. The abolition of initiation societies and excision ceremonies, and the acceptance by many parents of Western education for their children, are examples of changes which are not only conscious but intentional. More importantly, such a perspective does not explain why the Dyula *kabila*s, and indeed the Dyula community of Koko, have survived at all, despite altering. A sense of continuity is illusory only if viewed literally. Conversely, if this pattern of continuity is perceived as a full-fledged 'social fact', then it needs to be explained every bit as fully as change. Indeed, any discussion of change independent of patterns of continuity is incomplete if not invalid.

Among the Dyula, continuity is ultimately a moral notion which defines the parameters of their identity. However, the very polysemy of the modern name 'Dyula' implies that this sense of identity is by no means straight-forward. Each individual Dyula bears not one but a multitude of general identities. Some of these are subsumed under the rubric 'Dyula' in its more general senses: Moslem, 'northerner' and Manding-speaker. On the other hand, unlike many other 'Dyula', he is also an Ivoirian. He is also Dyula in a much more restricted sense, as a member of the Manding-speaking minority indigenous to the country east of the Bandama River. Not only is he a member of a specific community, such as Koko or Kadioha, but also of a specific *kabila* within that community.

This multitude of identities ranges from the broadly inclusive – 'Dyula' – to the narrowly restrictive – membership of a specific *kabila*. Obviously, such differences in scope imply differences in the kinds of social interactions which diverse identities tend to regulate. At the interpersonal level, individuals who share a common identity may be bound by reciprocal rights, duties and expectations. This is specifically the case for the most restrictive of identities, membership of a given *kabila*. Fellow *kabila* members expect assistance from one another, at least hospitality when they are traveling or when they choose to settle in another locality. This kind of mobility, both short- and long-term, has always been a fact of life for the Dyula, though never so much as today. In the short term, individuals move to seek better opportunities for medical care, to further their business interests, to deal with government officials or agencies at the local or national level or simply for the pleasure of visiting. In the long term, they seek better opportunities for formal schooling, to learn a particular trade or to establish more promising locales for business activities. *Kabila* members are not the only individuals who are expected to offer assistance and hospitality in such circumstances; kinsmen and friends outside the *kabila* are used in exactly the same way. Even so, the *kabila* serves as a vital mechanism for extending outside ties, linking individuals to the kinsmen and friends of fellow members as well as to their own.

Responses to change

Obviously, the more general the identity, the less it defines the content of interpersonal interactions and expectations. Appeals for assistance to a fellow 'Dyula' or 'Moslem' do not carry the same weight – if any at all – as appeals to a fellow *kabila* member. On the other hand, the very inclusiveness of such identities makes them relevant categories for political action on the basis of shared culture and/or shared interests. The emergence of *Koko Ton*, not only in Korhogo but also in the capital, demonstrates that broader identities can constitute a base for mobilizing groups and individuals in concrete situations. Of all of these identities, the category 'Dyula' is perhaps the broadest (in one of its senses, at least), not only because it bridges cultural, religious, national, regional and occupational identities, but precisely because of its polysemic ambiguity. By labeling himself a 'Dyula', an individual identifies himself in a general sense with 'Moslems', 'Manding-speakers' and 'northerners'. Used more specifically, 'Dyula' are not only natives of Ivory Coast but of a specific part of the country. The Dyula of Koko and Kadioha are 'Dyula' in all of these senses. Specific political contexts define which sense they wish to emphasize or ignore through implicit or explicit opposition ('Ivoirian' versus 'foreigner', 'northerner' versus 'southerner', 'Manding-speaker' versus 'non-Manding-speaker', etc.)

The categories 'Dyula' and '*kabila* member' represent different poles in a spectrum of identities, the first imprecise and ambiguous, the second precise; the first broad and inclusive, the second narrow and exclusive; the first 'political', the second 'interpersonal'. Yet in fact these two identities are closely linked and, in some contexts, inseparable. In its broader sense, a person's language, culture and religion make him a 'Dyula'. A 'Senufo' and even a 'southerner' can 'become Dyula'. But in a more restricted sense, a person is born Dyula by being born into a particular community, like Koko or Kadioha, and one cannot be born into such a community without being born into one of its constituent *kabilas*. *Kabila* membership is not only the most specific of the various social identities of the Koko Dyula; it is also the only one which implies all the other identities which all the Dyula of Koko and Kadioha can assume. Consequently, while identities such as 'Dyula' or 'Moslem' tend to be devoid of content at the interpersonal level, it is not conversely true that *kabila* membership lacks political content.

In different and to some extent opposite ways, *kabila* membership and 'Dyula' identity remain crucial to the day-to-day social life of the Dyula of Koko and Kadioha. These identities provide both links with the past and ways of dealing with the present. To the extent that each identity is more than a mere abstraction, a commitment to them constrains the nature of change in specific Dyula communities. In particular, the rights and obligations which link members of the *kabila* to one another, not simply as fellow members but as parents and children, elder and younger siblings and

168

so forth, need some mechanism of enforcement. Such a mechanism exists: the rigid hierarchy of seniority which ranks any two individuals in a given *kabila*, even twins, as 'senior' and 'junior' to one another. Juniors owe deference to seniors, while seniors are expected to fulfill their responsibilities towards juniors. Conflicts are resolved through meetings of the full *kabila* or of one of its constituent parts; decisions rest on the consensus of the group as a whole, with ostracism the ultimate sanction. The cohesion of the *kabila* as a whole depends on a virtually universal acceptance of the principle of seniority, that is to say, on a clearly recognized structure of authority and of the procedure for resolving conflicts. Until now, the principle of seniority has remained substantially unchallenged, but, as a consequence, authority and power are now almost completely divorced. The most senior members of virtually all *kabila*s are indigent senior males. Wealth and outside political influence are most often the privileges of certain middle-aged men. These men wield *de facto* authority in determining the *kabila*'s external relations concerning issues ranging from participation in *Koko Ton* to support for factions in the ruling party's local bureaucracy. Even so, the wealthy and the powerful must remain careful to display overt deference to the senior elders, who retain the ultimate right to veto the decisions of their juniors, a right which can nevertheless only be exercised at the risk of splitting the group. Internally, the authority of senior elders remains a great deal more than a polite fiction. One of the crucial arenas in which they can use this authority is marriage, particularly where the marriages of their own daughters and granddaughters are concerned. On the one hand, they can refuse to grant these women as brides to junior men who refuse to defer to their authority – or withhold legitimization to unions of women who refuse husbands chosen for them by their senior menfolk. On the other hand, by granting brides to economically independent junior men, they reinforce claims on their constituents, for goods and services as well as for deference.

In short, membership of a particular *kabila* continues to constitute a fundamental part of the personal identities of residents of Koko, Kadioha and other similar Dyula communities. Such identities are not mere empty abstractions. On the contrary, they involve real commitments by individuals to the principles of seniority, expressed in concrete terms not only by public display of deference and acceptance of procedures for conflict resolution within the group, but also by continued patterns of in-marriage within specific *kabila*s. At a different level, this concern with the maintenance of crucial identities has expressed itself in religious terms. This is particularly the case in Korhogo, where the *Koko-ka* consider themselves, and wish others to consider them, 'Dyula'. Yet to be 'Dyula' also means to be Moslem. Living as they do in a plural community where many individuals outside Koko also claim to be Moslem, the *Koko-ka* must maintain standards of conventional piety acceptable to their neighbors and co-

169

religionists. The ideological conservatism of the Dyula reflects, not so much a resistance to change, but rather the desire to maintain critical identities in the face of change. They are no longer traders living amidst farmers, nor Moslem islands in a 'pagan' sea; but they are still 'Dyula', still *Koko-* or *Kadioha-ka*, still members of particular clan wards. Such identities are part of the individual's most effective defenses against the faceless anonymity of the modern world.

Under present conditions, these identities cannot survive without a struggle. In the first place, the Ivoirian government is officially hostile to the 'extended family' – the *kabila* and the moral obligations of reciprocity between kinsmen which it represents – on the grounds that it is an impediment to economic development. This hostility is primarily embodied in the strictures of the Civil Code. So far, the Code has hardly had a dramatic effect on Dyula practice, especially since the government has not committed itself to a systematic implementation of its provision. However, the real threat to the *kabila*, and to the host of other identities which *kabila* membership implies, lies within rather than outside the community. Sharp differences in wealth have always existed in Dyula communities. The wealthiest members of any *kabila* are beginning to find the burdens of obligations to fellow kinsmen increasingly onerous. In the past, fortunes were accumulated through trade, a Dyula monopoly. The wealthy, more than anyone else, had a stake in maintaining a separate 'Dyula' identity restricted to members of specific Dyula communities. Nowadays, 'Dyula' traders in the region are not necessarily members of local Dyula communities. Wealthier traders from Koko or Kadioha obviously remain 'Dyula' in every sense of the word, but the temptation may easily arise to stress the professional rather than the 'ethnic' component of their 'Dyula' identity. The stereotype of the 'Wahhabi' in Koko, if not individual 'Wahhabi' themselves, involves precisely this menace. In any case, Dyula increasingly see the avenue to prosperity not in trade, but in education and access to the salaried elite. For the educated elite, the sources of wealth, prestige and influence lie increasingly outside the local Dyula community. At the same time, there is a tension between norms of elite behavior – patterns of consumption and rules of sociability – and the norms of behavior expected in communities like Koko and Kadioha. The Koko community has been quite successful in exorcising the overt 'Wahhabi' 'menace' and retaining the allegiance of wealthy traders (and even 'Wahhabis'!). In fact the covert reluctance of the educated elite to conform to the standards and expectations of their kinsmen poses a far more serious problem, with no easy solution.

The separation of wealth, based almost entirely on sources outside community control, and authority, based on the application of principles of seniority within the community, thus represents the greatest threat to the maintenance of those social identities which continue to govern the day-to-

Conclusions: Heraclitus' paradox

day interaction of Dyula in Koko and Kadioha. This polarity is even reflected in the patterns of polygyny. In Kadioha, polygyny is still largely a prerogative of the aged; in Koko, wealth is increasingly replacing age in distinguishing polygynous from monogamous husbands. In spite of such trends, the social rift between the relatively wealthy and educated and the relatively poor and illiterate (in French) is far from complete. The success of *Koko Ton*'s Abidjan branch in collecting contributions is a tribute to the elite's continuing commitment to their home community. The members of the elite still consider themselves *Koko-ka* and members of specific *kabila*s and frequently act accordingly, even if they sometimes feel that the burdens of such identities are onerous and if they fail to meet all the expectations of their poorer fellows. For the time being, the various identities by which the Dyula of Koko and Kadioha define themselves still imply a real moral commitment which can be translated into action.

In this book, I have attempted to show that a purely functional approach to change in social practices and institutions is, while, not incorrect, at least incomplete. At any given time, there is certainly a 'fit' between patterns of social organization and the functions they perform. Changing circumstances render certain functions obsolete and others imperative. The repercussions in the field of social organization may be direct; among the Dyula, for example, the joint family and the initiation societies for 'warriors' have disappeared. One can, of course, conclude that those features of any social system which survive change are 'multi-functional', but this tautology hardly carries the process of analysis very far. The weakness of a strictly functional approach is that it regards 'change' and 'continuity' as antithetical. The Dyula example suggests that the underlying reality is more paradoxical: aspects of society may change in fundamental ways while, in another and equally fundamental sense, remaining the same. The Dyula are still members of *kabila*s, still Moslems and indeed, still 'Dyula', though in none of these cases in quite the same way as a hundred years ago. *Kabila* membership, Islam and 'Dyula-ness' all embody identities, ways in which individuals define their present relationships with others in terms of the past. Such identities can only be labeled 'functional' in a very loose sense of the word. However, the maintenance of identities involves real functional prerequisites, such as the hierarchy of seniority and the preference for in-marriage within the *kabila* among the Dyula. The identities themselves, rather than the structural features of society which they sometimes require, represent the true link between the past and the present. Seen in this light, the apparent conservatism of any society implies not necessarily any reluctance to accept change, but rather a commitment on the part of its members to continue to define themselves as such. Such commitments are never a foregone conclusion. Members of any society may be tempted, and even eager, to shed their identities. Until now, the Dyula of Koko have

171

managed to hold such temptations in check. The inconsequential brook which trickles behind Korhogo's only cinema still separates Koko from the rest of the world.

Notes

1. Introduction: the people and the problem

1 Koko quarter also included members of various 'castes' – smiths, sculptors, brass casters and leatherworkers – all of whom except the latter were Senufo. In addition, a few speakers of the Fodonon dialect of Senufo (the majority of the chiefdom speaks the Kiembara dialect) also live in Koko and are apparently descendants of nineteenth-century inhabitants. In other words, the Dyula shared the quarter in the nineteenth century with other groups, including Senufo, whose members were all socially distinct from the inhabitants on the other side of the stream.

2 For example: 'Customs and values in tribal areas are part of a particular social context and cannot be compared with their counterparts in urban areas where they fall into another context.' (Mitchell 1966:45.)

2. Dyula and Senufo

1 Oral traditions collected among the Senufo of modern Pundya (Glaze n.d.) are consistent with the accounts told by the Dyula of Kadioha.

2 Administrative boundaries have since changed, and the eastern portion of the original district is no longer included in the modern préfecture of Korhogo.

3 These figures cannot be taken too literally. In particular, political events at the end of the nineteenth century contributed to the depopulation of certain chiefdoms (S.E.D.E.S. 1965, vol. 1:28).

4 The Dyula were also well aware of peoples living to the south, such as the Gouro and the Baoule, who were not Moslems either but known by terms other than *banmana*.

5 Manding-speaking 'pagans' have their own complex of secret societies: the N'domo, the Nama, the Kono, the Tyiwara, the Kore, and, above all, the Komo (Zahan 1960; Person 1968:59–63). Yet Dyula informants uniformly assert that their own (now defunct) initiation societies were part of the *poro* complex, borrowed from their Senufo neighbors, rather than associated with the initiation societies of their own distant Manding-speaking cousins.

6 Bravmann (1974) has demonstrated that this was equally true in Dyula communities to the east of Korhogo.

7 Certain other 'castes' occupied an intermediate position between Senufo and Dyula. These included not only the Dieli, leatherworkers who spoke their own language, but also Manding-speaking blacksmiths (Numu, Milaga and Somboro)

173

who were few in number and, except for the Milaga of Koko (assimilated to the Dyula in the nineteenth century), living in independent villages. In all of these cases, abandonment of traditional craft activities has invariably led to the very rapid adoption of Dyula identity.

8 However, the Dyula of Kadioha claim that, under French rule, they lost control over a number of Senufo villages which preferred to place themselves under the aegis of neighboring Senufo chiefs.

9 For the notion of 'ethnic boundary', see Barth (1969).

3. Warriors, scholars and traders

1 In this book, I have made the distinction between warriors and scholars (without quotation marks) and 'warriors' and 'scholars' (with quotation marks). The former refer to the specific occupations of particular individuals, the latter to hereditary social categories. All Dyula in the region were either 'warriors' or 'scholars' though many were neither warriors nor scholars. Warriors were usually (but not inevitably) 'warriors'; until quite recently, scholars were almost always 'scholars'. Nevertheless, an individual's chosen profession never in any way altered the social category to which he was ascribed.

   This dual division into 'warriors' and 'scholars' is common to other Manding-speaking peoples. The Malinke share the categories of *mory* and *tun tigi* (Person 1968:56, 136; N'Diaye 1970:14–26), while the Bambara kingdoms were similarly divided into Banmana 'warriors' and Marka 'scholars' and traders (Bazin 1972).

2 This was the case if a *mory* accidentally saw certain secret masks. He was then obliged to pay a fine, heavy in the case of a freeman, light in the case of a slave, and undergo a summary initiation.

3 Chiefs did, in fact, have a reputation as powerful witches (*subaga*), and as such their authority was felt to rest on some supernatural powers. On the other hand, scholars disposed of charms which conveyed other kinds of supernatural powers. In this domain, the chief was far from holding any monopoly.

4 Such activities were primarily the domain of the *tun tigi*, but individual 'scholars' were not prevented from taking part. One old 'scholar' in Kadioha confided to me that his grandfather had specialized in brigandage!

5 Wilks (1968:185) also found cases where elder brothers who were established traders financed the establishment of Koranic schools by a younger brother, but this was in Kong, a far more active locus of both trade and scholarship.

6 This near-exclusive reliance on bought or captured slaves acted as a leveling device in Dyula society; the heirs of a wealthy man could not count indefinitely on the slaves they had inherited, who formed an essential part of any rich man's fortune.

7 The Senufo term for tobacco, '*sara*', is identical to the Dyula term, while terms in other Voltaic languages are clearly not cognates (M. and L. Duponchel 1972).

8 See Meillassoux (1964:267–90) for a discussion of the trade from the Gouro point of view.

9 For the concept of 'landlord' in West African trade, see Hill (1966); Launay (1979).

4. Clansmen and kinsmen

1 The usage of terms to designate various segments of the descent group varies greatly from community to community among the Dyula, not to mention other

Manding-speaking peoples. Commonly-used terms include *so, lu (du* in certain dialects) and *gba*. In Bondoukou, for example, *lu* designates the joint family, while a *so* refers in principle to a somewhat larger segment (Tauxier 1921:216). Even this distinction is not without ambiguity. In a survey of six *kabila*s, Tauxier (1921:218) found only thirty-four *lu*s for twenty *so*s, or somewhat less than two *lu*s per *so*; in other words, many *so*s contained only one *lu*. In Koko and Kadioha, the term *so* is in fact synonymous with *kabila*, and there exists no term at all to designate the joint family, despite its real importance.

5. The mechanics of marriage

1 Certain non-Moslem African societies – for instance the Tswana (Schapera 1957) – also practice patrilateral parallel-cousin marriage.
2 A second generation Dyula resident of Ouagadougou did in fact identify patrilateral parallel-cousin marriage as a 'Moslem' practice. Most of his neighbors were Mossi, the majority of whom are not Moslems, but who are also patrilineal. In this case, marriage patterns could effectively distinguish 'Moslems' from 'pagans'.
3 For overall rates for men, see Table 11, p. 152. It was unfortunately impossible to tabulate comparable rates for women.
4 This preference for matrilateral cross-cousin marriage has a much wider distribution among Manding- and Soninke-speaking peoples (Cisse 1970:77; Pollet and Winter 1971:416; Luneau 1974:297–8; Schaffer 1980:50) than does parallel-cousin marriage as practiced by the Dyula.

6. The seeds of change

1 The French did not abolish forced labor until after World War II, and it was one of the major issues around which Houphouet-Boigny rallied opposition to the French (Morgenthau 1967:116–218; Zolberg 1969). In the field, I found many old men who were still bitter about it. Indeed, their concern that any census data I collected might be used against them and their families was one of the major obstacles I faced in conducting research.
2 See Abner Cohen (1969) for a discussion of the similar situation of the Hausa in Ibadan.
3 A French agronomist working in Korhogo once stopped a Senufo man along the road and asked through his interpreter whether he spoke French. 'Speak French?' the man replied. 'I don't even speak Dyula!' In sociological terms, this answer was not a *non sequitur*. For the ordinary Senufo farmer, speaking Dyula is the first step towards a more urban, and even cosmopolitan, way of life; speaking French implies a much fuller exposure and commitment to the world of the towns.

7. Occupation, migration and education

1 See, for example, Gibbal (1974); Oppong (1974).
2 For obvious reasons, the 'northern' populations of Ivory Coast lagged far behind in rates of secondary school education as well (Clignet and Foster 1966:50–72).
3 This reluctance is compounded by the inability of most civil servants to meet the expectations of their kinsmen and at the same time maintain patterns of consumption expected of men of their social standing; see Gibbal (1974).

8. Being Dyula in the twentieth century

1 Dyula from Kadioha or Koko ought to be counted among the 'Malinke'. However, because their communities of origin are situated in 'Senufo' territory, they may erroneously have been counted among the 'Voltaics'. In any case, it is clear that Manding-speakers are the most likely Ivoirians to leave their region of origin, with Senufo in second place.

2 Culturally, their homogeneity is much more pronounced; the very real differences which existed before the colonial period are tending to lapse in favor of a more unitary 'Dyula' immigrant culture. See Abner Cohen (1969) for a comparable account of the emergence of a unitary 'Hausa' culture among immigrants to Ibadan.

3 For a fuller discussion of the ritual cycle of weddings, see Launay (1975:chapter V): for *saraka*, see pp. 132–3.

4 The only cases which come to mind are 'orange peel' marriages of menopausal women to elderly villagers. These women continued to live in Koko, providing their largely absent husbands with food and lodgings when they visited town from time to time. I can think of no case where a Koko-born woman actually moved to a village to live with her husband.

9. Dyula Islam: the new orthodoxy

1 On this occasion, the scholar's criticisms were not aimed at Wahhabis in particular.

2 The distinction between 'town' and 'village' scholars applies, not necessarily to their place of birth, but where they are currently practicing. No scholar born in Koko would choose to practice in a village (though one, for instance, accepted the post of *imam* in the small town of Dikodougou), but an ambitious village-born scholar will naturally seek to make his reputation in town.

3 For an invaluable and detailed account of the ideology and history of the West African 'Wahhabi' movement, sympathetic to its point of view, see Kaba (1974).

4 See, for example, Dermenghem (1954); Gellner (1969).

5 See Abun-Nasr (1965:27–57).

6 There were too few 'Wahhabis' in Koko to allow me to judge whether this image had a substantial basis in fact. This would be a crucial issue for a sociology of the 'Wahhabi' movement. However, this does not really affect the analysis of the reaction of Koko's residents to the Wahhabiyya. This image need not be 'true', but merely credible.

7 Wealthy traders do enjoy a higher standard of living than their ordinary neighbors – indeed, they would be judged miserly otherwise. However, the differences between their patterns of consumption and those of ordinary Dyula are usually a matter of degree rather than of kind as is the case with civil servants, who must have their refrigerator, their car, their servants, their air conditioning, etc., whether or not they can really afford it. If traders must also resist the demands of kinsmen, this is rather to keep their trading capital intact than to consume conspicuously. For obvious reasons, such motives are far more readily accepted by the Dyula, who see the consumption patterns of civil servants as 'unnecessary' compared to their own pressing needs.

8 For a more extensive discussion of this ritual and the circumstances of its propagation in Koko, see Launay (1977a).

10. Kinship in a changing world

1 The underlying rationale is very explicitly stated in Abitbol (1966).
2 In another survey of the region, reported rates of polygyny among the Dyula were somewhat lower: 44.1% of husbands were polygynously married, with a mean of 155 wives per 100 married men (S.E.D.E.S. 1965, vol. 1:50). Even these lower rates are high by African standards (see Dorjahn 1959:102–3) and substantially higher than those reported for the Senufo in the same survey.
3 In this respect, differences between the two Cisse *kabila*s and other, smaller groups were negligible.
4 The Cisse of Koko were again atypical: only 42.3% of wives from outside the *kabila* conformed to either of these preferences.
5 The discrepant rates for the Cisse of Kadioha are undoubtedly a function of their inordinately high rates of in-marriage (see Table 11, p. 152).
6 Though Dyula of Koko and Kadioha marry few wives from ethnic groups outside the region, there is also a hierarchy of preferences for interregional inter-ethnic marriages along lines of social distance. 'Northern' ethnic groups from the savanna, particularly Moslems such as Fulani or Songhai, are 'closer' than 'southerners'. Even among 'southerners', women from matrilineal societies (essentially Akan-speakers) are considered inferior as wives to women from patrilineal societies in southwestern Ivory Coast.
7 Obviously, villages with a small Dyula population are in a different situation, and must take wives from other villages.

Bibliography

Abitbol, E. 1966. La famille conjugale et le droit nouveau de mariage en Côte d'Ivoire. *Penant* **712**: 303–16

Abun-Nasr, Jamil. 1965. *The Tijaniyya* London: Oxford University Press

Amselle, Jean-Loup. 1971. Parenté et commerce chez les Kooroko. In *The development of indigenous trade and markets in West Africa*, ed. Claude Meillassoux, pp.253–65. London: Oxford University Press

Amselle, Jean-Loup. 1977. *Les Negoçiants de la Savane*. Paris: Anthropos

Barth, Frederik. 1954. Father's brother's daughter marriage in Kurdistan. *Southwestern Journal of Anthropology* **10**: 164–71

Barth, Frederik. 1969. Introduction to *Ethnic groups and boundaries*, ed. Frederik Barth, pp. 9–38. Bergen-Oslo and London: Universitets Forlaget and George Allen and Unwin

Barth, Frederik. 1973. Descent and marriage reconsidered. In *The character of kinship*, ed. J.R. Goody, pp.3–19. Cambridge University Press

Bazin, Jean. 1972. Commerce et prédation: l'état de Ségou et ses communautés marka. Manding Conference, School of Oriental and African Studies, University of London (unpublished)

Bernus, Edmond. 1960. Kong et sa région. *Etudes Eburnéennes* **8**: 239–324

Bernus, Edmond. 1961. Notes sur l'histoire de Korhogo. *Bulletin de l'Institut Fondamental de l'Afrique Noire* **XXIII**: 284–90

Binger, Louis Gustave. 1892. *Du Niger au Golfe de Guinée*. 2 vols. Paris: Hachette

Bovill, E.W. 1968. *The golden trade of the Moors*. Second edition. London: Oxford University Press

Bravmann, René. 1974. *Islam and tribal art in West Africa*. Cambridge University Press

Caillé, Rene. 1968. *Travels through central Africa to Timbuctoo*. 2 vols. London: Frank Cass (first published 1830)

Cantrelle, P. and M. Dupire. 1964. L'endogamie des Peul du Fouta-Djallon. *Population* **19**: 529–58.

Chauveau, Jean-Pierre. 1972. Note sur la place du Baoulé dans l'ensemble ouest-africain précolonial. Abidjan: Office de la Recherche Scientifique et Technique d'Outre Mer (rexograph)

Cisse, Django. 1970. *Structures des Malinké de Kita*. Bamako: Editions Populaires

Clignet, Remi and Philip Foster. 1966. *The fortunate few*. Evanston: Northwestern University Press

Bibliography

Cohen, Abner. 1965. The social organization of credit in a West African cattle market. *Africa* **XXXV**: 8–20

Cohen, Abner. 1966. Politics of the kola trade. *Africa* **XXXVI**: 18–36

Cohen, Abner. 1969. *Custom and politics in urban Africa*. London: Routledge and Kegan Paul

Cotten, Anne-Marie. 1969. Introduction à une étude des petites villes en Côte d'Ivoire'. *Cahiers de l'O.R.S.T.O.M.*, sér. Sciences Humaines **VI**: 61–70

Delafosse, Maurice. 1955. *La langue Mandingue et ses dialectes*, vol. 2. Paris: Paul Geuthner

Dermenghem, Emile. 1954. *Le culte des Saints dans l'Islam Maghrebin*. Paris: Gallimard

Dorjahn, Vernon. 1959. The factor of polygyny in African demography. In *Continuity and change in African demography*, eds. William R. Bascom and Melville J. Herskovits, pp. 87–112. Chicago: University of Chicago Press

Duchemin, Jean-Paul and Jean-Pierre Trouchaud. 1969. Données démographiques sur la croissance des villes en Côte d'Ivoire. *Cahiers de l'O.R.S.T.O.M.*, sér. Sciences Humaines, **VI**: 71–82

Duponchel, M. and L. Duponchel. 1972. Le tabac en Côte d'Ivoire. Abidjan: Office de la Recherche Scientifique et Technique d'Outre Mer (rexograph)

Fisher, A.H. and H.J. Fisher. 1970. *Slavery and Muslim society in Africa*. London: Hurst

Fyzee, Asaf A.A. 1964. *Outlines of Muhammadan law*. Third edition. London: Oxford University Press

Gellner, Ernest. 1969. *Saints of the Atlas*. Chicago: University of Chicago Press

Gibbal, Jean-Marie. 1974. *Citadins et villageois dans la ville Africaine*. Paris: Maspéro

Glaze, Anita. n.d. History of Fodon-Pundya. m.s.

Goody, Esther. 1973. *Contexts of kinship*. Cambridge University Press

Goody, J.R. 1964. The Mande in the Akan hinterland. In *The Historian in Tropical Africa*, eds. Jan Vansina, Raymond Mauny and L.V. Thomas, pp. 193–218. London: Oxford University Press

Goody, J.R. 1968. Restricted literacy in northern Ghana. In *Literacy in traditional societies*, ed. J.R. Goody, pp. 199–264. Cambridge University Press

Goody, J.R. 1969. Inheritance, social change, and the boundary problem. In *Comparative studies in kinship*, ed. J.R. Goody, pp. 120–46. Stanford: Stanford University Press

Goody, J.R. 1971. *Technology, tradition and the state in Africa*. London: Oxford University Press

Hilaire, J. 1968. Variations sur le mariage. *Penant* **720**: 147–94

Hill, Polly. 1966. 'Landlords and brokers: a West African trading system. *Cahiers d'etudes Africaines* **VI**: 349–66

Hiskett, Mervyn. 1973. *The sword of truth*. New York, London and Toronto: Oxford University Press

Hodgkin, Thomas. 1966. The Islamic literary tradition in Ghana. In *Islam in tropical Africa*, ed. I.M. Lewis, pp. 442–60. London: Oxford University Press

Holas, B. 1966. *Les Sénoufo*. Second edition. Paris: Presses Universitaires de France

Ivory Coast. 1964. *Journal Officiel*, October 27

Jobson, Richard. 1968. *The golden trade*. London: Dawsons of Pall Mall (first published 1623)

179

Bibliography

Johnson, Marion. 1972. Manding weaving. Manding Conference, School of Oriental and African Studies, University of London (unpublished)

Kaba, Lansine. 1974. *The Wahhabiyya*. Evanston: Northwestern University Press

Kati, Mahmoud. 1964. *Tarikh el-Fettach*, translated by O. Houdas and M. Delafosse. Paris: Adrien Maisonneuve (first published 1913–14; written in the seventeenth century)

Khuri, Fuad. 1970. Parallel cousin marriage reconsidered. *Man* n.s. **5**: 597–618

Launay, Robert. 1975. Tying the Cola: Dyula marriage and social change. Unpublished Ph.D. dissertation. University of Cambridge

Launay, Robert. 1977a. The birth of a ritual: the politics of innovation in Dyula Islam. *Savanna* **6**: 145–54

Launay, Robert. 1977b. Joking slavery. *Africa* **47**: 413–22

Launay, Robert. 1978. Transactional spheres and inter-societal exchange in Ivory Coast. *Cahiers d'Etudes Africaines* **XVIII**: 561–73

Launay, Robert. 1979. Landlords, hosts and strangers among the Dyula. *Ethnology* **XVIII**: 71–83

Levtzion, Nehemiah. 1973. *Ancient Ghana and Mali*. London: Methuen

Levy, Reuben. 1962. *The social structure of Islam*. Second edition. Cambridge University Press

Lewis, Barbara. 1970. The Transporters' Association of the Ivory Coast; ethnicity, occupational specialization, and national integration. Unpublished Ph.D. dissertation. Northwestern University

Lewis, Barbara. 1971. The Dioula in Ivory Coast. In *Papers on the Manding*, ed. Carleton T. Hodge, pp. 273–307. The Hague: Mouton

Lewis, I.M. 1966. Introduction. In *Islam in tropical Africa*, ed. I.M. Lewis, pp. 1–96. London: Oxford University Press

Luneau, Rene. 1974. Les chemins de la noce: la femme et le mariage dans la société rurale au Mali. Unpublished Ph.D. thesis. University of Paris V

Marty, Paul. 1922. *Etudes sur l'Islam en Côte d'Ivoire*. Paris: Leroux

Meillassoux, Claude. 1964. *Anthropologie economique des Gouro de Côte d'Ivoire*. Paris and The Hague: Mouton

Meillassoux, Claude. 1975. Etat et conditions des esclaves à Gumbu (Mali) au XIXe siècle. In *L'Esclavage en Afrique Précoloniale*, ed. Claude Meillassoux, pp. 221–51. Paris: Maspéro

Mitchell, J. Clyde. 1966. Theoretical orientations in African urban studies. In *The Social anthropology of complex societies,* ed. M. Banton, pp. 37–68. London: Tavistock

Morgenthau, Ruth Schachter. 1967. *Political parties in French-speaking West Africa*. Oxford: Clarendon

N'Diaye, Bokar. 1970. *Les castes au Mali*. Bamako: Editions Populaires

Oppong, Christine. 1974. *Marriage among a matrilineal elite*. Cambridge University Press

Palmer, H.R. 1963. *Sudanese Memoirs*. London: Frank Cass (first published 1928)

Park, Mungo. 1954. *Mungo Park's travels in Africa*. London and New York: Dent and Dutton (first published 1799)

Patai, Raphael. 1955. Cousin right in Middle Eastern marriage. *Southwestern Journal of Anthropology* **11**: 371–90

Person, Yves. 1961. Tradition orale et chronologie. *Chaiers d'Etudes Africaines* II: 462–76

Person, Yves. 1964. En quête d'une chronologie ivoirienne. In *The Historian in*

Bibliography

Tropical Africa, eds. Jan Vansina, Raymond Mauny and L.V. Thomas, pp. 322–38. London: Oxford University Press.

Person, Yves. 1968. *Samori: une révolution Dyula,* vol. 1. Dakar: I.F.A.N.

Person, Yves. 1975. *Samori: une révolution Dyula,* vol. 3. Dakar: I.F.A.N.

Pollet, Eric and Grace Winter. 1971. *La Société Soninke (Dyahunu, Mali).* Brussels: Editions de l'Institut de Sociologie, Universite Libre de Bruxelles

al Qayrawani, ibn Abi Zayd. 1968. *La Risâla,* fifth edition, translated by L. Bercher. Algiers: Editions Populaires de l'Armée (written in 996)

Richter, Dolores. 1980. *Art, economics and change: the Kulebele of northern Ivory Coast.* La Jolla California: Psych-Graphic Publishers

Rouch, Jean. 1956. Migration au Ghana 1953–55. *Journal de la Société des Africanistes* **26**: 33–196

Roussel, Louis. 1967. *La Côte d'Ivoire population 1965.* Abidjan: Ministry of Planning (cited in Barbara Lewis 1970:42)

Schaffer, Adam. 1980. *Mandinko: the ethnography of a West African Holy Land.* New York: Holt, Rinehart and Winston

Schapera, Isaac. 1957. Marriage of near kin among the Tswana. *Africa* **XXVII**: 139–59

S.E.D.E.S. (Société d'Etudes pour le Développement Economique et Sociale). 1965. *Région de Korhogo: etude de développement socio-économique,* vol. 1, *rapport démographique;* vol. 2, *rapport sociologique.* Abidjan: Ministère des Finances, des Affaires Economiques, et du Plan

Tauxier, Louis. 1921. *Le noir de Bondoukou.* Paris: Leroux

Vendeix, M.-J. 1934. Nouvel essai de monographie du pays sénoufo. *Bulletin du Comité d'Etudes Historiques et Scientifiques de l'A.O.F.* **XVI**: 578–652

Wheelwright, Philip. 1964. *Heraclitus.* New York: Atheneum

Wilks, Ivor. 1966. The Saghanughu and the spread of Maliki law: a provisional note. *Research Review* (I.A.S., Legon) **II**: 67–73

Wilks, Ivor. 1968. The transmission of Islamic learning in the Western Sudan. In *Literacy in traditional societies,* ed. J.R. Goody, pp. 162–97. Cambridge University Press

Zahan, Domonique. 1960. *Sociétés d'Initiation Bambara: le N'Domo, le Koré.* Paris and The Hague: Mouton

Zolberg, Aristide. 1969. *One-party government in the Ivory Coast.* Princeton, New Jersey: Princeton University Press

Index

Abidjan, 86, 108, 110, 118–19, 120, 168, 171
agriculture, 19, 25, 39–41, 86, 90, 91, 92
Akan, 1, 13, 14–15, 177n6, *see also* Baoule
apprentices, 94–5, 105, 120, 147–8
artisans, modern, 91–6, 105, *see also* tailors

Bamako, 80, 82, 129
banmana, 17–18, 112, 164, 173n 2.4
Baoule, 14–15, 20, 31, 67, 79, 81, 107, 173n 2.4, *see also* Akan
Binger, Louis Gustave, 8, 21, 22, 79
Bondoukou, 3, 20, 35, 124, 175n 4.1
Boron, 3, 14–15, 16, 20, 44, 45, 131
Bouake, 86, 108, 129
Bouna, 3, 20, 39
bron, 52–3, 101

Caillé, Rene, 8, 79
'castes', 19, 173n 2.7, *see also* Dieli
chauffeurs, 91–4, 102
chiefs, 19, 26, 29–30, 32–3, 52, 53, 63–4, 73, 174n 3.3
Cisse, Sabati, 26, 31
Civil Code, *see* Ivory Coast, Civil Code
civil servants, 86, 91, 92, 97, 104–5, 115, 119, 135–7, 141, 175n 7.3, 176n 9.7
clan names, *see* patronyms
cloth, *see* trade, cloth; weaving
cola, *see* trade, cola
Coulibaly, Gbon, 31, 80, 88, 112
Coulibaly, Nanguin, 16

descent: matrilineal, 18, 62, 73–3, 139, 177n 6; patrilineal, 18, 48–50, 51–2, 54, 58–9, 62–3, 72
descent groups, *see* kabila
diatigi, see hosts (*diatigi*)
Dieli, 14, 17, 19, 117–18, 120, 173n 2.7
Dikodougou, 85, 98, 99, 100, 142–3, 176n 9.2
divination, 37, 130
divorce, 140, 154–5

dyeing, 44, 84
Dyendana, 14–15, 16, 23, 114
dyula, meanings of, 1–3, 106–8, 111–13, 167–8
Dyula (language), *see* Manding (language)

education: Arabic, 26, 34, 36–7, 103–4, 136; Western, 101–5, 136–7, 150, 153, 165, 170, 175n 7.2
excision, 125–6, 165

family, joint, 43, 45–6, 56–7, 59, 93–4, 95 6, 138, 145–6, 150, 165
Faraninka, 14, 15, 23
Fodonon, *see* Senufo
French (language), 103, 175n 6.3
funerals: Dyula, 37, 100, 115, 117, 132, 135, 146; Senufo, 41, 83–4

Gagnoa, 108–9
gba, see kabila, subdivisions of
Ghana, 2, 8, 13–14
gold, *see* trade, gold
Gold Coast, *see* Ghana
Gouro, 44, 67, 79, 80–1, 173n 2.4, 174n 3.8
Guinea, 13, 87, 107, 108, 109, 129

Hajj, *see* pilgrimage
Hausa, 2–3, 175n 6.2, 176n 8.2
hosts (*diatigi*), 4, 28, 68, 115, 160, *see also* strangers (*lunan*)

imam, 5, 26, 29, 37, 52, 63, 88, 100, 125, 176n 9.2
inheritance, *see* Moslem law, of inheritance
initiation societies: Dyula, 18, 26, 30, 33, 63, 74, 125, 165, 173n 2.5, 174n 3.2; Manding, 173n 2.5; Senufo, 18, 30, 112, 125, 173n 2.5
Islam, 17–18, 23, 25–6, 34–6, 62, 107–8, 112–13, 123–37, 165, 166, 167, 169–70, 175n 5.2, *see also* Moslem law; scholars, Islamic

183

Index

Ivory Coast, 2–3, 13–14, 79, 81, 83, 86, 97, 101–2, 105, 107–11, 116, 129, 175n7.2, 177n6: Civil Code, 139–45, 150, 170; colonial rule in, 31, 79–81

joking relationships, 27, 70
jons, see slaves, *jons*

kabila, 28–9, 36, 38–9, 48–54, 56, 58, 68–70, 73–5, 92, 100–1, 104, 114, 115, 138, 166–71; authority in, 50–4, 64–5, 74–5, 96–7, 105, 138, 147, 148–9, 156–7, 163, 169; and individual identities, 110–11, 147–9, 167–71; marriage within, 55, 61–6, 71–2, 75, 110, 138, 147, 150–7, 169, 177; as political unit, 32–4; ritual functions of, 52–3, 100–1; specialization of, 46–7, 63, 165; subdivisions of, 29, 50–1, 66, 151, 174–5n 4.1
Kadioha (chiefdom), 15–16, 20, 27, 30–2, 63, 64, 74
Kadioha (village), 5–6, 8–9, 14, 16, 27, 32–3, 35, 38, 50, 61, 64, 65, 67, 69–70, 79, 80–1, 85, 90–1, 96, 106–7, 148–9, 165, 167, 168, 169, 170, 171, 173n 2.1, 175n 4.1, 176n 8.1, 177n 5 and 6; education in, 101–5; emigration from, 97–101, 109–11, 114, 146–8, 154–5, 166; Islam in, 124, 126–7; marriage in, 141–5, 150–63; occupations in, 91–3
Kapele, 23, 35, 143
karamokos, see scholars, Islamic
Katia, 23, 67, 143
Kenedougou, 30, 31, *see also* Sikasso
Kiembara, *see* Senufo
kin, cooperation among, 55–9, 62–3, 64–5, 93–4, 95–7, 145–6, 147–9, 167
Koko (quarter of Korhogo), 4–9, 22, 27, 33, 35, 38, 50, 67, 69–70, 85–9, 90–1, 96, 111–22, 149, 164–72, 173n 1.1, 175n 4.1, 176, 177n4 and 6; education in, 101–5; emigration from 97–100, 110–11, 146–8, 154–5, 166; factions in, 120, 121–2, 128–9, 153; Islam in, 124–37, marriage in, 141–5, 150–63; occupations in, 91–5: *see also* Korhogo (town)
Koko Ton, 118–20, 122, 148, 168, 171, *see also Lamogoya*
Kong, 3, 8, 15–16, 20, 22–3, 30, 35, 38, 39, 42, 44, 124, 128, 174n 3.5
Kooroko, 3, 82, 87–8, 165
Korhogo (chiefdom), 5, 8, 16, 23, 27, 32, 64, 121
Korhogo (town), 3–9, 14, 27, 86–9, 90, 97, 112–13, 116, 120–2, 146, 153, 164; as administrative center, 79, 84, 160; civil marriage in, 141–2; immigration to, 87, 98, 112–14, 116, 124, 146, 160; *see also* Koko (quarter of Korhogo)
Korhogo-ka, 109–11, 116, 149

Lamogoya, 116–19, 148, *see also Koko Ton lu, see kabila*, subdivisions of
lunan, see strangers (*lunan*)

magic, 37, 130–1
makafo, 52, 69
Mali (empire), 1–2, 13
Mali (modern), 2, 13, 44, 67, 80, 81–2, 85, 87, 107, 108, 129
Malinke, 1–2, 17, 24, 61, 107, 108, 174n 3.1, 176n 8.1, *see also* Manding-speaking peoples
Manding (language), 1, 17, 18, 175
Manding-speaking peoples, 1–3, 13–14, 17, 18, 20, 61, 82, 83, 87–8, 107–14, 120–1, 158–9, 160, 167, 173n 2.5 and 2.7, 174n 3.1, 175n 4.1 and 5.4, 176n 8.1, *see also dyula*; Kooroko; Malinke
Mandinko, *see* Malinke
Maninka, *see* Malinke
marriage: between communities within region, 69–70, 116, 158–61; choice of spouse in, 60, 64–5, 70–1, 141, 144, 150, 153; civil, 136, 140–5; with grandmother, 70–1; within *kabila*, 55, 61–6, 71–2, 75, 110, 138, 147, 150–7, 169, 177; with kin outside *kabila*, 68–70, 157–8, 159; within local community, 70–2, 157–8, 159; with Manding-speakers from outside region, 158–9, 160; with matrilateral cross-cousin, 68–9, 175n 5.4; polygynous, 68, 139, 140, 161–3, 171, 177n 2; prestations, 62, 115, 132, 135; prohibitions, 60–1; ritual, 100, 115, 132, 135, 146–7, 176n 8.3; with Senufo, 60–1, 72–3, 159; with slaves, 48–9, 65, 66–8; of widows and divorcees, 70–2, 151, 153–4, 157, 162, 176n 8.4
migration, 97–101; to Korhogo, 87, 98, 112–14, 116, 124, 146, 160; within northern Ivory Coast, 98–100, 154, 155; precolonial, 23–4, 49–50, 97, 146, 166; to southern Ivory Coast, 81, 98–100, 107–11, 116, 124, 146–8, 165, 166
mory, see 'scholars' (*mory*)
Moslem law, 34–5, 37, 55, 62, 70; of inheritance, 18, 43, 56, 59, 140; marriage prohibitions, 60–1, 65
mosques, 5, 37, 88, 125

Nafana, 15
Ngandana, 16, 20
Nielle, 20–2

Parti Démocratique de la Côte d'Ivoire

184

Cambridge Studies in Social Anthropology

187

Cambridge studies in social anthropology

Also published as a paperback